THE FANTASY SPORTS BOSS 2017 FANTASY BASEBALL DRAFT GUIDE: EARLY OFFSEASON EDITION

BY MICHAEL E. KENESKI

TABLE OF CONTENTS

EDITOR'S NOTE

To Our Readers:

Every year we always start out by saying the same thing right around this time and that is "I can't believe fantasy baseball is already almost here." The offseason is shorter than ever what with the always intense winter meetings and Arizona Fall League putting potential sleeper names out there for the following year. Of course once 2016 was in the books, our staff got right into working on the 2017 Fantasy Sports Boss Fantasy Baseball Draft Guide which just keeps on getting bigger and bigger. Now moving into the 300-page range, our work is increasingly getting more and more positive attention from both the industry as a whole and from you the readers. We strive for nothing short of the best for all of you in profiling the players in a clear and concise manner that makes your draft day decisions so much easier to make. While most publications give you a few sentences on each hitter or pitcher, we know you want more which is why we pride ourselves on the lengthy write-ups on every potential impact player in fantasy baseball. Nowhere else will you find up to a half-page on one player which we have all throughout the draft guide and our work will only get more thorough as we continue on. Again we reiterate our gratitude and thanks for supporting us going back over ten years now and we look forward to helping you all throughout the 2017 season on our website as well (www.thefantasysportsboss.com). Good luck this season and we will see you at the finish line.

Sincerely,

Michael E. Keneski

"The Fantasy Sports Boss"

www.thefantasysportsboss.com

2017 TEN BURNING QUESTIONS

Perhaps our most popular feature in these pages outside of the position rankings and analysis is our annual "Ten Burning Questions" where we look at the most pressing and important storylines and themes heading into the new fantasy baseball season. While some of these questions are annual staples such as "who goes number 1?" and "who makes up the first round?" we also have some new topics that need to be sorted out before the first draft pick is made. So with that said, here are the ten key questions and answers that will at least help clear up some of the muddle before the first pitch is thrown or the first swing is made.

1. Q: Mike Trout number 1 again for 2017?

A: While Trout has done nothing to shed his label as the number 1 player in the game, there are at least two challengers to his throne for being the top pick in 2017 fantasy baseball drafts. You can make the case that Houston Astros second baseman Jose Altuve is deserving of the honor as he comes off a ridiculous 2016 performance that saw glowing numbers everywhere. Trout bested Altuve in three of the five standard categories (HR, RBI, runs) but the latter plays a more shallow position which is not a minor issue. Obviously you can't go wrong with either guy but Trout still gets the slight nod.

Then there is Boston Red Sox outfielder Mookie Betts who himself had a beyond spectacular 2016 that saw him pull ahead of Trout in THREE of the five standard league categories (average, HR, RBI). Betts also scored ONE fewer run then Trout which gives him ammunition to say he should be the top pick. With Boston giving Betts a better supporting cast then Trout gets with the Angels, this is a serious debate. Again in the end, we would go with Trout given the fact he has a longer track record of producing at this extreme level but there would be no criticism from here if you selected Betts.

2. Q: With the top three established, who are the remaining 9 players that should make up the rest of Round 1 in mixed league standard drafts?

A: Third base is very prominent in Round 1 as Josh Donaldson, Kris Bryant, Nolan Arenado, and Manny Machado all should hear their names called among the initial 12 picks in your draft. Joining them should be Paul Goldschmidt, Clayton Kershaw, Anthony Rizzo, Miguel Cabrera, and Bryce Harper.

3. Q: Bryce Harper still in Round 1 despite a 2016 performance that could only be described as a letdown?

A: Listen this is still Bryce Harper we are talking about so let's not get too cute here. Yes Harper saw his offensive numbers tumble by more than a little last season (an ugly .243 average and just 24 home runs) but this is still the same guy who went absolutely nuclear on opposing pitchers the year prior (42 homers, 99 RBI, .330 average). Harper got a bit too whiff-happy in 2016 but he did run more than ever (career-best 21 steals) and injuries kept him to only 506 at-bats which made the counting numbers in home runs, RBI, and runs appear deceptively lower. Remember that Harper is still only going to be 24 during the 2017 season and his tools are as good as any the game has ever seen. While you won't need a top five pick this season to get him, Harper should not last past the end of Round 1.

4. Q: With there surely being some borderline Round 1 guys who just missed the cut, let's go another round deeper to see who would make up the rest of your Top 24.

A: In addition to the 12 who made our first round grade, we would then go with the following to complete Round 2: Joey Votto, Charlie Blackmon, Carlos Correa, Edwin Encarnacion, Rougned Odor, Robinson Cano, Freddie Freeman, Xander Bogaerts, Max Scherzer, Corey Seager, Trea Turner, and Daniel Murphy.

5. Q: How on earth do you decide between Donaldson, Arenado, Bryant, and Machado?

A: It is amazing how potent the top tier of the third base position is these days and once Trout-Betts-Altuve go off the board, those four likely will go next in various orders. Honestly you can't go wrong with any of these massive offensive performers but there has to be some sort of ranking among them. The way we figured it out was to place them in order from 4 down to 1 in each of the five standard categories. We assigned points based on their respective finishes, with 4 going to finishing first and 1 for last. Using this method, the totals came out as follows:

Arenado: 16

Bryant: 15

Donaldson: 12

Machado: 9

So what you have here is a decision between Arenado and Bryant as they are separated by just one point. We believe most in the fantasy baseball community would go with Bryant despite finishing a point behind in our exercise and that honestly is the right call. Bryant has the best stolen base potential among this foursome and he also has position eligibility at first, third, and the outfield which the other three don't come close to matching. From there go Arenado-Donaldson-Machado in that order.

6. Q: Gary Sanchez can't be this good can he?

A: It was a performance that went down in the history books in terms of being one of the greatest rookie debuts in history as New York Yankees catching prospect Gary Sanchez looked like Babe Ruth in slugging 20 home runs in just 229 at-bats. Instantly the hype meter went into overdrive for 2017 drafts given the fact Sanchez' hitting numbers were as rare as it gets when it comes to the always shallow catching position. With Sanchez literally on almost every sleeper list for this coming season, his draft price figures to end up in the silly range (maybe as high as the late second round). This is a dangerous situation for those who are in fact willing to pay the extreme price as Sanchez never came anywhere near his 2016 level of performance coming up the minor league ladder and opposing pitchers will now have had a full winter to dissect any weakness he may have. While Sanchez is clearly a rare talent, you never want to get into a bidding war on a player who has not even had HALF of a season in the majors under his belt. Remember Yasiel Puig a few years ago? Or Carlos Correa last March? Or how about Anthony Rendon in 2015? These three are all cases where a young player came up and went nuts at the dish and in the process, sent their draft stocks the following season into the stratosphere. All three struggled in that subsequent season (with Puig and Rendon turning out to be monster busts) and this is why Sanchez is probably not worth investing in given the current price tag. A wonderful talent for sure but Sanchez is more likely to hit 25 home runs this season then 35.

7. Q: Trea Turner belongs in the same boat as Gary Sanchez then wouldn't he?

A: Different player and different situation. As we noted earlier, Turner should not last past the second round in most fantasy baseball drafts this season as he comes off a 2016 debut that was as good as it gets. Just like with Sanchez, there was little to no adjustment period for Turner in terms of unleashing the full array of his talents. Those talents include a bat that can hit .300-plus, the power to contribute some in the home run category, and the extreme speed to challenge for a stolen base title right away. We saw all of this on display in his 73-game debut for the team as Turner batted .342, cracked 13 home runs, and stole 33 bases. Just like that, Turner has put himself into firm second round consideration in 2017 drafts and one can understand why. Throw in eligibility at second base and the outfield and Turner has just as much hype attached to him as Sanchez coming into the new season.

Now while we said to tread carefully when it comes to Sanchez, we are more accepting of drafting Turner in the second round this season given his five-category game and multi-position eligibility. Sanchez doesn't have eligibility outside of catcher and he doesn't make five-category statistical contributions like Turner does. Yes the price will be extreme but Turner seems like money well-spent this drafting season.

8. Q: 2016 Daniel Murphy: Legit or Fluke?

A: This is no doubt a very popular topic of conversation going into 2017 drafts as Murphy's spectacular MVP-worthy 2016 was almost too good to be true. While Murphy had never been much of a home run hitter prior to last season (previous high of 14), he exploded to the tune of 25 long balls. In addition, Murphy almost won the batting title with another career-high-by-a-mile average of .347. Add in 88 runs scored and 104 RBI and Murphy was ridiculous throughout the year. So was it a completely legit performance? The way we answer questions like this is to go with some commence sense and look at the outlier aspect of it. Clearly Murphy was way over his head statistically across the board and it wasn't like he went to a better ballpark leaving the Mets for Washington as both places favor pitchers. Yes Kevin Long's tip to have Murphy set up closer to the plate seems to have unleashed some burgeoning power but we think the guy is more likely to be around 20 home runs then 25 going forward since opposing pitchers will likely be more careful throwing to him. Also batting in front of Bryce Harper for a full season gave Murphy all the juicy fastballs he could handle and you see what happened. So in conclusion, yes we think a good deal of what Murphy accomplished last season was legit but also a bit of a fluke. Does that help? If not just wait until the third round to draft him and you will be good.

9. Q: Giancarlo Stanton no longer a top-24 guy?

A: In order to be a firm top-24 hitter or pitcher in yearly fantasy baseball leagues, both performance and durability have to be part of the equation. While Miami Marlins outfielder Giancarlo Stanton certainly has the production down pat in terms of his awesome power, durability is a different story as he has played in more than 125 games just once in the last five years. That means you simply can't depend on Stanton providing you with even remotely a full season of numbers and this is a big negative in terms of investing in him for 2017 fantasy baseball. Again we have no qualms with the major home run and RBI potential Stanton has in his bat but counting on health here is proving to be foolhardy.

10. Q: Staying in Miami with the Marlins, who is the real Dee Gordon?

A: That question will be answered more clearly as Gordon has to show that his PED bust last season means his 2015 All-Star campaign was not chemically-enhanced. By now it is old news that Gordon was nothing but a failed prospect who couldn't hit when first arriving with the Los Angeles Dodgers and then took off in 2015 with the Marlins when he turned into a batting champion overnight (.333), while also scoring 88 runs, and stealing 58 bases. This allowed Gordon to be drafted on average in the late second round prior to 2016 and the rest as they say is history since the PED suspension came soon after the year began. When Gordon returned after the 80 games, his hitting was quite shaky as he batted just .268 and he also showed rate numbers that were well of his 2015 standards. While Gordon still piles up the steals, one now has to debate whether he can replicate his pre-PED production.

In terms of where we stand on this, we do like the fact Gordon's draft price will come much cheaper this time around. The steals potential is still massive and Gordon is likely to put up a high amount of runs scored as well. We won't be buying into the 2015 average though as Gordon is likely back to being a shaky hitter there off the juice. If you can get Gordon in Round 5 or later, then you did well.

2017 FANTASY BASEBALL ROOKIE REPORT

As much as we all love the fantasy baseball sleeper, the fantasy baseball rookie pretty much goes in conjunction with that draft darling group. It is the rookies after all who are filled with promise and upside and who also have the potential to yield some tremendous fantasy baseball value with varying degrees of a draft price. Just like we see every season, there will be some hits and misses from this group as some hitters/pitchers adjust to the Major League game quicker than others. What you surely want to do is be aware of the prospects that will likely make their debuts at some point during the season so that you have the familiarity in terms of how they can help your team. So without further delay, here are the top rookies to know for 2017 fantasy baseball.

1. Dansby Swanson (SS, Atlanta Braves) ******SEE SHORTSTOP RANKINGS FOR PROFILE. *****

2. Alex Bregman (3B, Houston Astros)******SEE THIRD BASE RANKINGS FOR PROFILE.*****

3. Lucas Giolito (SP, Washington Nationals): Widely considered to be the number 1 pitching prospect in all of baseball, don't let a somewhat rough 2016 debut with the Nats (6.75 ERA in 21.1 innings) sway you from thinking anything less of the future ace. With K/9 rates over 9.00 both at Double-A and Triple-A, Giolito only has to work on his control to unleash the top-end stuff.

4. Yoan Moncada (3B, Boston Red Sox): While he struggled badly in his cup of coffee debut with the Boston Red Sox at the tail end of 2016, there is no disputing the massive potential of this smooth-swinging Cuban. What really makes Moncada a particularly swell prospect in fantasy baseball is that his speed is just as impressive as the raw power. Future 20/20 player at the very least.

5. Jose De Leon (SP, Los Angeles Dodgers): The Los Angeles Dodgers saw their rotation decimated in 2016 as they went in without Zack Greinke after losing him during free agency and then saw ace Clayton Kershaw miss a huge chunk of the year with injury. That necessitated the call-up of top power pitching prospect Jose De Leon in September which served as a "run to the waiver wire" moment in the fantasy baseball community. Power is the name of the game here as De Leon put up monster K/9's at Double-A (12.33) in 2015 and then at Triple-A (11.57) last season prior to his promotion. While De Leon struggled in his four-start cameo with the Dodgers in pitching to a 6.35 ERA and 1.53 WHIP, there is no denying the fact that the 24-year-old has major ability and he should be planted firmly on most sleeper lists for drafts this spring. The initial stumble with the Dodgers didn't go according to plan but that will just help keep the price from getting out of hand at the draft table. Go get him.

6. Andrew Benintendi (OF, Boston Red Sox): *******SEE OUTFIELD RANKINGS FOR PROFILE.******

7. Al Reyes (SP, St. Louis Cardinals):   The St. Louis Cardinals know how to develop prospects, as they annually are lauded for having one of the best farm systems in the game of baseball. They bolstered that assessment in 2016 when they unveiled top pitching prospect Alex Reyes to spectacular results. In the heat of a pennant race, Reyes looked like an ace starter as he struck out batters at a 10.17 K/9 clip and posted a dominant 1.57 ERA in 46 innings. An extreme groundball pitcher, Reyes's home run rate was ridiculous at 0.20. Of course the requisite control problems went along for the ride (4.50 BB/9) like it does for most young power arms but Reyes looks like he fits with Julio Urias as quite possibly the best pitching sleeper for 2017 fantasy baseball. We are making it a point to get Reyes on all of our teams this season and so should you.

8. David Dahl (OF, Colorado Rockies)******SEE OUTFIELD RANKINGS FOR PROFILE.******

9. Austin Meadows (OF, Pittsburgh Pirates): The Pirate outfield is crowded right now with Andrew McCutchen, Gregory Polanco, and Starling Marte, but Meadows can hang with them given his five-tool potential. Meadows' 20/20 skill-set would fit in seamlessly with the Pirates' athletic outfield to say the least. Get ready to move Meadows up by a lot on your draft board if the Pirates trade one of their starting outfielders.

10. Clint Frazier (OF, New York Yankees): The big prize the Yanks got in the Andrew Miller deal, Frazier possesses massive raw power that could eventually make him a 40-home run guy in that ballpark. He also has the speed to steal bases as well.

11. J.P. Crawford (SS, Philadelphia Phillies): Has good patience at the dish for a young player but the glove is currently ahead of the bat. Crawford does possess good speed that will make him an immediate steals help and the power is starting to come along as well.

12. Brendan Rogers (SS, Colorado Rockies): Big-time power here and the comparisons are already being made to Troy Tulowitzki. A bit strikeout-heavy for now but Rogers will be up before 2017 is out. Where he plays will be the interesting development since Trevor Story is already in at SS.

13. Bradley Zimmer (OF, Cleveland Indians): There are some pros and cons here as Zimmer has incredible speed to steal 25 bags right out of the gate in the majors. Unfortunately there also are sizable holes in the swing which lead to a boatload of strikeouts and an ugly batting average. Think Chris Young or Grady Sizemore here.

14. Orlando Arcia (SS, Milwaukee Brewers)*******SEE SHORTSTOP RANKINGS FOR PROFILE.*******

15. Victor Robles (OF, Washington Nationals): Needs more seasoning given the extremely young age (20) but Robles is already showing the contact skills to be a batting average help and the speed to pick up steals at a decent clip. The power has not shown itself yet though and that issue will determine just how high Robles' ceiling goes.

16. Andrew Espinoza (SP, San Diego Padres): The Padres netted Espinoza from the Boston Red Sox in the Drew Pomeranz deal and needless to say, they did very well in that transaction. Yes Espinoza's numbers were ugly last season but that is what happens when any prospect is just 18-years-old. There is high-end stuff here such as a high-90's fastball that elicits a bunch of swings and misses; not to mention very good secondary stuff. The ceiling goes high here but Espinoza is more of a 2018 story.

17. Aaron Judge (OF, New York Yankees):*****SEE OUTFIELD RANKINGS FOR PROFILE.******

18. Hunter Renfroe (OF, San Diego Padres): Renfroe is older than most of the prospects on this list and we have to take his PCL numbers last season with a bit of a grain of salt. However there is very good power here that will likely be his calling card at the major league level.

19. Ian Happ (OF, Chicago Cubs): You get a little bit of everything when it comes to outfield prospect Ian Happ. The Cubs farmhand can hit some home runs, steal some bases, and play both the outfield and the infield. Happ won't exactly blow up any one category away but his overall game should make him at least a utility guy very soon.

20. Gleyber Torres (SS, New York Yankees): The Cubs were so stacked with middle infield prospects that they were able to deal the highly regarded Torres to the Yankees in the Aroldis Chapman deal. The power is just now starting to show up to join the very good speed and Torres also has a terrific glove. A future star.

21. Josh Hader (SP, Milwaukee Brewers): The strikeouts were silly here last season in the minors and the rebuilding Brewers really have no reason outside of the arbitration clock to not give the kid a long look in spring training. Could be the next top power starter in the game.

22. Reynaldo Lopez (SP, Washington Nationals): Got blasted in his short came with the Nats in 2016 but Lopez' 100-mph fastball won't keep him on the farm for long. Lopez is your typical young power pitcher who can blow batters away but who also can't control where his pitches go.

23. Jeff Hoffman, SP, Colorado Rockies): Yeah we hate the atmosphere and future home ballpark in Coors Field but Hoffman is the latest power-arm to develop in the Colorado Rockies' system. Hoffman misses a ton of bats with a power fastball and terrific curve but the upside is capped given the locale.

24. Manuel Margot (OF, San Diego Padres): Good average and contact guy who has not shown much power yet. It is debatable if the power will arrive but Margot can help on the bases and also is a top defender.

25. Jesse Winker (OF, Chicago Cubs): Already Winker has advanced hitting skills in terms of possessing a low strikeout rate and a line-drive swing that makes him an average asset already. The power is also starting to come along as well which could net Winker a promotion sometime during the summer or earlier if the need arises.

2017 FANTASY BASEBALL DRAFT SLEEPERS

The paradox of the fantasy baseball draft sleeper has been well-established by now. A classic sleeper often hints at above-average ability, while also possessing a sizable ceiling and room for growth. It is these variables that make such players some of the most sought after hitters and pitchers in fantasy baseball drafts and at the same time, wind up carrying some immense risk. The latter is due to the fact that while the draft sleeper has shown hints of major ability, it is far from a guarantee they will adjust right away to the major league game. For every Ryan Braun or Mike Trout, there are 15 other cases of guys who simply were not ready for the "show" and who found themselves back in the minor leagues for more seasoning. So as we do every year in this space, we remind you to consider the cost on any prospective sleeper you want to invest in and also at the same time, try to not flood your roster with players from this type of class. The bust factor remains very high here but at the same time, some tremendous value can also be had if you are lucky. So without further delay, here at the top sleeper candidates for 2017 fantasy baseball, with the benchmark being players that have the best chance of producing numbers beyond their draft slot.

Wilson Contreras: Still carrying catcher eligibility for 2017 fantasy baseball, the smooth-swinging Wilson Contreras has an immense amount of potential value attached to his name. With good power that seems to translate to 20 home runs and with expected daily playing time as he also can start in the outfield, Contreras should be squarely on all your sleeper lists.

Tommy Joseph: While he was not much of a power hitter in the minors, Phillies first baseman Tommy Joseph added that skill to his game during his 2016 debut with the team. Overall Joseph swatted 21 home runs in just 347 at-bats and he makes for a nice upside play for your CI or UTIL spot.

Jose Peraza: This kid should be right at the top of your sleeper list this season as the Cincinnati speedster has potential five-tool ability at second base or the outfield. Right out of the gate Peraza can steal 25 bases and hit .300. He also is adding power as he develops which checks almost all of the offensive columns going into the season.

Devon Travis: We have already seen glimpses of upper-level ability from Toronto Blue Jays second baseman Devon Travis over the last two seasons. That is when he was not sidelined by ongoing shoulder trouble. While Travis has had trouble staying on the field, his bat seems capable of 20 home runs and some steals for a dirt-cheap price tag at the draft.

Whit Merrifield: The Kansas City Royals will open up a battle for the second base job in spring training this February and the speedy Whit Merrifield has a good chance to come out on top. Having stolen a ton of bases in the minors, Merrifield has hit as high as .340 while coming up the Royals minor league ladder.

T.J. Rivera: All New York Mets second base prospect T.J. Rivera has done in the minors leagues is hit for a .300-plaus average at every stop and he has a chance to be the team's starting second baseman for 2017 if Neil Walker is not re-signed.

A.J. Pollock: The draft price will come down by a sizable margin for 2017 fantasy baseball but Arizona Diamondbacks outfielder A.J. Pollock's ability remains second round-worthy. 2016 was a complete throw out for Pollock given the fact he missed most of the year with injury but his blockbuster 2015 numbers should be a reminder that he can be an outfielder 1.

David Dahl: Any young hitter coming up in the Colorado Rockies system is automatically a sleeper and this is especially true for the team's former first round pick. Outfielder David Dahl already began to show a burgeoning power/speed game last season in his cameo debut for the team and 20/20 is not out of the question for 2017.

Michael Brantley: Like with A.J. Pollock in Arizona, a decent price tag suddenly attaches itself to Cleveland Indians outfielder Michael Brantley. An outfielder 1 on ability, Brantley will come cheaper this season after dealing with shoulder problems for almost all of 2016. The guy is one of the best pure hitters in baseball and he has 15/15 ability as well in his power/speed game.

Hector Neris: The Philadelphia Phillies should have gone with the hard-throwing Hector Neris and not the mediocre Jeanmar Gomez to close games from the start of 2016. After Gomez eventually got exposed, Neris got the much-deserved promotion to the ninth inning where he did well. Capable of big-time strikeouts, Neris will be a high ceiling and solidly priced closer this season.

Robbie Ray: While Robbie Ray's 4.90 ERA was far from impressive, 218 K's in 174.1 innings certainly caught the attention of the fantasy baseball community.

Ray looks like he is on the verge of stardom and once he gets his ERA down into the 3.00-range, ace-level could be possible.

Aaron Nola: While Nola's composite 4.78 ERA last season looked quite ugly, the underlying numbers pointed to a young pitcher that is capable of being a top-of-the-rotation arm soon. Nola looked like an ace the first two months of the year before going into the tank due to injuries and fatigue but a 9.81 K/9 rate as a rookie is very impressive. Don't forget that Nola was also a 2011 first round pick (7th overall) of the Phillies so there is a lot of pedigree here. Look past the ERA.

David Phelps: A very good setup man for the Miami Marlins in 2016, the interest meter went up by more than a little when he moved into the rotation down the stretch of the season. Phelps pitched great in that role, averaging a K/IP and his stuff seemed to play well there. We don't know if Phelps will stay in the rotation or move to the bullpen for 2017 but if he ends up in the former, there is a decent amount of upside to work with.

Lance Lynn: Having missed the entire 2016 season after falling victim to Tommy John surgery, many in the fantasy baseball community will forget about St. Louis Cardinals starter Lance Lynn. Keep in mind Lynn was a 200-K power pitcher who came close to ace status before the surgery. While his always shaky control will be more of an issue in coming back from the Tommy John, Lynn is shaping up as a swell value.

Edwin Diaz: Boy do the Seattle Mariners have a closing talent on their hands. Right from the start of his 2016 rookie season, Edwin Diaz began collecting strikeouts by the boatload (mammoth 15.33 K/9) which made him the easy choice to replace the struggling Steve Cishek in the ninth inning. Turning just 23 this March, Diaz has the dominant K rate and overpowering stuff to be a top closer for years.

Carter Capps: Expected to be fully recovered from Tommy John elbow surgery, flame throwing Carter Capps is expected to begin the 2017 season as the San Diego Padres closer. Remember that Capps looked like the next great dominant closer prior to his elbow going bad, rocking a ridiculous K/9 that went over 16.0 in 2015. Could instantly become a top five closer overnight.

2017 FANTASY BASEBALL DRAFT BUSTS

Fantasy baseball draft busts are like getting sick. You don't realize what is happening at first inside your body but soon you become ill and laid out in bed for days. The fantasy baseball draft bust often starts out as a minor annoyance. A slow start or slump begins out of the gates. A nagging injury sends a player to the bench or to an early DL stint. Then that injury becomes a major problem that results in weeks or months out of action. Or the slump becomes so bad that the player gets benched or sent to the minors. Before you know it there is disaster all around on your roster and your team is floundering. You rue the mistaken draft pick and curse your luck. You have been infected fully with a fantasy baseball draft bust and it is quite an unpleasant experience you just surely would not want to have again. So as we venture toward 2017 fantasy baseball, we are back to try and identify those pitchers and hitters who stand the best chance of making things go all wrong for you this season. For sure there will be other busts that show up out of nowhere but the following players all have red flags or warning signs you should take as a clue to ignore them at the draft.

Gary Sanchez: Sanchez' selection for the bust team has everything to do with his expected expensive draft price and nothing else. There may not be a more sought after sleeper in 2017 drafts then the power-hitting catcher who set all sorts of records in his two-month debut with the team last season. While we don't doubt the ability of Sanchez, there is no way he will be able to match the home runs rates he set in 2016 and with everyone after him in the draft, the price tag is set to be way overinflated. As we have seen in cases such as this with Yasiel Puig and Anthony Rendon in the past, often these inflations end up badly.

Brad Miller: How formerly light-hitting infielder Brad Miller was able to crack 30 home runs last season for the Tampa Bay Rays is one of life's great mysteries. When we see outlier numbers such as this, it is always a good idea to pretend like it never happened. Miller is surely going to see a giveback when it comes to home runs this season as pitchers will now be much more careful attacking him and again we find it hard to believe he can match those numbers for a second year in a row.

Dustin Pedroia: Always on notice as a prime bust/erosion candidate going into 2016, longtime Boston Red Sox second baseman Dustin Pedroia managed to stay almost fully healthy last season which allowed his previously slipping numbers to rebound. Of course asking an aging Pedroia to stay that healthy two years in a row is foolish and the wear-and-tear of playing second base tends to cause offensive statistics to erode quicker than at other positions. When we see late-career upticks in numbers, always assume it was a one-year anomaly.

Hanley Ramirez: After years of injuries and seeing his offensive numbers drop sharply, Boston Red Sox first baseman Hanley Ramirez managed to reverse those trends in 2016 as he cracked 30 home runs while staying on the field consistently. Just like we mentioned with Dustin Pedroia, asking Ramirez to repeat such good luck on the health front is a tall order and the burst in power does not seem sustainable. Another case of a player's name brand exceeding expected production.

D.J. LeMahieu: There is arguing the fact that Colorado Rockies second baseman D.J. LeMahieu is a major batting average and runs asset in fantasy baseball but his 2016 batting title figures to cause his draft price this season to go above where it should be. The problem is that outside of runs and average, LeMahieu is quite ordinary as he doesn't have much power and his steals dipped last season to mediocre levels. Throw in the fact LeMahieu won't likely approach his lofty 2016 average and there are too many issues to look past here.

Neil Walker: Anytime a second baseman hits 23 home runs at second base, the reflexive reaction would be to go after him in fantasy baseball given the lack of depth at the position. Well in the case of Neil Walker, this is a mistake for a number of reasons. While respect should always be given for such good power, Walker is coming off back surgery that historically has sapped a hitter's strength going forward. With Walker likely set to lose some home runs this season due to the surgery, his overall fantasy baseball outlook becomes very murky since he doesn't offer any speed or prime average contributions.

Noah Syndegaard: This one is obvious as New York Mets ace Noah Syndegaard is the best example of what a prospective Tommy John elbow surgery candidate looks like. Young and possessing a blazing repertoire, Syndegaard already has had a few Tommy John scares in his young career. It simply is not natural for a pitcher to consistently throw as hard as Syndegaard does and eventually the elbow is going to snap. It is only a matter of time before this takes place.

Aaron Sanchez: Leading the American League in ERA at 3.00 is no small feat when you call the AL East your division and Rogers Center in Toronto home.

That is just what Aaron Sanchez accomplished last season for the Blue Jays in his first full campaign as a starting pitcher and there was a lot to be impressed about. However there is major trouble brewing here as Sanchez went way above his previous innings high by more than 100 and that alone spells injury trouble and/or eroded numbers for 2017. In addition, Sanchez got quite a bit of good BABIP luck to the tune of a .267 mark which likely won't be repeated. When adjusted for the luck, Sanchez' XFIP ERA was a higher 3.75. The injury risk remains real here given the jump in innings and that should cement Sanchez as a guy to avoid.

Kyle Hendricks: While Kyle Hendricks has been a very good SP 4-type of pitcher the last few seasons, 2016 saw him go to a whole new level as he pitched to a crazy 2.13 ERA. Of course there was BABIP luck involved and quite a bit as Hendricks' number came in at a very fortunate .250. When corrected from luck, Hendricks' XFIP ERA was a much higher 3.59. Again good pitcher but not a great one as his 2016 numbers showed.

Stephen Strasburg: Another year and another series of injuries for Washington Nats ace Stephen Strasburg. Simply out, Strasburg can't ever make it through a season unscathed when it comes to his health and 2016 was no different as he came down with a flexor scare in his elbow. Already with a Tommy John surgery in his past, Strasburg is simply not worth the aggravation considering how his draft price is so annually high.

Gerrit Cole: Along the same lines as Noah Syndegaard, Pittsburgh Pirates ace Gerrit Cole seems like another Tommy John candidate waiting to happen. Unlike Syndegaard, Cole struggled noticeably in 2016 as he his velocity was down, his K rate sank, and his health betrayed him with shoulder injuries. While Cole avoided surgery, he is clearly trending in the wrong direction and his still-elevated price tag is a non-starter for us.

Rick Porcello and J.A. Happ: We group both Happ and Porcello together as they each shockingly won 20 or more games last season despite coming into 2016 as nothing but below-average Major League starters. It all came together for both and in the AL East of all places last season which added to the surprise of it all. Again in unexplained situations such as this, advanced numbers tell the story and both were not good there. Happ's .268 and Porcello's .269 BABIP were clearly in the lucky zone and since both guys have mediocre mid-7.00 K/9 rates, their margin for error is quite thin to begin with. Now when their luck goes to the mean in 2017, the runs will start piling up again as they historically have for these two. Avoid both at all costs.

Junior Guerra: This is an easy one as Guerra came out of the Mexican League and immediately morphed into an "ace" pitcher at the major league level as a rookie. Sorry but that just doesn't happen without a bunch of BABIP luck and that is what took place with Guerra in 2016. While his surface ERA of 2.81 was impressive, Guerra's .250 BABIP was insanely lucky. Driving this point home, Guerra's XFIP of 4.29 showed how he really was not as good as his 2.81 ERA showed. This one could get real nasty in a very quick manner to begin 2017.

Craig Kimbrel: Over the last two seasons, former consensus number 1 closer Craig Kimbrel has lost the aura of invincibility. For one thing, a number of elbow scares have been a reminder of Kimbrel's high Tommy John risk. Then there is the matter of Kimbrel losing a bit of velocity which caused his ERA to go above 3.00 for the first time in his career in 2016. Another one trending the wrong way.

Francisco Rodriguez: Age and slipping velocity are conspiring to make K-Rod one of the biggest risks among all closers. That is saying something when you consider that closers are the least-dependable class of player in fantasy baseball. You have to know when it is time to move away from aging players before things get really ugly and we appear to be at that point now with Rodriguez.

Dellin Betances: The last memory of Dellin Betances last season was his horrible September performance in his second month as a closer for the Yankees that might have the front office re-thinking the idea of the guy being the team's long-term ninth inning solution. Even if the Yanks don't bring back Aroldis Chapman in free agency (which has been rumored), Betances needs to answer the question of whether he has the mental acumen to succeed as the closer. While his raw stuff is as good and overpowering as any arm in the majors, Betances has also had a huge workload for a reliever over the last three years which makes him also an injury risk. This one is not as safe an investment as it might look.

2017 FANTASY BASEBALL POSITION ELIGIBILITY REPORT

One of the most crucial and often overlooked aspects of evaluating players in yearly fantasy baseball drafts concern position eligibility. Of particular importance to a hitter, the more positions a player qualifies for, the greater the potent his potential value may be. Every season key players go into the year with eligibility they didn't have at the start of the previous year and on the flip side, they also can lose it at certain spots as well. So with that in mind, here are the eligibility setups for some prime fantasy baseball hitters for the 2017 season.

Jean Segura-2B/SS

Ben Zobrist: 2B/OF

Daniel Murphy: 1B/2B

Logan Forsythe: 2B

Javier Baez: 2B, SS, 3B

Jedd Gyorko: 2B, SS, 3B

Howie Kendrick: 2B, OF

Buster Posey: C

Jonathan Lucroy: C

Wilson Contreras: C, OF

Kris Bryant: 3B, OF

Mark Trumbo: OF

Carlos Santana: 1B

Wil Myers: 1B

Todd Frazier: 1B

Chris Davis: 1B

Matt Carpenter: 1B, 2B, 3B

Kendrys Morales: UTIL

Brad Miller: 1B, SS

Victor Martinez: UTIL

Jose Bautista: OF

Travis Shaw: 1B, 3B

Brandon Moss: 1B, OF

Antony Rendon: 3B

Martin Prado: 3B

Eugenio Suarez: 3B

Eduardo Nunez: SS, 3B

Danny Espinosa: SS

Jose Ramirez: 3B, OF

Danny Valencia: 3B, OF

Brandon Drury: 3B, OF

David Freese: 1B, 3B

Yangervis Solarte: 3B

Lonnie Chisenhall: OF

Hernan Perez: 3B, OF

Marwin Gonzalez: 1B, 3B

Steve Pearce: 1B

Logan Morrison: 1B

Whit Merrifield: 2B

Jeff Marte: 1B, 3B, OF

Tyler Saladino: 2B, SS

Jurickson Profar: 3B

Chris Coghlan: 2B, OF

Nick Franklin: OF

Miguel Sano: 3B, OF

Chris Owings: SS, OF

Trea Turner: 2B, OF

Brock Holt: OF

Eduardo Escobar: 3B, OF

Manny Machado: SS, 3B

Jonathan Villar: SS, OF

2017 POSITION RANKINGS AND PROFILES

CATCHER POSITION OVERVIEW

The catcher position remains somewhat of a mess for 2017 fantasy baseball, as the defections of big bats like Carlos Santana, Mike Napoli, and Victor Martinez over the years have taken a ton of offensive productivity away from this already shallow group, but things could be looking up due to the arrival of two high upside bats. The promotions last season of top catching prospects Gary Sanchez and Wilson Contreras by the New York Yankees and Chicago Cubs respectively brought two upper-level hitters to a position in dire need of offensive impact. Not since Buster Posey have we seen such prominent catching prospects like we have with Sanchez and Contreras and both should be among the more popular sleepers for 2017. Add in the return from injury of Kyle Schwarber (who retains catcher eligibility in most leagues after missing all but two games in 2016 due to injury) and the re-eligible Evan Gattis and all of a sudden the catcher spot is not one big disaster as it often has been.

The draft strategy however remains to avoid picking a catcher early if you play in a league that plays only one starter. We have seen this mistake all too often over the years and 9 times out of 10 it turns out bad. While we would love to have a Posey, Sanchez, or Contreras, you can do just fine with a value play like Wilson Ramos, Matt Wieters, or Stephen Vogt.

Buster Posey: It was standard operating procedure when it came to the offensive performance of San Francisco Giants catcher Buster Posey in 2016. Considered the number 1 catcher in fantasy baseball for a few years now, Posey batted .288 with 14 home runs, scored 80 runs, and drove in 82. While Posey lost 5 home runs from 2015, nothing in his rate stats was out of the ordinary. Posey's reputation as one of the best pure hitters in baseball remains intact as he is a .307 career hitter and he has put up at least 18 home runs in four of the last six seasons when he has accumulated 400 at-bats. With a 10.4 BB/9 rate and a very low 11.1 K/9, Posey can hit .280-plus in his sleep which makes him an incredibly rare commodity to own in terms of fantasy baseball. Of course the biggest issue with Posey on an annual basis is the draft price and how much you as a prospective owner are willing to pay. On average going in the third round of mixed leagues the last 4-5 years, Posey is a bit overpriced when you consider the offensive numbers of the guys picked around him are likely much more potent. Again having a catcher who can hit like Posey gives you a clear advantage over the rest of your league but at the same time it can also hurt you in terms of letting some big-numbered batters at other positions wind up onto other teams. The value says to pass on Posey and snag a catcher value play in the later rounds.

2017 PROJECTION: .300 18 HR 84 RBI 83 R 5 SB

Gary Sanchez: Buckle up and hold on because the fight at all draft tables this season is going to be beyond intense in terms of getting your hands on New York Yankees overnight star catcher Gary Sanchez. In what can only be described as a truly insane debut, Sanchez broke all sorts of rookie records in clubbing 20 home runs and collecting 42 RBI in just 229 at-bats. Sanchez tied the all-time MLB record for the fastest player in history to 20 home runs to begin a career and a .299 batting average that was only depressed by a final week slump went along for the ride. In going back down memory lane a bit, Sanchez was a much hyped prospect from the beginning but he also ran into a few detours along the way to the majors due to injury and misconduct (he was suspended twice for behavioral/disciplinary reasons). Even prior to his promotion last year, Sanchez had only 10 home runs and a modest .282 average in 313 Triple-A at-bats, which makes what he did with the Yankees so spectacular. At the same time though, you have to fully accept that Sanchez will NEVER approach numbers on a per game basis like that ever again and his draft price for 2017 is likely going to be grossly inflated. This is especially true when you get the very rare catcher who can hit the way Sanchez can. Keep in mind that for all the glowing numbers, Sanchez struck out in 24.9 percent of his at-bats last year and he also got a lucky boost from his .317 BABIP. With apparent holes in his swing, opposing pitchers will study those Sanchez weaknesses all winter and be ready to exploit them from the jump in 2017. Remember we have seen recent examples of overnight stars such as Yasiel Puig or to a lesser extent Carlos Correa a year ago who then struggled during their sophomore campaigns and Sanchez stands a good chance of joining this group. Now understand we are not saying Sanchez is going to be a bust this season in terms of the totality of his numbers. Instead what we're saying is that for his expected second or third round ADP, Sanchez's numbers stand a good chance of not making the grade in terms of that lofty draft spot. If you can get Sanchez in Round 5 or later then by all means dive right in but he was in such outlier territory a year ago that this has a better chance of going in the disappointment bin then in the spectacular one.

2017 PROJECTION: .280 24 HR 74 RBI 65 R 4 SB

Jonathan Lucroy: After an injury-marred and somewhat disappointing 2015 campaign, veteran backstop Jonathan Lucroy saw his fantasy baseball draft stock slip when it came to 2016 drafts. Those who were able to snag Lucroy at his depressed cost made out like gangbusters though as he set a career-high in home runs with 24 and once again was a batting average asset in hitting .292. Lucroy surely benefited by being traded from the Milwaukee Brewers to the Texas Rangers at the Aug. 1 deadline as he wound up in a better power park overnight and the results showed as he smacked 11 of his home runs in just two months time there. With one more year to go on his contract, Lucroy will now have a full season in Texas to take advantage of that offensive haven that the place has always been and that alone will keep him in the top 3 range among fantasy baseball catchers. Lucroy is aging a bit as he turns 31 in June and perhaps we are seeing a tiny bit of effects from that after his 18.4 K/9 rate was his highest since 2011. That is a just a mild nitpick however as the guy seems like a very safe investment again this season.

2017 PROJECTION: .288 21 HR 84 RBI 77 R 5 SB

Kyle Schwarber: Well that didn't go according to plan. Arguably one of the most sought after players for 2016 fantasy baseball was Chicago Cubs slugging catcher/outfielder Kyle Schwarber, given his massive power and precious eligibility behind the dish. As a result, Schwarber's draft price soared which made his almost complete washout for 2016 (as a result of an early April knee injury) tough to stomach. Now 100 percent recovered from his torn ACL, the hype machine is churning again as he should retain catcher eligibility in most leagues given that he only played in two games last season. While Schwarber has a big strikeout problem that could make hitting above .270 a challenge, he should easily reach 30 home runs and 80 RBI if the health holds up. Again the catcher eligibility is the key here which inflates the value of Schwarber since you don't get this type of offensive numbers from a guy who dons the tools of ignorance. The question that needs to be answered is if Schwarber will have eligibility here at the start of the year after his miniscule 2016 season only had him in the outfield. It is possible Schwarber will get a complete "do over" in leagues this season in terms of repeating his 2016 eligibility but even if he starts off without the "C" next to his name, it is likely Schwarber will gain it back eventually since the Cubs still plan on having him catch some. Give him another chance.

2017 PROJECTION: .267 26 HR 89 RBI 84 R 1 SB

J.T. Realmuto: Another guy we hit a home run on for 2016 fantasy baseball was Miami Marlins ascending catcher J.T. Realmuto. In fact Realmuto was the catcher we told you all to draft in terms of once again preaching our strategy of picking an upside backstop in the later round. Realmuto was every bit available in the final rounds of almost all drafts prior to last season and in some cases, he went unclaimed altogether. Instead we saw the potential here due to the fact that Realmuto hinted at very good contact skills for a catcher to go along with possessing speed not seen here since Jason Kendall. Realmuto wound up doing a nice Kendall impression as he hit .303 with 11 home runs and 12 stolen bases last season in a tremendous value campaign. Easily leading all catchers in steals, Realmuto was a rock of consistency with the bat all year as he struck out in just 18.3 percent of his at-bats (justifying our good contact assessment). Turning only 26 in March, Realmuto should absolutely be able to reprise those numbers, with perhaps just a dip in his average after posting a lucky .357 BABIP. Kid is perfectly legit and draft accordingly.

2017 PROJECTION: .289 12 HR 50 RBI 62 R 11 SB

Willson Contreras: The never-ending conveyor belt of top-shelf prospects coming out of the Chicago Cubs farm system continued unabated during the 2016 season as the team unveiled smooth-swinging catcher Willson Contreras in June. Reminding many of Buster Posey, Contreras was a batting average monster in the minor leagues as he hit .333 at Double-A in 2015 and then followed that up by beginning last season with a scorching .353 at Triple-A. The Cubs had no choice but to promote Contreras and the kid did pretty darn well for himself as he batted .282 with 12 home runs and 35 RBI in just 283 at-bats. While Contreras did whiff in 23.7 percent of his at-bats, his hitting profile is incredibly rare at catcher and again brings forth accurate comparisons to Posey in terms of being a perennial .300 stick with power. Better yet, Contreras may end up having more power then Posey as he is just scratching the surface there and could very well be in the 25-home run range before too long. As an added bonus, Contreras gained outfield eligibility as Joe Maddon added versatility to his name as he does with almost every hitter on the Cubs roster. In terms of how much Contreras will catch this season, this is still up for debate as Kyle Schwarber also returns from injury. The only thing that matters though is that Contreras retains eligibility there for another year and his upside is huge. While most in the fantasy baseball community will chase Gary Sanchez, the better investment is the cheaper but still filled with upside Contreras.

2017 PROJECTION: .288 20 HR 75 RBI 62 R 6 SB

Wilson Ramos: Long on fantasy baseball potential but short on results for years, veteran catcher Wilson Ramos was mostly ignored when 2016 drafts got underway last spring. It was tough to blame the fantasy baseball community from looking past Ramos (even at a very thin position) due to the fact the guy was an annual tease who hinted at a potent offensive game but who ultimately let everyone down with poor numbers and an insane amount of injuries. Ramos was also coming off a 2015 campaign where he hit a pathetic .229 with 15 home runs in 504 at-bats. Now the one thing that many overlooked though with Ramos entering into last season was the motivation factor, as he was slated to be a free agent upon the conclusion of 2016. As we have seen countless times, the allure of impending dollars was more than enough to jumpstart Ramos' bat and before you knew it, he was sitting there with career-bests in home runs (22) and batting average(.307) by the end of September. Unfortunately Ramos couldn't quite get through the last two weeks of the season untouched by injury as he suffered a torn ACL in his knee that cost him the playoffs for the Nats. The timing was terrible of course with free agency on tap but Ramos still figured on receiving a lucrative contract given his very rare offensive numbers from behind the dish. A few things to note though before making an investment for 2017 is that Ramos' numbers last season clearly belong in the outlier bin and you also have to wonder if the motivation will be there once he gets paid. Finally, the injuries remain a huge problem for Ramos and you have to pretty much take into account a guaranteed DL stint at some point during the season. Throw in the rehab from his torn ACL and that is a ton of negatives to digest when it comes to Ramos' outlook. Try and go with someone a bit less volatile if possible as catchers already cause you enough angst.

2017 PROJECTION: .271 17 HR 73 RBI 53 R 1 SB

Salvador Perez: It is extremely rare when a catcher can accumulate more than 525 at-bats in a season given all the rest days off and the injuries that crop up with donning the tools of ignorance. That is what makes the incredible durability of Kansas City Royals backstop Salvador Perez so impressive. Perez stretched to four seasons in a row in 2016 when he piled up more than 525 plate appearances and that includes two years where he went over 550 which is unheard of in today's game. Being able to have that many opportunities to swing the bat obviously helps Perez' counting numbers and last season those came out to 22 home runs, 64 RBI, and 57 runs. The RBI total was actually a bit disappointing as Perez had reached the 70-plus mark the three seasons prior but there is no denying the extreme dependability you get here. What is interesting to note with Perez as well is how his hitting profile has changed since breaking into the majors in 2011. From that debut season all the way through 2013, Perez hit .290 or above but with little power. Those trends have reversed themselves since then as Perez has hit just .260, .260, and .247 the last three years but with a total of 60 home runs in that span. Again you are buying into the dependability here despite the disappointment his average couldn't keep up with the recent power uptick.

2017 PROJECTION: .261 20 HR 72 RBI 57 R 1 SB

Evan Gattis: With the recent defection of catcher-eligible assets such as Victor Martinez, Mike Napoli, and Joe Mauer, the position has become tougher and tougher to find usable bats for fantasy baseball purposes. The Houston Astros' Evan Gattis was also part of that defection in 2015 as he became the team's full-time DH but he regained eligibility in 2016 after coming back from a hernia injury that had him beginning the year on the DL. Entering into his fourth major league season, the book on Gattis has been pretty firm in terms of being a big power guy but also someone who is a sizable liability in the batting average department. While Gattis' average remained ugly last season at .251 (mainly through a very high 25.5 K/9 rate), he was a monster in the home run department as he recorded a career-best with 32. Getting that kind of power production from your catcher is a big deal in fantasy baseball where most backstops struggle to go past 15 homers and that statistic alone puts Gattis into near-top five status at the position.

2017 PROJECTION: .248 28 HR 70 RBI 55 R 1 SB

Yasmani Grandal: Just like with Wilson Ramos, Los Angeles Dodgers catcher Yasmani Grandal was a guy we always were recommending due to a combination of remaining upside and for the dirt cheap draft price. A top catching prospect while coming up the San Diego Padres system (where he was known more for average then power), Grandal has been pretty much an all-or-nothing guy with bat with his developing home run swing leading into the 2016 season. We said to give Grandal one last try though as he was just reaching his prime at the age of 27 and the power was really beginning to take hold. Fast forward a year and Grandal played to our predictions as he smacked 27 home runs and collected 72 RBI. Yes the average remained gross at .228 as Grandal's growing penchant for strikeouts seem to know no end (25.4 K/9) but these are Evan Gattis-type numbers for a guy who comes much cheaper at the draft table. While it seems like Grandal won't ever hit over .240, a charge toward 30 homers is possible.

2017 PROJECTION: .239 28 HR 75 RBI 45 R 1 SB

Yadier Molina: Future Hall of Fame St. Louis Cardinals catcher Yadier Molina has pretty much been left for dead in today's fantasy baseball world despite the fact he can still hit for average. There is no denying the fact Molina has a ton of mileage on him and he has not reached double-digits in home runs since 2013. However Molina remains as tough a guy to strike out as any hitter in today's game (10.8 K/9) and that is why he can hit .307 like he did last season at an advancing age. Molina is pretty much like Russell Martin in terms of putting up good counting stats in runs and RBI while also excelling in one other spot (for Martin it is home runs, for Molina it is average). The best part about Molina is that you likely can get him as late as the very last round of your draft and he still would provide you a decent season.

2017 PROJECTION: .290 7 HR 56 RBI 55 R 2 SB

Sandy Leon: It is very tough to come out of nowhere and put up a decent season when you are part of the Boston Red Sox organization but such a rare happening occurred in 2016 when it came to previously unknown catcher Sandy Leon. A longtime minor league veteran who washed out of the Washington Nationals organization, Leon eventually claimed the starting catching job over the woeful Christian Vasquez and Ryan Hanigan in the middle of the season. Leon ended up being a terrific value as he batted .310 with 7 home runs in 283 at-bats. That production came in Leon's age-27 season but the average was WAY out of whack with his minor league and early major league numbers in that category. Blame can go on an insane .392 BABIP which is impossible to sustain going forward and that means Leon will see his average dip by a mile this season when many in the fantasy baseball community will be drafting him based on his 2016 numbers. Leon has bust written all over him as he was a terrible hitter in the minor leagues and his track record points to him being at best a backup at the major league level. Draft him at your own peril.

2017 PROJECTION: .260 10 HR 65 RBI 57 R 1 SB

Brian McCann: By the time you read this, Brian McCann may be on a new team. After the massive emergence of Gary Sanchez midway through the 2016 season pretty much placed McCann into backup catching duty (with some DH starts thrown in), the New York Yankees were expected to offer him around in trade talks over the winter. As far as McCann's performance last season was concerned, he was able to stretch to 9 straight his streak of reaching the 20-home run mark as he hit that number right on the nose. While 20 home runs is never anything to sneeze at when found at the catcher position, the rest of McCann's numbers were shaky as he saw 43 fewer at-bats compared to 2015 due to the presence of Sanchez and thus, saw both his runs (56) and especially his RBI totals (58) slide. Forget the .242 average as McCann has been a big liability there for the last five years (just once hitting over .250 in that span) and as he turns 33 in February, that number figures to go even lower. When you cut to the chase here, McCann's 2017 value depends almost completely on getting dealt to another team who will use him as a starter again. If McCann does find a new home, add 10-15 RBI and 3-5 home runs to his 2016 ledger as you draft him as a top ten catcher. Failure to get moved would result in McCann having nothing but backup status at best.

2017 PROJECTION (banking on a trade): .245 22 HR 68 RBI 62 R 2 SB

Russell Martin: Well past his prime Toronto Blue Jays catcher Russell Martin just won't go away in terms of fantasy baseball as he overcome a horrific start to the year (.150 average in April, .230 in May) to once again post top-ten numbers at the position with 20 home runs and 74 RBI. Serving as one of the most durable catchers in the game, Martin's career .254 average continues to fall (.231 in 2016). On the plus side, Martin's counting stats in runs and RBI are as good as it gets among catchers and that helps overcome the average hit. Turning 34 in February, a decline can arrive at a moment's notice but the always affordable draft price makes Martin a decent buy for at least one more season.

2017 PROJECTION: .242 19 HR 75 RBI 65 R 3 SB

Matt Wieters: It took more than 2 full seasons but veteran catcher Matt Wieters finally put his 2014 Tommy John elbow surgery in the rearview mirror last year when he clubbed 17 home runs and collected 66 RBI in 464 at-bats. The former 2007 first round pick has never fully lived up to the massive hype that followed him to the majors when he debuted in 2009 but Wieters continues to hit for above-average power at the position which keeps him as a top ten fantasy baseball catcher. The average took a tumble to .243 last season but a lot of the blame for that falls on an unlucky .265 BABIP. With neural luck, Wieters is a firm .260 hitter to go with the good power. Turning 31 in May, Wieters is well past the upside portion of his career but his expected cheap 2017 draft price makes him a very good late round value pick.

2017 PROJECTION: .259 19 HR 73 RBI 56 R 1 SB

Stephen Vogt: After smacking 18 home runs in a semi-breakout season for the Oakland A's in 2015, Stephen Vogt was viewed as a solid and somewhat decently-priced catcher for 2016 fantasy baseball. Vogt was actually on a big pace in his breakout year before a terrible second half slump quieted a lot of prospective pop attached to his name last spring. Pretty much the same thing happened last season however as Vogt's .277 average in the first half dropped all the way to .222 in the second which cemented his status as a fade guy after the All-Star Break. Also the 14 total home runs Vogt hit were a bit under expectations as he lost four from the year prior despite getting an additional 21 at-bats. Vogt is older than you think at the age of 32 given the late start to his MLB career and so we wouldn't look in his direction at the draft until the very late rounds. Decent but far from impactful.

2017 PROJECTION: .253 15 HR 59 RBI 53 R 0 SB

Wellington Castillo: One of the better catching values entering into the 2016 fantasy baseball season was the Arizona Diamondbacks' Wellington Castillo. While Castillo took a tour through three major league organizations the year prior, he produced throughout the season in swatting 19 home runs and collecting 57 RBI in just 378 at-bats. Despite putting up above-average power at an offensively-starved position, Castillo fell through the cracks for 2016 drafts which is why we told you to pounce on the value. Being able to settle into one locale for an entire season, Castillo performed in a solid but unspectacular way with the bat. He would lose 5 home runs from the previous season in hitting just 14 but Castillo set a career-best in RBI with 68. Strikeouts are a big problem for Castillo however as he whiffed in 26.5 percent of his at-bats last year; a struggle that will make it almost impossible for him to hit over .260. Yes Castillo did bat .264 in 2016 but that was helped immensely by a very lucky .337 BABIP. In short, Castillo once again is a serviceable fantasy baseball backstop you can snag in the last 2-3 rounds of your draft but he works best as the second option in two-catcher formats.

2017 PROJECTION: .251 15 HR 67 RBI 56 R 2 SB

Cameron Rupp: In our never-ending search for catching values in fantasy baseball, we saw the sudden upside that presented itself in the form of hulking Philadelphia Phillies catcher Cameron Rupp. Having been tabbed the starter over longtime Phillies veteran Carlos Ruiz last spring training, Rupp's 6-1 and 240-pound frame screamed out "20-home run catcher." While Rupp did not get there in 2016, he still managed a decent year with 16 home runs, 54 RBI, and a .252 average. Good but not great numbers for sure but in two-catcher formats Rupp made the grade as a starting option. That is where his value resides for 2017 as well as Rupp is limited due to his insane 27.2 K.9 rate and for the fact he managed just 36 runs in 419 plate appearances last season. In single-catcher leagues though, you can ignore Rupp almost entirely.

2017 PROJECTION: .250 17 HR 53 RBI 46 R 1 SB

Yan Gomes: How quickly things can change when it comes to the value of a given player in fantasy baseball. In 2014 it looked like the Cleveland Indians had a new star catcher on their hands in Brazilian Yan Gomes after the smacked 21 home runs and batted .278 for the team at the age of 27. Over the last two years though, Gomes has fought a losing battle to injuries and his numbers took a massive tumble. The trouble started in 2015 when Gomes had an early six-week stint on the disabled list and then wound up hitting just .231 with 12 home runs in 389 at-bats. Still many were willing to give Gomes another chance for 2016 but it was more of the same as he hit the DL in July with a sprained AC joint in his shoulder and then suffered a broken wrist in September. In between Gomes' numbers sank even further to just 8 home runs and a .190 average in 262 at-bats. Now 29 and with a medical chart that is quiet in-depth, Gomes is impossible to trust as anything more than a backup in single-catcher leagues.

2017 PROJECTION: .251 12 HR 53 RBI 43 R 0 SB

Derek Norris: It was a strange season from Derek Norris in 2016 for a number of reasons. For one, Norris was actually the very rare catcher with a power/speed game as he smacked 14 home runs and stole 9 bases for the San Diego Padres. On the negative side, Norris' .186 batting average was a joke and that followed a .250 season the year prior. What needs to be mentioned though is that it looks like Norris had one of those overall "off" years as his K/9 of 30.3 was a career-worst and his .238 BABIP was as unlucky as a hitter can get. Without that much bad luck on the batted ball, Norris would likely have hit around .250 again which would have made his overall line more impressive with the power/speed game. Not the worst idea for your catcher 2 in two-backstop formats but Norris is not a starting-caliber guy in singles.

2017 PROJECTION: .246 15 HR 54 RBI 59 R 8 SB

THE REST

Kurt Suzuki: Having already quietly put together a solid MLB career, veteran catcher Kurt Suzuki was pretty good again in 2016 as he hit 8 home runs and batted .258 for the Minnesota Twins. In fact Suzuki's average should have been even higher as his unlucky .265 BABIP held him back a bit. Still Suzuki's production last year put him just in AL-only territory and at the age of 33, that doesn't figure to change for 2017.

Travis D'Arnaud: When you lose your starting catching job to a guy who was released in spring training and struggles to hit .200 (Rene Rivera), there really must not be anything nice to say about the guy's 2016 numbers. That sums it up for annually disappointing New York Mets catcher Travis D'Arnaud who was laughable when at the plate last season as he hit just .247, while also managing to collect 4 home runs and 15 RBI in 276 at-bats. Prior to last season, the disappointment regarding D'Arnaud centered on the fact he couldn't ever stay healthy but now it is both the DL stints and a bat that was as listless as any hitter in the game in 2016. Turning 28 in February, D'Arnaud is now past the prospect stage of his career and the Mets have shown they are ready to move on after trying to swing a deal for Jonathan Lucroy at last year's trade deadline. If the Mets don't address the catching spot during the offseason, D'Arnaud might get one last chance to save his career but the fact of the matter is that the guy looks like he doesn't even belong in the majors.

Francisco Cervelli: With very little attention, Pittsburgh Pirates catcher Francisco Cervelli has been a quietly effective hitter at a habitually weak offensive position in his career. In fact Cervelli has been the very rare catcher who can hit for average, as he batted .301 and .295 from 2014-15. The flip side is that Cervelli has zero power and more concerning is the fact the guy can't ever stay healthy. 2016 saw Cervelli limited to just 101 games as he battled maladies all over his body and his offense sank badly as he hit just .264 with 1 single home run. While Cervelli still has decent tread on his catching tires at the age of 31 (due to inconsistent playing time early on in his career), you simply don't get enough offense here to make owning him outside of deeper two-catcher formats worthwhile.

Nick Hundley: A free agent as of press time, aging catcher Nick Hundley enters into the open market coming off a mediocre 2016 season where he hit just 10 home runs and batted .260 for the Colorado Rockies. Once again missing a significant amount of time with injury, Hundley didn't exactly take advantage of the thin air in Coors Field to set himself up for a sizable payday. The .301 that Hundley batted in 2015 went down as the fluke it was (due to a lucky .356 BABIP) and so he should only be graded as the .260 hitter he was last season (again despite having the advantage of hitting in Coors Field). Having turned 33 this past September, there is no guarantee Hundley will even find a starting job this winter.

Chris Herrmann: A very light-hitting backup catcher with the Minnesota Twins from 2012-15, Chris Herrmann had some in the fantasy baseball community looking up his name last summer when he had a decent stretch with the bat for the first time in his career. While Herrmann was able to cram 6 home runs and a .284 average in his 166 at-bats, this is the same guy who struggled to even hit .220 in the minors.

Tyler Flowers: Turning 31 in March, Tyler Flowers has reached the point in his major league career where it is not a given he even is a starter anymore. Flowers performed solidly enough in 2016 as he hit 8 home runs and actually posted a career-best .270 average but a very lucky .366 BABIP was the reason for the latter. He will likely start again for the Atlanta Braves in 2017 unless the team makes a long-rumored deal to bring back Brian McCann. Even if Flowers starts, he is barely worth owning outside of maybe just NL-only formats.

Tucker Barnhardt: Former 2009 10th round pick Tucker Barnhardt took hold of the starting catching job for the Cincinnati Reds last season but the upside here doesn't seem like it goes very high. While Barnhardt was not terrible, his .257 average and 7 home runs in 420 at-bats left a lot to be desired offensively. We do like the fact Barnhardt takes walks (8.6 percent) and has a good K rate for a catcher (17.1 percent) which could lead to an average uptick but he has a lot to prove before an actionable move would be required.

Jeff Banty: The Los Angeles Angels might have something at catcher in former 2011 31st round draft pick Jeff Banty. The kid acquitted himself quite well in his 231 at-bat debut in 2016 as Banty hit 8 home runs but the .234 average shows that some work needs to be done before he can be looked at as a possible fantasy baseball option in two-catcher formats. Someone to watch early in the season.

Blake Swihart: The nice 2016 performance of Sandy Leon behind the dish for the Boston Red Sox have now left former first round pick Blake Swihart somewhat of a forgotten man going into the 2017 season. The fact of the matter is that Swihart showed he was not ready for the majors in his debut last year as he hit just .258 with 0 home runs in 74 at-bats before he was optioned back to the minors. Even back on the farm, Swihart was not impressive as he batted a woeful .243 at Triple-A with 1 home run in 122 at-bats. That made it 1 home run in almost 200 total at-bats which is obviously not impressive and Swihart also dealt with injuries that stunted his growth. Could get another chance in spring training but this is Leon's gig to lose given his performance last season.

Mike Zunino: There may not be a more pronounced home-run-or-nothing player in all of baseball than Seattle Mariners catcher Mike Zunino. Over the last three years, Zunino has really impressed with his power in hitting 22, 11, and 12 home runs but that has been matched with batting averages of .199, .174, and .207. Even with someone with the type of big-time power that Zunino has, you can't have that on your fantasy baseball team given the hurt he puts on you everywhere else.

FIRST BASE POSITION OVERVIEW

    In one of the most obvious statements to be made concerning fantasy baseball, the first base position remains ground zero for the most impactful and high-end power bats in the game. While third base recently has closed the gap some, first base is where you ideally want to double-dip in terms of using bats from this position filling your 1B and CI/UTIL spot. We always reiterate that despite the immense depth at the position, you want to have one of the stud options on your team by the end of Round 2 if you can. The five-tool outfielder/first base combo for the first two rounds is still the way to go but we also now will sign off on a top third baseman to go with the five-tool outfielder as your first two picks as long as you address first base in Round 3.

Paul Goldschmidt: Five-tool players in fantasy baseball are the gold standard when it comes to annual drafts and in almost every case, it is the outfield or middle infield where these first round superstars are mostly found. The first base position has seen one of their own end up in this hallowed class the last few seasons in terms of the Arizona Diamondbacks' Paul Goldschmidt. Already a five-tool first round star entering into the 2016 season, Goldschmidt somehow took his statistical game to new heights as he went nuts on the base paths to the tune of a career-high 32 stolen bases. Not since Derrek Lee have we seen this kind of stolen base production from a first baseman and Goldschmidt has even taking it past what the former Florida Marlin was able to accomplish. Goldschmidt's stolen base prowess is pretty much unheard of at first base and when those numbers are joined by excellence in the other four standard categories, it winds up putting him in play as a top five player in all of fantasy baseball. Regarding those other numbers, Goldschmidt's 24 home runs was down from the 33 he hit the year before but he countered that by scoring a career-high 106 runs. Throw in the 95 RBI and .297 average and there is nothing Goldschmidt can't do (and do at a high level) in fantasy baseball. Still in his prime at the age of 29, Goldschmidt should not last past the fifth pick in almost all mixed league drafts.

2017 PROJECTION: .300 27 HR 100 RBI 107 R 26 SB

Miguel Cabrera: I guess Miguel Cabrera is not declining after all. That was the narrative surrounding Cabrera as 2016 fantasy baseball drafts got underway last February after the all-time great slugger came in off two "down years." What was interesting though was the fact that while many were saying Cabrera had lost some of his top-2 overall ability at the dish, the dip in his offensive numbers in both

2014 and 2015 was due more to missing games with injury than anything else. Yes part of aging means a player will experience more physical troubles which Cabrera endured in both of those campaigns but his hitting was as good as ever outside of a drop in the home runs per game rate. Consider that Cabrera batted .318 in 2014 and then followed that up with a scorching .338 for the 2015 season. With Cabrera's BB/9 and K/9 rates remaining stable in both those seasons, it stood to reason that he could go right back to being a top tier slugger if the health cooperated. Well that is exactly what happened in 2016 as Cabrera was durable throughout the whole year and as a result, shot right back to his MVP production days in slamming 38 home runs, collecting 108 RBI, and batting .316. In other words, vintage Miguel Cabrera. When you further dig into the numbers, Cabrera's 17.1 K/9 and 11.7 BB/9 rates were as good as ever and while his .336 BABIP was well into the lucky zone, the Tigers first baseman has made a career out of posting high numbers there. While Cabrera is aging as he turns 34 in April, the guy is still every bit the monster first round masher he always has been and if you can snag him in the second round again (like you were able to in 2016 drafts), then all the better.

2017 PROJECTION: .315 35 HR 105 RBI 92 R 2 SB

Anthony Rizzo: Having graduated into the late first round of drafts for the first time in his career leading into 2016 fantasy baseball, it was a decent-sized "prove it" year for Chicago Cubs first baseman Anthony Rizzo in terms of validating his breakout 2015 campaign. Well Rizzo accomplished just that as he nearly matched those numbers to a "T" as he hit 1 more home run (32-31) added 8 RBI (109-101) and exactly duplicated the runs total (94 in both) when comparing his 2015 and 2016 statistics. If you were to nitpick on Rizzo, you could point out he was a disappointing non-factor on the base paths in swiping just 3 bags (this after stealing 17 the year prior) but that was far from a deal-breaker in putting him back into the late first round area code this spring. Rizzo won't turn 27 until August and so his current level production seems like it is of the "write it in ink variety."

2017 PROJECTION: .289 33 HR 114 RBI 96 R 7 SB

Edwin Encarnacion: While there has been some noticeable slippage in veteran slugging first baseman Edwin Encarnacion's batting average the last few seasons as a concession to age, his power game remains as massive as ever as he comes off a terrific 2016 where he clubbed 42 home runs and registered a career-best 127 RBI. While in the past Encarnacion was prone to getting nicked up at times, he has been a major source of durability the last two years in posting 624 and 702 at-bats which have no doubt helped boost the counting numbers. In fact Encarnacion has become a beacon of stability as he has reached at least 34 home runs in five straight seasons and he also has made it to the 100-RBI mark in four years during that same span. Encarnacion has in fact changed as a fantasy baseball stock the last few years, seemingly losing for good the 8-10 steals he once provided and also seeing his K/9 rate inch up as well (his 19.7 mark in 2016 was Encarnacion's highest since first breaking in with the Cincinnati Reds). Be that as it may, Encarnacion takes plenty of walks (12.4 %) which helps him be an asset in runs (90-plus in four of the last five seasons) to go with the power. While Encarnacion will never win a batting title since he has settled firmly in the .265-average range, his status as a clear top five fantasy baseball first baseman remains intact.

2017 PROJECTION: .266 37 HR 116 RBI 97 R 4 SB

Joey Votto: There is hot and then there was the insanity that became Joey Votto in the second half of the 2016 season. After Votto came out of the gates in one of the longest slumps of his career (.229 Mar./April, .200 May), there were whispers that age was beginning to take a toll on his numbers or that maybe past knee problems were cropping up again. Perhaps motivated by the slights, Votto went on an epic tear during the second half of the year as he batted an unbelievable .408 with 15 of his 29 home runs. While there is no denying the fact that Votto is starting to inch up there in age (he turned 33 this past September), his rate stats are as good as ever. Arguably the most patient hitter in the game (a point that has actually earned him some criticism in the fantasy baseball community), Votto did in fact swing the bat more last season as his BB/9 dropped to 16.0 from the insanely high 20.6 in 2015. He remained impossible to strike out as well, whiffing in only 17.7 percent of his at-bats. Votto has been a rock of consistency, especially the last two years where he has hit 29 home runs, collected at least 95 runs scored, and batted .314 and .326 respectively. Finally, Votto is still holding onto the 8-10 stolen bases he always has provided, which is an added bonus at a speed-starved position. Right there with Robinson Cano, Miguel Cabrera, and Jose Altuve, Joey Votto is as good a pure hitter as there is in today's game.

2017 PROJECTION: .310 27 HR 83 RBI 99 R 7 SB

Freddie Freeman: While no one could question his talent, Atlanta Braves first baseman Freddie Freeman was a guy many shied away from in terms of drafting for 2016 fantasy baseball. What was interesting is that the reasons for avoiding

Freeman really had nothing to do with the player himself and more to do with the comical "support" that the Atlanta front office had surrounded him with the two seasons prior to 2016. With the Braves in a complete rebuild as they looked ahead to opening their new ballpark in 2017, the lineup was left almost completely bare outside of Freeman. This would prove to be a very bad thing for Freeman's fantasy baseball value from 2014-15 for a number of reasons. The first was that opposing pitchers could pitch around Freeman liberally and attack the much weaker hitters in front and behind him in the order. That cut down on the opportunities for Freeman to not only hit home runs but it also put a major hurt on his counting numbers. Secondly, when Freeman did get something to drive, often there was nobody on base for him to collect RBI's with and when on base, he was left stranded too many times to count due to the ineptitude of the other Atlanta batters. As a result, Freeman was a guy that many in the fantasy baseball community (including our publication) told you to draft only as your CI or UTIL option as his numbers would fall short of the high offensive standards of first base. What happened next had to be considered a major surprise as Freeman did more than his best with what he had in the Atlanta lineup and proceeded to post a career-year that included highs in home runs (32), runs (102), and his best batting average since 2013 (.302). Freeman also managed to collect 91 RBI and for good measure swiped 6 bases. Put it all together and Freeman performed like a top tier fantasy baseball first baseman despite the challenges he once again faced in terms of support. Looking ahead to 2017, the Braves were expected to address their lineup issues in free agency and they also began to unveil some of their very talented prospects at the end of the prior season such as shortstop Dansby Swanson. Despite the fact it seems like Freeman has been around forever, he turned only 27 this past September which means he really is just starting his prime years. Considering how complete a player Freeman already is, that is quite telling in terms of how good the future looks. Upwards we go.

2017 PROJECTION: .308 30 HR 95 RBI 108 R 5 SB

Jose Abreu: It was a bit of a winding path but Chicago White Sox first baseman Jose Abreu pretty much supplied the expected numbers for his mid-first round grade in 2016 fantasy baseball. The Cuban masher had to get on his horse though in the second-half of the season to get there as he was uncharacteristically quiet in the first half. What needs to be noted though is that Abreu has slipped in the home run department after cracking 36 as a rookie; dropping to 30 and then 25 long balls the last two seasons. Be that as it may, Abreu made it 3-for-3 in 2016 with regards to reaching the 100-RBI mark and his .293 average was right where it should be when examining his advanced numbers. While you would like to see Abreu walk more (6.8 BB/9) he separates himself from other slugging first baseman in terms of not being an easy guy to whiff (career-best 18.0 K/9 last season). While the mid-first round grade is not likely to be repeated this season, Abreu seems like a very safe investment no matter where you get him considering his already impressive numbers and the fact he is in his prime at the age of 30.

2017 PROJECTION: .297 27 HR 104 RBI 79 R 1 SB

Eric Hosmer: While Kansas City Royals first baseman Eric Hosmer has burned more than a few in the fantasy baseball community as he developed at a young age in the major leagues, the former third overall pick in the 2008 draft had a semi-career season in 2016. We say semi-career season based on the fact that Hosmer set a personal best in home runs with 25 and in RBI with 104. On the flip side, Hosmer disappointed a bit as his average sank to a very mediocre .266 (down from .297 in 2015) and he lost 18 runs from the season prior (80-98). Hosmer has already made a career in terms of putting up numbers that are all over the map and so what he did in 2016 was just par for the course. He became a bit more of a free-swinger last season as his K/9 jumped up a bit to 19.8) and Hosmer's BB/9 slipped a bit to 8.5 which contributed to the average dip. Keep in mind though that Hosmer was likely pressing some as the Kansas City lineup was ravaged with injuries last season, an issue that had him take on more of the offensive load. Finally, the earlier double-digit steal totals that Hosmer posted from 2011-13 (11, 16, and 11 respectively) seem to be gone already at the age of 27 since he has not topped 7 in any of the last three years. As a result, draft Hosmer as a 4-category first baseman who still has a smidge of upside remaining.

2017 PROJECTION: .288 24 HR 98 RBI 88 R 6 SB

Wil Myers: Just when it started to look like Wil Myers would never live up to the sizable hype that surrounded him when he first arrived on the major league scene with the Tampa Bay Rays, the guy put it all together in a better-than-anyone-expected 2016 campaign. The key to Myers' breakthrough was the fact he finally stayed healthy after enduring lengthy DL stints ever year from 2013-15. Finally figuring out how to stay on the field, Myers' power and athleticism did its thing as he hit 28 home runs, stole 28 bases, scored 99, runs, and collected 94 RBI. About the only negative thing you could say about Myers' season was that his average was a underwhelming at .259 but that was never his strong suit to begin with (.257

career hitter). While Myers strikes out too much (23.7 K/9), he offsets that by drawing a high number of walks (10.1 BB/9). While we do hate the ballpark, Myers is still very young (26 this past December) and thus, he has some ceiling left to tap into. Also Myers hit 18 of his 28 home runs at home and batted over .300 there which means the dimensions of Petco Park should not be held as much against him. A 30/30 year is not out of the question given what we have seen but Myers has to prove he can continue to stay healthy. Health is the biggest issue here going forward as Myers has not shown he can consistently stay on the field but this kind of speed at first base is almost impossible to find (outside of only Paul Goldschmidt). In fact you can call Myers by the name of Goldschmidt-lite given the similar numbers outside of batting average and the Padres first baseman will come a few rounds cheaper.

2017 PROJECTION: .259 26 HR 90 RBI 92 R 25 SB

Chris Davis: With Mark Trumbo mostly manning the DH spot for the Baltimore Orioles in 2016, the first base job fell almost full-time to Chris Davis. Arguably the most potent pure power hitter in all of baseball, the story has remained steady here in terms of Davis hitting a massive amount of home runs, to go along with very good numbers in runs and RBI. Last season was par for the course as Davis smacked 39 homers, drove in 84, and scored 99 times. As anyone who has invested in Davis in the past knows however, the guy also comes with an extreme batting average negative (.250 for his career, .221 in 2016). Pretty much performing like Adam Dunn used to, Davis' 32.9 K/9 rate last season made it five of the last six years he has been over the 30.0 mark in that category. A classic "he is what he is" guy, Davis is a terrific power anchor for your team but he also can be annoying to draft due to the fact you need to make it your mission to fill out the rest of your roster with .300 hitters to overcome how bad his average hit will be to your team.

2017 PROJECTION: .234 40 HR 99 RBI 97 R 2 SB

Carlos Santana: While there is still a longing in the fantasy baseball community for Cleveland Indians first baseman Carlos Santana to go back to donning the tools of ignorance due to the fact his very potent bat would play even better at the annually shallow catcher position, the fact of the matter is that the 34 home runs he hit in 2016 would play very well anywhere on the field. The always unconventional Terry Francona surprised many by putting the slow as molasses Santana into the leadoff spot at the start of the season in referencing his high OBP and walk rates. While it the move certainly raised eyebrows, in the end Francona's strategy worked out about as well as could be given the numbers. While hitting leadoff obviously puts a bit of a hit on a player's RBI total, Santana still managed to drive in 87 and he also chipped in with 89 runs scored. A longtime batting average liability, it needs to be noted that Santana showed some tremendous strides with his hitting in 2016 as he posted a career-best K/9 rate of 14.4 percent; which ironically was the exact same number of his very high walk rate. Also while Santana's .259 average was not great, it was still miles ahead of the .230 marks that dotted his earlier years. Finally, Santana's .259 average should have been even higher but he suffered from a very unlucky .258 BABIP. In the end, Santana seems to have the batting leadoff approach down pat already and his big power makes him a very good UTIL or CI option.

2017 PROJECTION: .262 32 HR 86 RBI 92 R 4 SB

Hanley Ramirez: Boston Red Sox first baseman Hanley Ramirez is one of those rare players who really has had two distinct and completely different phases in his career. The first half of Ramirez' career centered on his incredibly productive time with the Florida Marlins where he exploded on the scene as a five-tool shortstop who became the number 1 pick in fantasy baseball leagues in a very short amount of time. The second half is where Ramirez currently is with the Red Sox in terms of being a power-driven slugger whose speed left the station years ago and whose average has tumbled along the way. Be that as it may, Ramirez is coming off a quietly very good 2016 campaign where his 30 home runs marked just the second occasion (and first since 2008) where he reached that power plateau. Ramirez also contributed a career-high 111 RBI and batted a solid .286 (this just a year after hitting .249 in 2015). While Ramirez no longer carries anywhere near the flash he once did when he was posting 25/25 seasons with the Marlins, he still stole 9 bases in 2016 to at least be a contributor in all five categories. Again it needs to be said that Ramirez will be 33 when the 2017 season gets underway and his K/9 rate has risen steadily over the years (his 19.4 last season was the fourth year in a row that showed an increase) as he sells out more and more for home runs. You also have to remember that until he finally stayed in one piece a year ago, Ramirez was nothing but an injury-marred mess every season form 2012-15. Another year older means that Ramirez stands a good chance of getting hurt again and his recent average fluctuations also mean he is no lock to hit over .280 either. This feels like a case of the fantasy baseball community trusting Ramirez again off his big 2016 but then age/injury crop up to make him a decent bust candidate this season. You have been warned.

2017 PROJECTION: .277 24 HR 90 RBI 77 RBI 7 SB

Brad Miller: After bombing out in the Seattle Mariners organization despite being given plenty of chances to show what he could do in his three-season stay in the Pacific Northwest, it appeared as though former 2011 second-round pick Brad Miller's major league career was already on life support. Enter the Tampa Bay Rays who never met a reclamation project they didn't think they could fix and then sat back and watched Miller slam 30 home runs (19 more than his previous high) for the team in 2016. Say what? In what was clearly one of the most unexpectedly great performances of the 2016 season, Miller literally crushed it for the Rays. In almost every way, Miller exceeded expectations and his previous hitting rates by a mile and that is what makes forecasting him for 2017 so difficult. On the surface, it is easy to surmise the "outlier effect" that Miller's 2016 qualifies for since he has never approached anything like that before. In fact when coming up the Seattle system, Miller was known more for a batting average talent and an ability to go maybe 15/15 with his power/speed. Now Miller doesn't run much anymore (only 6 steals last season), the average has been terrible from day 1 in the majors (.243 a year ago) but yet the power exploded at an unfathomable rate. It has become obvious that Miller is selling out for power like he never did in the minors, with his 2016 K/9 rate of 24.8 percent showing how much he is swinging for the fences. A .277 BABIP was unlucky which means Miller could be more of a .260 hitter going forward but either way it looks like it is home runs or bust now for the guy. That makes it somewhat of a razor thin margin in terms of turning a profit on Miller for 2017 fantasy baseball. Either he replicates the production from last season in the power department (which we have our extreme doubts about) or he goes into the bust bin. There are too many moving parts here for our liking so it is best if you avoid Miller altogether.

2017 PROJECTION: .257 24 HR 77 RBI 71 R 5 SB

Albert Pujols: While he didn't match the spectacular 40 home runs he hit in a comeback 2015 campaign, Los Angeles Angels first baseman Albert Pujols was still very solid last season in swatting 30 long balls and collecting 119 RBI at the age of 36. With Pujols' days of being a first round mashing monster having fallen by the wayside since 2012, the guy continues to hold onto his power as he continues on into his late 30's. There are still some obvious negatives though, such as the fact Pujols' runs don't go much over the 80 mark now and his average has been under .270 three of the last four years. While he has not fallen flat on his face yet (which looked like a strong possibility after his horrific 2013), Pujols should only be drafted as your CI or UTIL batter. Try and get some more upside there if you can however.

2017 PROJECTION: .259 28 HR 93 RBI 78 R 3 SB

Adrian Gonzalez: Long one of the better values at first base in fantasy baseball, the Los Angeles Dodgers' Adrian Gonzalez was a disappointment in 2016 as he failed to hit 20 home runs for just the second time in his last 11 seasons as veteran finished with a paltry 18 in 633 at-bats. Age was being blamed for the slip and there could be some merit to that as Gonzalez' K/9 rate of 18.5 last season was his worst mark there since 2008. Even more troubling was that Gonzalez' .328 BABIP was quite lucky and so his .285 average should have been a bit lower to go with the drop in home runs. Turning 35 in May, Gonzalez may not be aging as well as a David Ortiz and his outlook appears quite murky. Gonzalez' tough year in 2016 could very well be a one-year anomaly but without at least 20 home run, the total package of numbers leave a lot to be desired since he already is a negative in runs and steals. Decent draft price but select Gonzalez now only for your CI or UTIL spot.

2017 PROJECTION: .282 19 HR 91 RBI 72 R 0 SB

Mike Napoli: Part of the reason the Cleveland Indians had so much success in the 2016 season was due to hitting it big on some under-the-radar veteran signings such as the one-year deal for $7 million they gave to Mike Napoli to man first base. After being forced into a bit of a journeyman role for both the 2014 and 2015 seasons, Napoli showed he was not done yet as far as being a starting-caliber hitter in the major leagues in 2016. Power has always been the calling card for Napoli and he went nuts on that front in clubbing a career-best 34 home runs to go with personal bests in runs (92) and RBI (101). Napoli remains a hacking slugger through and through, as his K/9 rate of 30.1 went right along with his normal rates in that category. As a result of such a high K rate, Napoli's .239 average is far from a surprise and that has been the biggest knock on his career. A free agent as of press time, it makes too much sense for Napoli and the Indians to not extend their relationship for at least one more season. Resist the urge though to pay for what Napoli accomplished in 2016, as great as those numbers were. Having turned 35 on Halloween, Napoli will undoubtedly come back to earth some in 2017 considering his statistics from last season were in outlier territory. On the flip side, nobody will want Napoli at the draft which will once again make him quite attractive when you factor in the expected 20-25 home runs.

2017 PROJECTION: .234 26 HR 88 RBI 81 R 4 SB

Brandon Belt: Stop waiting for the breakout that is never going to come. An annual topic of conversation at fantasy baseball drafts each season was the whole "this is the year Brandon Belt puts it all together." Well the fact of the matter is that Belt has shown he is barely even worth using in your CI or UTIL slot as he comes off a mediocre 2016 season where he hit just 17 home runs in 655 at-bats and hit an uninspiring .275. Everything about Belt screamed out mediocrity and the fact he turns 29 in April should drive home the point that there is no ceiling left to his game. In actuality, Belt's numbers last season should have been WORSE as his .346 BABIP was VERY lucky and so the batting average should have been in the low-.260 range instead. While Belt does run a bit (9 steals), the overall body of work here is not great. Throw in the fact Belt's K/9 has shot over the very high 25.0 percent mark in two of the last three seasons and you should realize how pointless it is to go back to the well here yet again.

2017 PROJECTION: .271 18 HR 80 RBI 75 R 8 SB

Justin Bour: Looking like a young Adam Lind (very good power but can't hit a lick versus lefties), the Miami Marlins' Justin Bour has become an annually good buy at the draft table. While he missed a large portion of the 2016 season with a serious ankle injury, Bour produced when on the field as he hit 15 home runs in only 321 at-bats. This just after Bour first put himself on the fantasy baseball map in 2015 when he cracked 23 home runs in 446 at-bats for the Marlins. Bour does have drawbacks such as an average that will struggle to reach .270 but he is now just getting into his prime years. If you wait until the last few rounds to address your CI or UTIL spot, Bour is the perfect guy to target.

2017 PROJECTION: .265 22 HR 77 RBI 55 R 0 SB

Tommy Joseph: After bombing out at Triple-A in 2015 when he batted just .193 in 45 games, former Philadelphia Phillies 2009 second round pick Tommy John was not fooling around in 2016 when hit the baseball hard at all levels. After cracking 6 home runs with a .347 to begin the season at Triple-A, the rebuilding Phillies promoted Joseph in May. While Joseph didn't exactly tear it up in any one month, he consistently hit with power throughout so that by the end of the season, he sat there with 21 home runs in just 347 at-bats. The power was terrific and also surprising as Joseph never came near that type of home run per game rate in the minors. One can surmise that the 25-year-old Joseph grew into his power and also matured as a hitter last season and the nice debut no doubt will earn him the inside track to the Phillies' starting first base job for 2017 now that Ryan Howard's contract has run out. Even the .257 Joseph hit as a rookie would have been better if not for an unlucky .267 BABIP, so this stock has some legs to it. Joseph's fantasy baseball profile is well off the radar entering into 2017 despite the nice initial showing and that means you could turn a nice profit here in getting him in the late rounds.

2017 PROJECTION: .267 24 HR 70 RBI 65 R 2 SB

Josh Bell: While the Pittsburgh Pirates have been known for their monster stable of outfield prospects that have come through their farm system, they also have developed a pretty promising first baseman in Josh Bell. The former 2011 second round pick (61st overall) debuted in 2016 with some decent results; hitting .273 with 3 home runs in 152 at-bats. Clearly a small sample size, Bell has raw power that should have him around 25 home runs before too long. Even more impressive then the power perhaps is the fact Bell has a terrific approach at the plate that includes impressive K/9 rates for a young hitter and also for the fact he draws walks. Not striking out and accumulating a high number of walks is very rare when it comes to prospects who are known for power and that is what makes Bell a very intriguing sleeper pick for 2017 fantasy baseball.

2017 PROJECTION: .280 17 HR 62 RBI 55 R 4 SB

Chris Carter: The scouting report on mammoth slugger Chris Carter has pretty much been written ink since he first solidified a spot in the major leagues back in 2012. Pound-for-pound one of the strongest players in the game, Carter is your classic three-outcome hitter (walk, home run, or strikeout). It was more of the same on that front in 2016 as Carter slammed a career-best 41 home runs, walked in 11.8 percent of his at-bats, and put up an ugly .222 batting average. Overall it was actually one of Carter's best-ever seasons in the majors, as he also set career-highs in RBI with 94 and in runs with 84. The 32.0 percent K/9 was hideous but that is what you sign up for when you draft Carter. The same theme will hold true for 2017 as well so be sure you surround Carter with a string of .300 hitters elsewhere on your team if you do decide to invest in his powerful bat.

2017 PROJECTION: .220 36 HR 91 RBI 80 R 1 SB

Matt Adams: Yes he certainly looks the part but yearly disappointment Matt Adams has never translated his size to being even a decent home run guy. Now 28-years-old and a free agent as of this writing, Adams is running out of time in terms of solidifying himself as a starting first baseman in today's game. That means his fantasy baseball value is almost nil, despite the fact Adams did finally show some signs of life in 2016 by hitting 16 home runs in just 327 at-bats. Adams has really struggled with his health over the years however and his 24.8 K/9 rate last season is a problem for his batting average (.249). While the post-hype sleeper tag could apply here, Adams is not worth chasing to find out.

2017 PROJECTION: .257 17 HR 62 RBI 56 R 1 SB

Lucas Duda: It was nothing but a nightmare season for slugging New York Mets first baseman Lucas Duda in 2016. Counted on to anchor the lineup and provide needed power on the offensively-challenged Mets, Duda managed just a woeful .231 average and 7 home runs in 130 at-bats before he hit the DL in late May with a fracture in his back. Duda ultimately was not able to return to the Mets, which ultimately made his season almost a complete disaster. Now turning 31 in February, Duda is no longer considered a young player and the fact he already is dealing with what appears to be chronic back trouble is a major concern going forward. Even when he is healthy, Duda is a very limited player in that he helps only in home runs and RBI as he has zero speed and a .247 career batting average that is littered with ongoing struggles against lefties. While Duda is fully capable of 25-30 home runs if healthy as he sits in your UTIL or CI spot, we can no longer even count on him playing on a consistent basis. Fading.

2017 PROJECTION: .248 17 HR 65 RBI 61 R 0 SB

Greg Bird: Along the same lines as Kyle Schwarber with the Chicago Cubs, the power outlook on New York Yankees first base prospect Greg Bird was viewed through some very optimistic fantasy baseball sleeper glasses heading into the 2016 season. Also like with Schwarber, Bird showed off his big natural power in a cameo role with the Yanks filling in for an injured Mark Texeira during the second half of 2015 when he slugged 11 home runs in just 178 at-bats. While Bird was not slated to start for the Yanks entering into 2016 with Teixeira healthy to begin the season, the latter's history of ill health made it only a matter of time before the kid got another shot. Unfortunately again like Schwarber, Bird suffered a season-ending injury when he tore the labrum in his shoulder which required surgery during spring training. Fast forward a year and the outlook is once again rosy for

Bird as Teixeira is off into retirement and there is a wide open first base spot waiting for him. The power is immense and natural here which means Bird could hit an easy 25 home runs and collect 80 RBI right out of the gate. The 24-year-old has holes in his swing though as he showed when he struck out in 29.8 percent of his at-bats during his 2015 debut. That means an ugly average is likely going to be part of the early equation so don't go overboard on what the draft cost will be. Still the injury from last season will keep the price down a bit on Bird and that makes him even better in terms of a draft buy.

2017 PROJECTION: .258 24 HR 79 RBI 70 R 1 SB

Pedro Alvarez: After he was dumped by the Pittsburgh Pirates (concluding a six-year run with the team), Pedro Alvarez was forced to settle for a backup 1B/3B gig with the Baltimore Orioles for the 2016 season. With Manny Machado, Chris Davis, and Mark Trumbo all ahead of him on the depth chart, Alvarez was only able to scratch out 376 at-bats. Alvarez made the most of the light playing time though as he hit 22 home runs and collected 49 RBI. The power has never been in question when it came to Alvarez as he has hit 27 or more home runs in 3 of his last five seasons but instead the trouble resides in the veteran's always high K rate and pitiful batting averages. It was more of the same there last year as Alvarez whiffed in 25.8 percent of his at-bats and so it was no shock when the average went bad again at .249. A free agent as of press time, Alvarez needs to find a starting first or third base position to bring his value back to mixed league worthiness. If he finds such a designation, Alvarez could again approach 30 home runs and 80 RBI but again with the ugly batting average. Overall we have never been a big booster of the guy given the fact the poor averages swipe some of the power positives Alvarez supplies and 2017 should be no different.

2017 PROJECTION: .248 26 HR 73 RBI 63 R 1 SB

Adam Lind: Getting traded to the Seattle Mariners last winter was a huge blow to any prospective value Adam Lind had going into 2016. Spacious Safeco Field will do that to a slugger (just ask Mark Trumbo before his home run title last season with the Baltimore Orioles) and Lind was impossible to use for large stretches of the year as he finished with just 20 home runs and a .239 average in 430 at-bats. 20 home runs was actually a decent haul for Lind considering the ballpark but the guy will be turning 34 in July and has nothing to offer outside of power. In addition, Lind is not a full-time player as he can't be in the lineup versus a lefty given his career-long struggles there. The usage meter is at an all-time low now and considering the age, Lind is best left to the wire.

2017 PROJECTION: .255 19 HR 62 RBI 55 R 1 SB

Mitch Moreland: Another power hitter who routinely slips through the cracks in annual fantasy baseball drafts is the hulking Mitch Moreland. Few probably realize that the guy has hit 22 or more home runs in 3 of the last 4 seasons but it is the rest of Moreland's statistical package that leaves you wanting. For one thing, Moreland is just a .254 career hitter and that number was very ugly for him in 2016 as he batted a woeful .233 (despite calling the launching pad of Texas his home ballpark). Yes a .266 BABIP was partly to blame for the average hit but overall Moreland is a very limited player who helps only in home runs and RBI (even there his impact is not tremendous). No matter where he ends up in free agency, the dye has been cast on Moreland as a guy who is barely even a backup in most fantasy baseball leagues.

2017 PROJECTION: .248 20 HR 65 RBI 53 R 1 SB

Brandon Moss: Leave it to the St. Louis Cardinals to be the team that reinvigorate what looked like a dead career for slugging first baseman/outfielder Brandon Moss in 2016. After the already limited Moss struggled mightily in batting just .226 with 19 home runs in a year split between the Oakland A's and Cardinals in 2015, the latter felt he still had enough juice left in his bat to contribute to the team going forward. Moss proved the Cardinals right by turning right back into the potent power hitter he was from 2012-15 as he cracked 28 home runs and drove in 67 batters in just 464 at-bats. While his .225 average was once again very ugly, Moss was hitting .270 in late August before completely going into the tank the last five weeks of the season. Having turned 33 last September, age is still an issue here and overall Moss remains a guy with clear hitting limitations. He works best in five outfielder formats as the power is still very good but Moss' 30.4 percent K/rate turns his average into a major liability. Finally, there is no guarantee Moss will be a starter in 2017 no matter where he ends up as a free agent.

2017 PROJECTION: .230 23 HR 63 RBI 56 R 2 SB

THE REST

C.J. Cron: Held back by veteran-loving manager Mike Scoscia, Los Angeles Angels 1B/DH C.J. Cron finally got an extended look from the team in 2016 and he responded in a pretty positive manner in hitting .278 with 16 home runs in 445 at-bats. These were not earth-shattering numbers by any means but Cron can swing it well enough and should be able to at the very least duplicate his 2016 haul. While he seems allergic to walks (5.4 BB/9), Cron makes very good contact for a first baseman (16.9 K/9) which means an uptick in average this season is likely. The ceiling doesn't go much higher then what we have already seen but Cron's late-round price tag make him a solid backup first base option.

Ryan Zimmerman: Just when you thought things couldn't get any worse for the oft-injured and recently underperforming Ryan Zimmerman, the Washington Nationals first baseman was truly pathetic last season in hitting just .218 with 15 home runs in 467 at-bats. The 467 at-bats were Zimmerman's most since 2013 which speaks to how injury-prone he has been and now his hitting is completely abandoning him at the age of 32. After posting a career-worst K/9 of 22.3 AND BB/9 rate of 6.2 percent, Zimmerman is going in the wrong direction everywhere. Avoid at all costs.

Dae-Ho Lee: The Seattle Mariners took a low-risk chance on signing Korean slugger Dae-Ho Lee for 2016 and they had to be impressed by what they saw as he hit 14 home runs in part-time duty for the team. Lee is older than you may think at as he will turn 35 in June but the guy has some serious power that would make him interesting as a late round grab if he gets more playing time. That is something which will be determined in spring training and if the Mariners even bring him back as Lee is a free agent. A 23.3 K/9 rate is not great which showed up in Lee's shaky .253 average and that serves as a limit to any value he may have.

Joe Mauer: If you remove the name "Joe Mauer" and instead just look at the 2016 numbers, you would be correct in assessing him as nothing more than waiver fodder. This is what it has come to now for Mauer who pretty much lost all of his fantasy baseball value when he stopped catching. Increasingly injury-prone and aging as he turns 34 in April, Mauer struggles to hit even 10 home runs at this stage of the game.   Also where he once was an annual batting title challenger, Mauer is coming off a 2016 when he hit just .261 which followed his .265 mark in 2015. Nothing but a name now.

John Jaso: Ever since losing catcher eligibility a few years ago, Pittsburgh Pirates first baseman John Jaso has been a good OBP guy who works the count and can hit for a solid average. While these are skills that certainly have a place in real-life baseball, Jaso's utter lack of power (8 home runs in 432 at-bats in 2016) make him pretty useless in fantasy. Laud Jaso's pure hitting but keep looking for a backup first baseman.

James Loney: When the woeful San Diego Padres have no use for you at the major league level, no one would blame James Loney if he packed up his stuff and went home for good. Loney stuck it out though and was rescued from the bushes by the New York Mets who needed a long-term replacement at first base after Lucas Duda went down with a back injury. Showing the good pure hitting skills that always have been part of his game, Loney stabilized things for the Mets as he batted .265 with 9 home runs in 366 at-bats. Loney remains a strong defender as well and with his mini-comeback now in the books, the veteran should be able to latch one somewhere for 2017. Alas the same "good average/mediocre power" game of Loney remains and that makes him not worthy of being drafted as he moves into the final phase of his career.

Justin Smoak: Yes it was Justin Smoak who was the main piece that the Seattle Mariners acquired when they sent Cliff Lee to the Texas Rangers back in 2010. Believing that Smoak would be a 40-home run stud, the Mariners went all in on his 2008 standing as the 11th overall pick in that year's draft. It would be all downhill from there though as Smoak has proven to be nothing but a 20-home run bat who struggles to hit even .220 as he flamed out in Seattle and has been nothing but a backup first baseman in Toronto. Even though Smoak is still relatively young (he will be 30 to begin the 2017 season), his production is set in stone here which makes him someone to own just in AL-only formats.

Kennys Vargas: Having spent the majority of last season at Triple-A, Kennys Vargas is not someone you should concern yourself with in fantasy baseball terms. Yes Vargas has flashed some ability in cup of coffee stints in 2015 and 2016 with the Minnesota Twins but a 32.2 K/9 in 177 at-bats last season really show the limitations here.

Justin Morneau: Not ready to throw in the towel on his career just yet, Justin Morneau made his way back to the majors in 2016 with the Chicago White Sox last season where he got into 56 games and accumulated 281 at-bats. He did all right too as Morneau hit .261 with 6 home runs which should get him an invite somewhere for 2017 spring training. The power has not been great since his Minnesota Twin days and Morneau has been a big injury mess the last five years. A good career without a doubt but it is time to move on from the veteran for good.

Tyler Austin: With Mark Teixeira now into retirement, it will be a spirited spring training battle between Tyler Austin and Greg Bird to replace him for 2017. While Bird missed all of last season recovering from a torn labrum in his shoulder, Austin got a shot to show what he can do during the second half of the year. Austin certainly had a smashing debut as he cracked a home run in his first start for the Yankees but the rest of the year was tough sledding as he batted just .241 in 90 at-bats. An older prospect at 25, Austin was almost released by the Yankees after a rough 2015 but he stuck with it and got himself to the majors. The problem with Austin is that he is a strikeout machine at times (a ridiculous 40.0 K/9 in his debut campaign) and the power doesn't seem like it is anything special. He can also play the outfield though which at least gives Austin a better chance to stick with the Yankees. Someone to watch in spring training but don't chase during the draft.

Byung-Ho Park: We were not on board with the decent amount of hype that was attached to Minnesota Twins first base Korean import Byung-Ho Park heading into the 2016 season. While there was no doubting the pure power that Park had in his bat, we correctly predicted that his massive issues with strikeouts would make him impossible to use in fantasy baseball terms. That is exactly what happened as Park hit just .191 and struck out in 32.8 percent of his at-bats before the Twins demoted him to the minors in July. Park never made it back to the big leagues as he hit a still woeful .224 at Triple-A before suffering a tendon subluxation in his hand that required season-ending surgery. While the 12 home runs Park hit in 215 at-bats with the Twins was impressive, the 30-year-old was the definition of an all-or-nothing player who has almost no value in fantasy baseball leagues.

Ben Paulsen: Well that didn't go well. There was at least some intrigue surrounding Colorado Rockies first baseman Ben Paulsen going into the 2016 fantasy baseball season; mostly due to the Coors Field appeal. A somewhat mediocre prospect while coming up the Colorado farm system, Paulsen was downright horrific when given a chance to solidify the starting first base spot for the Rockies last season. Hitting just .217 in 39 games with 1 home run, Paulsen was optioned back to the minors where he is likely to stay to begin 2017. Look on by.

Yonder Alonso: The narrative of veteran first baseman Yonder Alonso being an empty power bat, despite his position being filled with monster offensive players, remained true in 2016. The former top prospect in the Cincinnati Reds system has simply never developed in terms of power and last season was no different as he hit just 7 home runs in 532 at-bats for the Oakland A's. Even Alonso's usually decent batting average was a negative as well as he put up a listless .253 mark. With no power and now an average that stinks, Alonso should not come off the wire for all of 2017.

Chris Colabello: An early 80-game PED suspension derailed Chris Colabello after only 10 games of regular season in 2016 and the annoyed Toronto Blue Jays front office sent him right down to the minors when his sentence was through. Colabello managed to hit just a pathetic .185 on the farm and so you have to think his major league career could be in serious jeopardy.

Billy Butler: Even the budget conscious Oakland A's had enough with the incredibly light hitting of DH/1B Billy Butler in 2016, designating him for assignment late in the year after hit a pathetic .274 with all of 4 home runs in 221 at-bats. Butler would latch on with the New York Yankees for the final 29 games (where he actually showed some life by hitting .345) but the dye has been cast now regarding how he is barely even a major league player at this stage of his career. Could get a shot somewhere else for 2017 but Butler should not be on any fantasy baseball team this season.

SECOND BASE OVERVIEW

For the first time in over 5 seasons, Robinson Cano was not a first round pick in 2016 drafts as he came off a somewhat rough 2015. Cano certainly came all the way back last season as a top-end hitter however but his age and continued nerves in the fantasy baseball community regarding his home park will likely keep the Seattle slugger in the second round conversation. However Houston Astros dynamic second baseman Jose Altuve went in the late first round in some drafts a year ago (a spot we told you he deserved while others said the opposite) and off his ridiculous fantasy baseball MVP campaign in 2016, it will likely take a top-3 pick to get him this time around. In fact we believe Altuve is worth the number 1 overall pick despite the knee-jerk habit of going with Mike Trout there. Altuve is the true definition of a five-tool monster, whose rise to the 20-plus home run plateau for the first time in his career last season further elevated his already sky-high status. Then there is the ridiculous performance of the Washington Nationals' Daniel Murphy who put up an MVP year in 2016. His numbers puts Murphy in second round territory but there could be fears that what he did a year ago was an outlier. Even though we suggest going first base/third base/five-tool outfielder as some combination with your first two picks, you MUST take Altuve if you have any shot at him. Failing to get Altuve, your best bet is to wait for value here past the third round where very effective options like D.J. LeMahieu, Ian Kinsler, Jason Kipnis, and Matt Carpenter should be available. Also be sure stolen bases are attached to any of your middle infield picks.

Jose Altuve: Just when you thought the spectacular offensive performances of Houston Astros second baseman Jose Altuve couldn't get any better, the 5'7 dynamo goes out and puts forth what can only be described as a fantasy baseball MVP campaign in 2016. Already firmly established as a batting title hitter who also possesses some of the best stolen base speed in the game, Altuve unveiled a new trick last season when he reached career-highs in home runs with 24, runs with 108, and RBI with 96. You almost had to shake your head at how insanely great Altuve was last season as he also filled up the other two standard ROTO categories by stealing 30 bases and almost winning a batting title with a .338 average. Put all those numbers together and Altuve was the clear number 1 player in all of 2016 fantasy baseball. Want some more ridiculous numbers? Try a K/9 rate of 9.8 or a BB/9 of 8.4. Or that Altuve has hit over .320 in four of his last five seasons (with two of those years going over .340) Turning just 27 in May, Altuve is really just now entering into his prime years which is crazy to think given the monster numbers he is already putting up. The only possible issue we may have with Altuve is that the 24 home runs reek of an outlier performance but then again the guy is so incredibly skilled that nothing is impossible for him by the looks of it. While many in the fantasy baseball community will reflexively go with Mike Trout number 1, there is a firm case to be made that Altuve deserves the nod. You won't get an argument from us.

2017 PROJECTION: .322 20 HR 88 RBI 110 R 35 SB

Daniel Murphy: What on earth was that? By almost any measure, what Washington Nationals second baseman Daniel Murphy accomplished in the 2016 fantasy baseball season can be considered nothing short of phenomenal. In fact it was downright silly how crazy good Murphy was with the bat from the start of the year all the way through September as he fell just short of the NL batting title with a .347 average, while also setting a career-high in home runs with 25 and in RBI with 104. Throw in 88 runs scored to go with 5 steals and Murphy was on the short list as fantasy baseball MVP. Of course this magical run for Murphy began getting put into motion during the 2015 postseason with the New York Mets. After hitting just 14 home runs during the regular season (which was actually a career-high at the time), Murphy went to work in the cage prior to the start of the playoffs with hitting coach Kevin Long to try and generate more power with his swing. Long reportedly had Murphy move a bit closer to the plate so that his swing would get through the strike zone with increased velocity, which he theorized would add more home runs to his bat. 7 home runs that postseason and 25 more later in 2016 show that Long's strategy worked with beyond outstanding results. Even prior to the power uptick, Murphy was generally considered one of the better pure hitters in baseball while with the Mets as he routinely put up some of the best K/9 rates in the game and he also seemed to constantly put the bat on the ball. Still Murphy was mostly a .290-.300 hitter before going nuts last season which didn't hint at the .347 mark to come. Now of course there was some BABIP luck involved as it would be for anyone hitting for such a great average as Murphy was in the very lucky realm there at .349. While that number is very well into the lucky range (.around .300 is neutral), keep in mind that from 2011 through 2014, Murphy's BABIP was .315 or higher in each of those seasons. So we can conclude that Murphy is one of those guys who can stay ahead of the BABIP curve since he has decent speed and again always puts the bat on the ball. Now as far as the power is concerned, 25 home runs is a big outlier number compared to Murphy's career rates and so the easy assumption would be to move him back toward the 20 mark or lower for 2017. While the trends do say to go this way, keep in mind that since Long made the correction with Murphy's swing, the homers have flown out at a consistent rate since. Also Murphy hitting in front of Bryce Harper all season resulted in seeing a ton of fastballs after his teammate came off his own video game-like 2015 campaign. Since that particular lineup setup is almost guaranteed again for 2017, Murphy will continue to see a steady stream of fastballs to drive all over the park. So when combined together, Murphy has a better chance of being in the 20-25 home run range then going back to the teens. About the only thing you can knock Murphy about is his vanishing speed, as he swiped only 5 bags a year ago. Murphy did have a two-year burst where he swiped 36 bags from 2013-14 but those days seem finished for good. So while we don't expect a .347 batting average again, we also think Murphy can be a huge force with the bat in 2017 based on the advanced numbers and the lineup situation in Washington.

2017 PROJECTION: .322 23 HR 101 RBI 91 R 6 SB

Robinson Cano: As we already mentioned in the second base overview, for the first time in years, Robinson Cano was not a first round pick in 2016 drafts. This was no shock really when you consider that Cano's numbers both in 2014 and 2015 were down more than a bit from his monster days with the New York Yankees. The fact that both those seasons were Cano's first in Seattle and spacious Safeco Field was no coincidence either. It was both the downturn in numbers and the ballpark that sent Cano's stock sliding sharply in drafts last March and again that made sense given what he had produced the two years prior. Well Cano certainly changed that narrative in 2016 as he exploded back to his old near-MVP self, cracking a career-high 39 home runs, setting another personal best in runs with 107, and reaching the 100-plus RBI mark (103) for the first time since his last year with the Yankees. Throw in the .298 average and Cano was as good a four-category producer as anyone in fantasy baseball last season. Why the sudden uptick? The key here was that Cano apparently was dealing with a chronic sports hernia both in 2014 and the first half of 2015 which hurt his numbers. The hernia apparently caused a stomach ailment that also curtailed Cano's production but he had that issue remedied at the 2015 All-Star Break. Almost immediately after the procedure, Cano began pounding the baseball again as he batted a scorching .331 with 15 home runs during the second half of that season. Cano's mega-production set the stage for a full comeback to top tier status last season and the rest as they say is history. Getting back to the numbers, Cano's 14.0 K/9 rate in 2016 was right in line with his Yankee years, meaning age is not a factor yet in his offensive game. He is in fact walking less than ever before though and the ballpark issue means Cano's days of being a .310 or above hitter are over. Also Cano's days of running are finished as well since he has swiped just 2 total bases the last two seasons. Other than that however, Cano seems safe to fully invest in for 2017 fantasy baseball, despite the fact he will go into the year at an advancing age of 34. Perhaps the best part here is that despite coming off a career-best power season, Cano will not likely go back to his old first round days given some fears in the fantasy baseball community about the age factor and ballpark.

2017 PROJECTION: .299 33 HR 102 RBI 104 R 1 SB

Ian Kinsler: It seems like hitters are aging better and better these days as we watched David Ortiz go off into retirement with an MVP-worthy performance last season at the age of 40. While he is not that old, Detroit Tigers second baseman Ian Kinsler is aging nicely himself, as he comes off a performance last season that deserved some quiet MVP mention. While Kinsler was still a decent hitter from 2013-15, his overall numbers were slipping on the surface as his power and stolen bases fell under 18 in every one of those seasons. As a result, Kinsler was drafted in 2016 as a fallback second baseman when the other big names were off the board. Well those who yawned when they drafted Kinsler got the last laugh as he morphed back into his old Texas Ranger days by hitting 28 home runs (his most since cracking 32 in 2011), scoring 117 runs (again his most since 2011), and batting .288 at the top of the Tigers lineup. While Kinsler still doesn't run much, he is not a zero yet in that category as he swiped 14 bags. Throw in the 83 RBI Kinsler collected and his 2016 haul was a pleasant surprise. Still under contract with the Tigers for 2017, Kinsler will enter the year another year older at 34 and his long history of injuries is something that can't ever be ignored. In Kinsler's defense, he has been very durable since leaving the Rangers for the Tigers but his health still has to factored into the draft price. Kinsler's 16.9 K/9 rate last season was perhaps a hint that he may be losing a smidge of ability as a pure hitter but again the numbers were so terrific overall that this is quibbling. What you always do in situations where a guy goes off unexpectedly is to draft him with numbers in mind that are dialed back some. This is the smart way to go to prevent yourself from overpaying and it is a strategy that is correct way to go with Kinsler for 2017.

2017 PROJECTION: .284 20 HR 81 RBI 100 R 15 SB

Brian Dozier: Yes we admit it. We told you all to avoid Minnesota Twins second baseman Brian Dozier for 2016 drafts and 42 home runs, 104 runs, and 99 RBI's later, there was plenty of egg on our faces. The reasoning we were so down on Dozier entering into the year was pretty obvious. The guy had just put a 2015 performance in the rearview mirror where his stolen bases slipped sharply and his .236 average stretched to 4 seasons out of 4 where he could not even bat .250. While the 28 home runs were nice, such an ugly average takes some starch out of the power numbers as any fantasy baseball veteran would tell you. With four MLB seasons in the books, we felt there was enough of a sample size to draw our "try and avoid drafting" conclusion but Dozier's insane 2016 numbers said otherwise. Getting back to the numbers, not only did Dozier set a career-best in home runs by 12, his overall hitting improved as well which was perhaps even more important to his value. Dozier's final .268 average was almost like he hit .300 considering the very bad struggles he previously had in this area. In addition, Dozier upped the steals to 18 (gaining 6 from 2015) which again boosted his bottom line fantasy baseball standing. Now of course we have to throw a bit of cold water on Dozier's performance by pointing out the outlier aspect that is in play here. Dozier was far-and-away above his career norms both in home runs and batting average and so this needs to be factored into what you will pay for him in 2017. We can easily see Dozier slide back to 30 homers and a .250 average and that could be a bad development based on where you like will have to draft him this spring. This is why some discipline will be needed here when weighing an investment in Dozier and ideally, we would be apt to not chase the career year since that usually leads to disappointment.

2017 PROJECTION: .257 34 HR 90 RBI 101 R 16 SB

Rougned Odor: No matter what Texas Rangers ascending second baseman Rougned Odor accomplished in his terrific 2016 breakout season, there is no doubt that the first memory most will have of him last year was the Mike Tyson right he delivered to the kisser of Toronto Blue Jays outfielder Jose Bautista. The pugilism aside, Odor showed last season he is the real deal in terms of talent and you can argue there may not be a second baseman filled with more future potential then the Cuban. After all you don't see many 22-year-olds go out and hit 33 home runs, steal 14 bases, and collect 88 RBI in their second major league campaign. With a good 3-4 years before Odor reaches his prime, one can imagine a future five-category monster. While Odor's .271 average could use some work (blame goes on a very impatient 3.0 BB/9 rate), the sky literally is the limit here.

2017 PROJECTION: .282 35 HR 95 RBI 96 R 16 SB

Matt Carpenter: Another hitter who began the 2016 season under the "prove it" heading was St. Louis Cardinals 2B/3B Matt Carpenter. What Carpenter needed to prove was whether or not the out-of-the-blue 28 home runs he hit in 2015 were in fact legitimate or a major outlier. Consider that Carpenter's previous high in home runs was a modest 11 and there certainly was reason to question how legitimate those 28 bombs were. In terms of whether or not Carpenter accomplished this became a somewhat muddled endeavor since he missed a chunk of the season with a strained oblique. Despite the missed time, Carpenter still managed to hit 21 home runs in almost exactly 100 fewer at-bats. While Carpenter's HR pace was a bit off from what he accomplished in 2015, he was in line to finish with around 25 long balls if he stayed completely healthy. That means Carpenter has solidified his status as a mid-20's home run hitter going forward for the time being. As far as the rest of his numbers were concerned, Carpenter's batting average has been either .272 or .271 each of the last three years; numbers that were down quite a bit from the .300 marks he toted when first arriving in the majors. It is easy to see that Carpenter has given away some average in exchange for more power as swings more for the fences but that is a trade-off we can accept for fantasy baseball purposes. While there is zero speed to speak of, Carpenter is a near-lock for 100 runs scored and 80-plus RBI if he avoids the disabled list. There is little overall volatility here and Carpenters retains eligibility at both second (where you want to play him) and third base. Steady as it gets.

2017 PROJECTION: .273 24 HR 78 RBI 99 R 2 SB

Dee Gordon: One of the biggest bombshells during the early portion of the 2016 fantasy baseball season was the 80-game PED suspension of Miami Marlins second baseman Dee Gordon. Coming off a spectacular 2015 campaign where Gordon won the batting title with a .333 average, scored 88 runs, and stole 58 bases, his fantasy baseball stock skyrocketed to the second round of drafts last March. As a result of the high draft cost, those who owned Gordon took a tremendous hit in losing him for 80 games with the season barely underway. When Gordon finally returned, he looked like a stripped-down version of his 2015 self which added to the trouble. With a final mediocre average of .268 that brought back memories of his early struggles in that category with the Los Angeles Dodgers, it made many wonder if the PED's were primarily responsible for Gordon's impressive numbers the year prior. That is a question which will be answered more definitively in 2017 but at the very least Gordon should be good for a very high amount of stolen bases and runs. Whether he can hit for a good average again is the ultimate question but there is a decent buy-low opportunity at hand here that might be worth looking into.

2017 PROJECTION: .275 2 HR 43 RBI 84 R 46 SB

DJ LeMahieu: While he deserved to get destroyed for cowardly sitting out games the last week of the season in order to clinch the NL batting title, there is no denying the fact that Colorado Rockies second baseman DJ LeMahieu has graduated into one of the very best offensive players at the position. Batting .348 and scoring 104 runs at the top of the Rockies lineup, LeMahieu's statistical profile is that of your classic leadoff hitter. When you move past the average and run totals however, the rest of the LeMahieu package is not all that great. The fact he hit just 11 home runs while calling Coors Field home was disappointing and swiping just 11 bags also doesn't move the excitement needle that much. What we can also see is that LeMahieu's .348 average needs to be thrown out, as it is almost impossible to replicate such a lofty number the very next year. The expected regression in his average alone knocks down LeMahieu's 2017 fantasy baseball stock considering the mediocre power/speed numbers. Also keep in mind the Coors Field splits are very much at work here as LeMahieu batted .391 with 7 home runs at home, while dropping to .303 and 4 long balls on the road. Again the batting title will likely inflate LeMahieu's 2017 draft price a bit too much and the lack of numbers of elsewhere leave him as someone who will likely be overrated.

2017 PROJECTION: .318 12 HR 67 RBI 100 R 14 SB

Dustin Pedroia: While he is clearly a step or two below his past MVP days, Boston Red Sox second baseman Dustin Pedroia showed in 2016 that he is not done yet being a solid fantasy baseball contributor. Now an aging 33, Pedroia's biggest challenge the last few seasons has been winning the battle against injuries. It is a battle that Pedroia has failed to conquer at times but last season was an exception as he amassed 698 at-bats (which was the second-highest total of his career). That allowed Pedroia to boost back up his counting numbers as he scored 105 runs, hit 15 homers, and collected 74 RBI. Better yet, Pedroia was back to hitting line drives all over the park as his .318 average was his highest since batting .326 back in 2008. It was an all-stars-are-aligned season for Pedroia for sure but don't lose sight of the fact he remains a major injury risk given the combination of his 5-9 size and the wear-and-tears of playing second base. As a reminder of his age and fragility, Pedroia underwent a scope of his knee upon the end of the season but he is expected to be 100 percent for spring training. While Pedroia's days of stealing bases are pretty much over (just 7 steals in 2016), his hitting rates are still in line with his career norms which lends credence to his .318 average. As long as you tread carefully here given the age, Pedroia works nicely as one of the suddenly more affordable starting-caliber fantasy baseball second baseman in the game.

2017 PROJECTION: .300 14 HR 70 RBI 92 R 8 SB

Jason Kipnis: While he may not carry the flash and excitement he once did when stealing 30 bases and hitting for power, Cleveland Indians second baseman Jason

Kipnis is still pretty darn good as evidenced by his big 2016 campaign. Doing his part on the AL Central Champions, Kipnis logged career-bests in long balls with 23 and runs scored with 91. Kipnis was no slouch everywhere else as he also supplied 82 RBI, 15 stolen bases, and a .275 average. While it is true Kipnis is no longer the guy who stole 30 and 31 bases back in 2012-13, he has offset losses there by upping the power as he moved into his prime. With the Cleveland lineup performing very well last season, Kipnis also saw a nice jump in runs, which is a category that often gets overlooked. In actuality, Kipnis is a borderline five-tool second baseman if the average ticks back up a bit but his draft price has never been cheaper as many in the fantasy baseball community reflexively move away from him after the steals started to ebb. Turning 30 in April, Kipnis is pretty set now in his numbers for the next few seasons and that puts him squarely in top ten among fantasy baseball second baseman. More toward the bottom of the top ten but still in that group regardless.

2017 PROJECTION: .281 17 HR 80 RBI 88 R 16 SB

Jose Peraza: Since the Cincinnati Reds were pretty much in a rebuilding year from the start in 2016, you wonder why it took them so long to fully unveil multi-talented infield prospect Jose Peraza. Having already been a prime prospect piece in two majors traded that took him from the Atlanta Braves to the Los Angeles Dodgers and then into the Reds organization, the talent is obvious there. For one thing, Peraza has major speed to burn and he showed this skill in swiping 21 bases in just 72 games with the Reds in his 2016 debut. Better yet, Peraza is a terrific hitter and no one-trick pony as he hit a scorching .324 with 3 home runs in his cameo. The hitting talent is quite advanced here as Peraza doesn't strike out (12.9 K/9) and his speed is going to cause a bunch of problems on the bases. Already qualifying at second base, shortstop, and the outfield, Peraza should be front-and-center on your sleeper list this season.

2017 PROJECTION: .300 8 HR 45 RBI 65 R 37 SB

Javier Baez: Yes it is possible to not even technically be a starting player but still have fantasy baseball value. Filling such a classification is former Chicago Cubs 2011 first round pick (11th overall) Javier Baez. Despite Addison Russell manning shortstop and Ben Zobrist holding down second base, Baez still got into enough games to amass 450 at-bats where he hit 14 home runs and stole 12 bases. Perhaps more encouraging for Baez' long-term prospects was the fact he also started to make strides in his previously insane K/9 rate. Baez couldn't possibly be any worse here after posting 41.5 and 30.0 marks his first two years in the league where he made had cameo stints. Doubts even began to grow about Baez' ceiling due to all those strikeouts and some even whispered he may be a Quad-A guy. Baez showed in 2016 that was not his calling however as he lowered his K/9 to a much more adequate 24.0; a sign that he is beginning to get comfortable against major league pitching. He still needs a bunch of work in terms of patience (3.0 BB/9) but at least Baez is headed in the right direction overall with his plate approach. The overall talent here is obvious as Baez can hit the baseball a mile and he also has the speed to be a good stolen base guy as well. Playing time needs to materialize a bit more consistently for Baez in 2017 for him to attain those levels but an opportunity could arise in the Cubs' outfield where he also made some appearances last season. This is a fantasy baseball stock that is now pointing firmly upwards again.

2017 PROJECTION: .275 17 HR 65 RBI 63 R 16 SB

Starlin Castro: After coming up with the Chicago Cubs with great fanfare and five category production at the very young age of 20, it appeared as though Starlin Castro was headed for stardom at shortstop. Over the next few seasons though, Castro began putting forth a string of seasons that were good but overall below expectations which eventually led to a falling out with team brass. For one thing, Castro's initial 20-stolen base speed began to vanish and his defense became a sight not to be seen. Soon the Cubs were pulling the plug on Castro last winter when they dealt him to the New York Yankees for reliever Adam Warren in what was widely viewed as a salary dump. The trade was also looked at as a condemnation of Castro who was still only 25 at the time of the deal. However when it came to fantasy baseball, the trade of Castro into the launching pad of Yankee Stadium actually made him quite interesting again. Manning second base full-time (while still retaining shortstop eligibility for one more season), Castro came through for those who bought low on him as he hit a career-high 21 home runs before suffering a season-ending hamstring injury in mid-September. Looking at the rest of the numbers, Castro's speed seems gone for good as he swiped just 4 bags and he has collected a total of just 13 in the last three seasons combined. Still the uptick in power helped overcome the loss of value in that category and Castro should continue to be graded as a 20-homer guy as long as he calls Yankee Stadium home. In addition, Castro's .273 batting average was not overly impressive and he now has hit under .275 in three of the last four seasons. Finally, Castro no longer carries eligibility at shortstop which is a semi-decent blow to his value given there is less depth there then at second base. Overall though Castro is a top ten fantasy baseball second baseman who is still in his prime at the age of 27 and who comes at a decent price at the draft table given all the negative commentary on him during his Cub years. Dependable but no longer very flashy.

2017 PROJECTION: .275 22 HR 71 RBI 67 R 5 SB

Ben Zobrist: There was a not a free agent infielder that more teams fought over in free agency in the winter prior to the 2016 season then veteran Ben Zobrist but it was the Chicago Cubs who ultimately reeled in the veteran second baseman. Long praised for his ability to play all over the field while putting up decent offensive numbers, Zobrist began his age-35 season scorching the baseball to the tune of hitting 13 first half home runs with a .283 average. The law of averages took hold during the second half as Zobrist dropped to 5/.256 in those categories but the entirety of his season kept the guy as a daily fantasy baseball play for at least another year. What needs to be mentioned now is Zobrist is far from the guy who could threaten 20 homers and 20 steals like he did during his early Tampa Bay days but the guy still offers enough numbers elsewhere t stay relevant. In fact Zobrist is now considered to be more of an "intangibles" guy given his leadership and excellent glove as well. While 18 long balls and 94 runs scored are terrific numbers for someone who is second base-eligible, the .272 average was nothing but mediocre. Zobrist also stole just 6 bases as his days of helping in that category seem done for good. The fact of the matter is Zobrist is still not showing decline despite being in his mid-30's, as both his BB/9 (an extremely good 15.2) and K/9 (also very impressive at 13.0) show. The flash has faded since the steals have dried up but Zobrist can make the grade as a low-end starting second baseman in fantasy baseball or as a backup outfielder.

2017 PROJECTION: .270 17 HR 74 RBI 88 R 5 SB

Devon Travis: Many in the fantasy baseball community tend to have short-term memories when it comes to players and this is especially true if such a hitter or pitcher is young of age. Often a hot stretch of intriguing play followed by injury or an extended slump can quickly dull any fantasy baseball momentum that might have been building. This was such a scenario for Toronto Blue Jays second baseman Devon Travis over the last two seasons as he ran the gamut from being highly sought after to becoming waiver wire trash. Winning the second base job out of spring training 2015, Travis became an overnight sensation that April by hitting .325 with 6 home runs and 19 RBI in only 80 at-bats. It certainly looked like Travis was setting himself up to possibly be the next big thing at the always volatile second base position but then the calendar flipped to May which was when all the trouble began. A rough .189 performance that month was soon followed by a bout of shoulder soreness that eventually landed Travis on the DL. While he did make it back in July for a short 21-game stint, more shoulder pain sent Travis back to the DL for good and soon surgery was performed that offseason which prevented him from being ready at the start of 2016. After what seemed like endless waiting, Travis was activated from the DL in May and proceeded to go right back to hitting the baseball hard but with much less attention paid to his accomplishments. Batting .300 with 11 home runs in 432 at-bats, Travis showed his shoulder was sound and that he was ready to be a key contributor both for the Jays and his fantasy baseball owners. As far as the advanced numbers were concerned, Travis showed an overall nice approach at the dish, which has helped him hit for average at a still very young age (he won't turn 26 until February). A 20.1 K/9 rate looks just fine but Travis does need to show some more patience since he walked in just 4.6 percent of his at-bats last season. With age usually comes more patience and that will further solidify Travis as a decent average guy going into the future. Depending on where the Jays hit Travis this season, his counting numbers in runs and RBI should be helpful as well given how potent the lineup is. In terms of the power, we don't really know yet how high that ceiling goes but Travis has shown he can hit the baseball hard which makes 20 home runs not out of the question. Travis also possesses good speed but it has not translated yet on the base paths (just 4 steals in 2016). What should really be interesting about Travis for 2017 fantasy baseball is the fact no one is really talking about him since April 2015 is slipping out of the minds of many. That means a very good profit could be made here if you choose to go with Travis as your starting second baseman.

2017 PROJECTION: .292 17 HR 62 RBI 65 R 8 SB

Jedd Gyorko: If you are a struggling young pitcher or hitter who is on the border of flaming out, be sure to sign with the St. Louis Cardinals where everything comes out smelling like roses. Power-hitting infielder Jedd Gyorko could attest to this after he saved his fledgling career by smacking a personal-best 30 home runs for the team in 2016 while playing all over the diamond. This after the San Diego Padres gave up on Gyorko to the point that they demoted him back to the minors for a short time during the 2015 season. While Gyorko's power has never been questioned, his annually hideous batting averages drew the ire of San Diego management and that ultimately was what helped expedite his departure. Enter the Cardinals who bought low on Gyorko and them helped him unleash his best offensive season yet to this point at the age of 28. While Gyorko still posted an ugly batting average of .243, he actually made nice strides at the dish since his 21.9 K/9 rate was a career-best and he also drew a good amount of walks as shown by a very good 8.4 BB/9. When these two skills are combined together, an uptick in average is almost a guarantee. What prevented this from happening last season though was the fact Gyorko had a very unlucky .244 BABIP. In fact Gyorko's

BABIP was one of the lowest marks in baseball for a hitter with more than 400 at-bats and at a neutral .300, he would have had a chance to hit around .270 which is obviously a more digestible number. While 30 home runs is the maximum you could expect from Gyorko going forward, that is still a massive total for an infielder. Keep in mind though that there is literally zero speed here as Gyorko has not stolen a base the last two seasons. You ideally want to get a decent amount of your team steals from your infield so this is not a minor problem. On overall numbers alone however, Gyorko has graduated into firm daily usage.

2017 PROJECTION: .260 34 HR 67 RBI 65 R 0 SB

Jonathan Schoop: The Baltimore Orioles have found their second baseman both of the present and the future as Jonathan Schoop improved on an already decent breakout in 2015 by cracking 25 home runs last season for the team. Scoring 82 runs and also driving in the same number of batters, Schoop shown firmly that he is a power guy all the way. On the flip side, there is zero speed here as Schoop has 3 total steals the last two years and so he pretty much is the AL-version of St. Louis' Jedd Gyorko. Schoop has a slightly better average than his counterpart (.267) but a pathetic 3.2 BB/9 rate last season shows that he is a hacker all the way. Unless Schoop starts being a bit more selective at the dish, he won't hit more than .275 at best. We reiterate that it is tough not getting steals from your middle infielders but if you got a Billy Hamilton in the outfield, by all means take a chance on the still improving 25-year-old.

2017 PROJECTION: .266 24 HR 84 RBI 74 R 1 SB

Brandon Phillips: The end of the Major League journey is almost near for Cincinnati Reds second baseman Brandon Phillips. At least in fantasy baseball terms, Phillips has reached the stage where no one wants to go near the guy anymore in terms of ownership, as he goes into the new season at the advanced age of 35. While Phillips shocked even his most ardent supporters in 2015 by posting a semi-comeback year (.294/12-HR/23-SB), he came back to earth last season as we warned he would. Small late-career upticks in numbers are usually just a one-year blip and then the bottom begins to fall out the next year at an irreversible rate. Phillips began this movement in 2016 as he hit just 11 home runs, drove in 64 batters, and swiped 14 bases. Combined with a good .291 average, Phillips' numbers on the surface were not terrible but underneath one would see that his K rate inched up and the walk rate went the wrong way. This is an indication Phillips is currently in the erosion stage and that should be more apparent in 2017. While we have been big boosters of Phillips over the years, we can't say we recommend him for anything other than NL-only formats.

2017 PROJECTION: .281 12 HR 68 R 62 RBI 10 SB

Anthony Rendon: Yes nothing can ever change the fact that Anthony Rendon was quite arguably the biggest fantasy baseball draft bust of the 2015 season but he did do quite a bit to mend the scars in 2016. As far as that nasty trip down memory lane, pretty much nothing went right for the Washington Nationals infielder after he was one of the most sought after young players in the game coming off a five-category breakout the year prior. Going as high as the late first round in many drafts, Rendon got injured in spring training which forced him to begin the year on the DL. From there it was all downhill as Rendon was pathetic with the stick in hitting .264 with just 5 home runs and 1 measly stolen base in 355 at-bats (he would hit the DL a second time as well). Having instantly become the butt of many jokes in the fantasy baseball community, Rendon's stock really couldn't go any lower as 2016 drafts got underway. As we have seen countless times before though, the talent won out for the former sixth overall pick in the 2011 draft. Looking much more like the 2014 star-to-be,. Rendon hit 20 home runs, crossed the plate 91 times, and collected 85 RBI for the NL East winners. Rendon also began to run again as he swiped 12 bases. Nothing earth-shattering by any means as the 20 home runs did come in a massive 647 at-bats but at least Rendon stayed healthy which was the most important aspect of his season. Yes the average was a disappointment again at .270 but Rendon is capable of upping that mark to the .280-range given his good K/9 (18.1) and BB/9 (10.0) rates. Not sure how much higher the home run and stolen base elevators will go but we are still talking about a young (27 in June) player who has some upside left. Sure Rendon is not nearly as appealing as he once was but that means a decent profit can now be turned here given the affordable price tag.

2017 PROJECTION .271 21 HR 88 RBI 97 R 14 SB

Neil Walker: At least for the first month of the 2016 season, it looked like the New York Mets made out just fine in swapping out Daniel Murphy for Neil Walker at second base. That is because Walker matched Murphy with a monster April as he slammed 9 home runs, collected 19 RBI, and hit .307 which were career-best rates on a per game basis. It was obvious Walker would cool however and from May onward, he went through some extreme peaks and valleys with his hitting. For example Walker was downright putrid in June with a .214 average but then was absolutely locked in during August as he hit a ridiculous .389.

Unfortunately the August hot stretch was not allowed to go into September as Walker was forced to undergo season-ending back surgery. The real shame was that Walker was not able to add to his career-high tying 23 home runs and his .282 batting average was his highest since 2010 which shows how effective a season the veteran was having. Outside of the home runs, pretty much everything else was right in line with Walker's hitting norms but back surgery is a huge red flag moving forward as we can go on forever giving you examples of guys who were never the same off such a procedure. While still young at the age of 30, Walker is now a big injury risk given his back condition. His draft price is always affordable despite the yearly solid numbers but even at that cheap rate, Walker is someone who looks like he peaked in 2016 prior to his back going out.

2017 PROJECTION: .273 19 HR 71 RBI 67 R 2 SB

Josh Harrison: After barely hanging on in the major leagues as a light-hitting utility man for the Pittsburgh Pirates for three years, Josh Harrison came out and posted a nice breakout season in 2014 that saw hit bat .315 with 13 home runs and 18 stolen bases while carrying eligibility at second, third, and the outfield. It was the power/speed numbers that really caught the eye of the fantasy baseball community but we said from the beginning that Harrison's 2014 belonged clearly in the outlier "let's see him do it again" bin. Well over the next two years, Harrison was not able to do it again as he hit just 4 home runs and stole 10 bases in 418 at-bats in 2015 which pushed him back into being a mostly ignored commodity once again. He did some more running in 2016 as Harrison swiped 19 bases but the power continued to underwhelm as he hit only 4 home runs for the second year in a row. On the positive side, Harrison has batted over .280 for three straight years and he retains eligibility at second, third, and the outfield in most leagues. A serious groin injury ended Harrison's year early last season but he really wasn't missed given the light output of numbers. Having turned 29 last July, Harrison is past the age where we can expect any improvement over what he is doing now. That leaves him only as a backup bat you can plug in when injuries strike or on light schedule days.

2017 PROJECTION: .282 5 HR 41 RBI 59 R 17 SB

Logan Forsythe: A typical Tampa Bay Rays player is veteran infielder Logan Forsythe. Having eligibility both at first and second base, Forsythe is a solid hitter but overall is a guy who doesn't do any one thing well in terms of standard fantasy baseball numbers. The 29-year-old did hit 20 home runs in 2016 but with a mediocre .264 average that showed his limitations. Forsythe also was nothing special in runs, RBI, or steals which keeps his starting usage to AL-only formats. With a 22.4 K/9 rate that is getting up there and a lucky .318 BABIP that shows his .264 average last season should have even been lower, Forsythe doesn't carry much intrigue to say the least.

2017 PROJECTION: .267 17 HR 59 RBI 72 R 8 SB

THE REST

Joe Panik: As he earned plaudits for what turned out to be a very nice full-season debut in 2015, San Francisco Giants second baseman Joe Panik became a bit of a fantasy baseball sleeper entering into last year. We say Panik was bit of a sleeper due to the fact that he didn't exactly light the world on fire with his 8 home runs and .312 average in 2015 but it was a nice debut nonetheless as he was lauded for advanced hitting skills at a young age. Well 2016 was not so good as Panik fell across the statistical board by more than a little. The very good batting averages that Panik put forth in the minors and in his first forays with the Giants unraveled to the tune of a .239 mark last season. Even worse, Panik failed to make inroads anywhere else as he hit just 10 home runs in 526 at-bats (a worse rate per game than the year prior). While he will only be 26 by the time the 2017 season gets underway, Panik looks like another Scooter Gennett, which is not saying much in fantasy baseball terms.

Scooter Gennett: While we always have loved the name, Scooter Gennett has not been someone you wanted to deal with in terms of fantasy baseball given the empty batting averages he has put up since becoming a regular in 2013. Consider that going into last season, Gennett's high in home runs was 9 and his best finish in steals was just 6. That is what made it so surprising to see Gennett somewhat break out in 2016 with 14 and 8 respectively in those categories; a performance that had him moving into backup second base territory in mixed leagues. With Gennett just starting to reach his prime years, perhaps it should not be a total shock that he tapped into some more power. Be that as it may, Gennett seemed to make it a point to ditch his disciplined plate approach in order to gain more power and that trade-off showed with his slipping .263 average. In fact Gennett should have hit even lower but he caught a break with a somewhat lucky .315 BABIP. He showed a decent rise in his K/9 rate (career-worst 21.0) to cement this trend. A free agent as of press time, Gennett is still nothing but an AL or NL-only second baseman wherever he ends up given the fact his jump in home runs and steals last season belong in the outlier bin until proven otherwise.

Howie Kendrick: Another one of our favorites, Philadelphia Phillies second baseman Howie Kendrick really struggled badly with the bat in 2016. Always one of the best value plays at second base throughout his career, what you always loved about Kendrick was the way he contributed in all five standard ROTO categories without blowing up any one of them which helped keep the cost down. 2016 was not one of those years though as Kendrick's always good batting average sank to .255. It was a staggering drop in that Kendrick batted at least .285 in his nine of his previous 10 MLB seasons. A neutral .301 BABIP showed that Kendrick's average was no fluke and so at the age of 33, we can start to surmise that some erosion is at work here. While his 8 home runs and 10 steals were pretty much in line with his career numbers in those categories, the Dodgers were only playing Kendrick on a part-time basis the second half of the year which spoke to their concerns about his production. Kendrick still does a nice job drawing walks (9.2 BB/9) and his 17.7 K/9 was also very solid, which means a mini-bounce back could be in order for 2017 now that he gets a fresh start in an offensive park with the Phillies

Ryan Schimpf: It took until the age of 28 but power-hitting second baseman Ryan Schimpf finally made it to the big leagues in 2016 and needless to say, he caught the attention of the fantasy baseball community when he slammed 20 home runs in just 330 at-bats. Having hit a combined 35 home runs between Triple-A and his stint with the Padres, Schimpf is your classic hacking slugger who will strike out a ton. That means there is batting average liability being paired with all those home runs and Schimpf was that guy in his debut as he batted just .217 due to a ridiculous 31.8 K/9 rate. The all-or-nothing approach of Schimpf is why it likely took so long for him to make the majors and honestly there should be little reason for you to invest here unless your league doesn't count batting average. Since 90 percent of fantasy baseball leagues do in fact feature batting average as a category, Schimpf's struggles there and lack of any speed to help offset the damage done by all the strikeouts make him one to avoid.

Whit Merrifield: With the Kansas City Royals suffering an insane amount of injuries that ravaged their lineup last season, the door opened up for some of the team's prospects to show what they could do. Second base farmhand Whit Merrifield was one of these players and he did a decent job in his 81-game run with the team by hitting .283 with 2 home runs and 8 stolen bases in 332 at-bats. Merrifield's calling card is speed and the stolen bases that flow from it as he has swiped as many as 32 bags in the minors. This is where Merrifield will make hay in fantasy baseball as he has just single-digit power and his average was mediocre coming up the team's farm system. This makes Merrifield more of an AL-only grab for now.

Brett Lawrie: The same career theme held in place for Brett Lawrie in 2016 with the Chicago White Sox. Given yet another clean slate fresh start with the White Sox, Lawrie continued his pattern of getting hurt (this time a hamstring injury that sent him to the DL for weeks) and posting underwhelming offensive numbers (12-HR/7-SB/.248 average). A free agent as of press time, we have seen this disappointing show out of Lawrie before and your patience should have run out a long ago.

Jace Peterson: The Atlanta Braves have given two years in a row now to infield prospect Jace Peterson and needless to say, they have to feel nothing but letdown from the guy who they traded Justin Upton for. While he stole a ton of bases early in his minor league career, that skill has not revealed itself at the major league level yet for Peterson who swiped just 5 bags in 115 games for the team last season. If Peterson is not stealing a high number of bases, he is almost useless as his average is poor (.239 and .254 the last two years) and there is little power to speak of. We're not impressed.

Jurickson Profar: After losing two full seasons due to a series of serious shoulder injuries, former top Texas Rangers prospect Jurickson Profar began to show what all the hype was about in the first place before his progress was disrupted. With Profar's summer promotion having few expectations attached to it, the Rangers sat back to see if the skills were still there. The performance by Profar was a mixed bag as he got off to a hot start but then went through a prolonged slump that resulted in final underwhelming numbers of 5 home runs, 2 stolen bases, and a .239 average in 307 at-bats. The Rangers have not said what their plans are for Profar this season but anything from being the team's starting second baseman to serving as a utility guy are in play. Keep in mind Profar will still only be 24 by the time the 2017 season gets underway and so as a result, he should be targeted as a late-round sleeper at a rock-bottom price.

T.J. Rivera: Sometimes a player just knows how to swing the bat and this is a skill that New York Mets infield prospect T.J. Rivera clearly excels at. While Rivera has been a minor league stalwart since 2011, what he has done at every level is hit for a very good batting average. Consider that in 2014, Rivera hit .358 at Single-A and then followed that up with a .358 mark in Double-A. Rivera continued to pulverize Double-A pitching at the start of 2015 as well (.341) which then got him promoted to Triple-A where he batted .306. See a trend here?

Finally last season was more of the same as Rivera was hitting .353 at Triple-A before being promoted to the Mets to help replace the injured Neil Walker. Showing that the level of competition was no factor in his performance, Rivera hit .333 with the Mets in 33 games with 3 big home runs down the stretch. With Walker not a sure thing to return to the Mets in free agency the opportunity could be there for Rivera to grab hold of the starting second base job. He would instantly be a batting average boost, while also contributing a few home runs as well. Rivera ideally looks like an NL-only play but his bat deserves another close look this spring.

Jed Lowrie: At one time a useful middle infielder for mixed league fantasy baseball, veteran Jed Lowrie has become nothing but an injury-prone journeyman at the age of 32. Before having his 2016 season finished early due to ligament foot surgery, Lowrie managed only 2 home runs in 338 at-bats for the Oakland A's. Lowrie has not reached double-digits in home runs since 2013 and his .258 career batting average shows how limited an offensive player he is. Shouldn't be owned in anything but the very deepest of leagues and even that could be pushing things.

Kolten Wong: A popular sleeper as recently as 2015, St. Louis Cardinals second baseman Kolten Wong is already in jeopardy of being left behind by the team given the listless play he has shown them the last three seasons. Looking more and more like a Quad-A player, Wong's very enticing power/speed game from the minors has not shown itself at the major league level to a consistent degree. Consider that the former 2011 first round pick has batted just .249, .262, and .240 his first three years in the league and one can easily see that Wong's hitting leaves a lot to be desired. The real shame of it all is that Wong has good power for a middle infielder and he also has the speed to collect a decent amount of stolen bases as well. With Aledmys Diaz and Jedd Gyorko both taking off last season in the middle infield, Wong is suddenly being squeezed out of a starting spot though. The talent is still bubbling underneath the surface as Wong went 11/20 in the HR/SB categories in 2014 but a fresh start somewhere else might be how he can finally unleash those talents for good.

Brock Holt: The only reason you ever want to own utility man extraordinaire Brock Holt is simply due to the fact he qualifies almost everywhere on the field outside of pitcher and catcher. That has value in fantasy baseball daily leagues since you can plug him in all over the place when light schedule days arrive and for the fact you don't need to have a glut of backups on your roster filling one or two positions. The fact of the matter though is that Holt is a very mediocre hitter who is lucky if he approached the high single-digits in home runs and steals. While he has hit for average before, Holt only managed a .255 mark last season which hurts his value even more. Just draft Holt for the versatility and don't expect much of anything else.

Chase Utley: Once again a free agent at press time, the end could be approaching for second baseman and former first round stud Chase Utley. While he was expected to be a backup infielder for the Los Angeles Dodgers last season, injuries opened up more playing time then expected for Utley. He generally responded pretty well by hitting 14 long balls and scoring 79 runs in 565 at-bats. Alas Utley's average is now a clear problem as he batted just .252 and his speed has long since left the station (2 steals). With a K/9 that has now gone over the 20.0 mark (20.4), Utley is well on his way down the erosion track. He will be 38 by the time the 2017 season gets underway and will likely be a firm backup wherever he ends up.

Rob Refsnyder: A favorite of New York Yankee fans, second base prospect Rob Refsnyder got his first extended look with the team in 2016. While Refsnyder didn't exactly light the world on fire (0-HR, /.250 average), he batted .316 at Triple-A last season and has shown some decent pop in the minors as well. The Yankee infield is crowded right now with Starlin Castro at second base and Didi Gregorious at shortstop but Refsnyder also can play the outfield which at least gives him a chance to stick as a backup utility guy. In fantasy baseball terms however, there is no value here unless injuries open up a spot for Refsnyder to play on a daily basis.

Aaron Hill: Having made a career out of driving us all crazy with numbers that never went according to plan, Aaron Hill is now nothing but an aging journeyman who will only be a backup on whatever major league team employs him in 2017. With just 10 home runs and a .262 average in 429 at-bats last season, there is nothing left to talk about here.

Derek Dietrich; While he can hit a bit, Derek Dietrich is nothing but waiver wire junk due to an utter lack of impact in any fantasy baseball standard league category. Not even guaranteed a starting job for 2017, Dietrich and his empty average pretty much are useless.

SHORTSTOP OVERVIEW

While the golden days of Derek Jeter, a young Alex Rodriguez, Nomar Garciaparra, and Miguel Tejada are a clear era of the past, the shortstop position all of a sudden is quite potent again as there has been a big arrival of youthful high-end hitters such as Carlos Correa, Corey Seager, Francisco Lindor, and Xander Bogaerts over the last three seasons. In addition to those new stars, there also were some incredible values which revealed themselves last season in the form of Jonathan Villar, Aledmys Diaz, Didi Gregorious, Javier Baez, and a resurgent Jean Segura. In other words, you don't need to pay top dollar for Correa or Seager if you choose to address this spot later. Again like with Jose Altuve at second base, you don't let a Seager or Correa pass you buy if he is sitting there available when you pick at the end of Round 1 or better yet in Round 2. Always be flexible with your draft but if those two are gone, then go value in the early middle rounds where there will be more options than ever to choose from.

Carlos Correa: Other then maybe his mother, nobody loved Houston Astros shortstop Carlos Correa more than the 2016 fantasy baseball community. After all there was not a single player in the entire game that was more sought after at the draft given the massive combination of five-tool ability, qualifying at the very shallow shortstop spot, and for the insane amount of upside that still remained. Despite not even playing a full season the year prior in his 2015 debut, Correa sailed into the first round of drafts last spring given his incredible debut performance. This is what happens when you're a former number 1 overall draft pick (2012) and then come up to the majors to hit .297 with 22 home runs and 14 stolen bases in 432 at-bats as Correa did in 2015. While no one would even possibly try to knock Correa's ridiculous talents, the fact of the matter was that his 2016 production did not justify the first round price tag. In 228 more at-bats, Correa actually hit FEWER total home runs with 20 and his 13 steals were a major letdown given the additional chances to pad that number. Correa's .274 batting average was also quite disappointing and in fact that number would have been worse if Correa hadn't gotten some luck with his .328 BABIP. Yes the overall production of Correa was lacking last season but only in terms of where he was picked. When you really look at the big picture, Correa was still quite good and you must keep in mind he turned just 22 this past September. That is an incredibly young age for a hitter to be playing in the majors and so any sort of "sophomore slump" Correa went through last season should not be a total surprise. Digging into the advanced numbers a bit more, Correa shows nothing but optimism as he drew walks at a very high 11.4 BB/9 clip last season and his 21.1 K/9 rate is also very impressive for a youngster. Thus is stands to reason that the best is still to come for Correa and the fact he should slip into the second round of drafts this spring makes him even more appealing. There is no doubt in our minds that Correa is one of the brightest and most talented offensive players in the game and his status as a potential five-tool monster is still very much written in stone.

2017 PROJECTION: .281 25 HR 100 RBI 95 R 16 SB

Corey Seager: While we have been forced to speak too often in these pages about many disastrous cases of reaching too high for unproven but very high-end talented hitters (Yasiel Puig, Anthony Rendon, etc.), we actually had a case of a player making good on his elevated draft price in 2016 when it came to Los Angeles Dodgers shortstop Corey Seager. At only 22-years-old, Seager proved he was every bit worth the late second round price tag he carried in 2016 drafts as he smacked 26 home runs, scored 106 runs, and batted .308. Seager's performance conjures up memories of a young Troy Tulowitzki in Colorado but without the added benefits of operating in a power park. The pure hitting skills are immense already as Seager struck out in just 19.4 percent of his at-bats last season and many think he can challenge for a batting title real soon. Nothing seems beyond Seager's grasp outside of an impactful stolen base total (just 3 total steals a year ago) and that means he is worth whatever you pay for him at the draft once again.

2017 PROJECTION: .315 28 HR 79 RBI 110 R 5 SB

Jonathan Villar: What on earth? Who knew that instead of drafting Carlos Correa in the first round in 2016, you could have gone with Jonathan Villar off the waiver wire instead and ended up with the much better statistical season. The fact you would have likely been kicked out of your league for taking Villar even as high as Round 8 last season tells you how unexpected his insane five-category bonanza season was. Previously a failed Houston Astros prospect who batted just .243 and .209 his first two years in the majors, the light bulb for Villar seemed to go off in 2015 while he was playing for the team's Triple-A affiliate. It wasn't until Villar got a much-needed fresh start with the Milwaukee Brewers (after coming over via trade) for the 2016 season that the speedster's full potential began to manifest itself. The rest as they say is history as Villar went nuts to the tune of setting career-highs in all five standard league categories. Operating out of the team's leadoff spot, Villar batted .285, scored 92 runs, and ran all year long to the tune of an MLB-leading 62 stolen bases. Perhaps the most shocking development of all was the fact Villar smacked 19 home runs and collected 63 RBI. Considering that from 2013-15, Villar hit a TOTAL of 26 home runs between the minors and majors, one can see just how spectacular a feat that was. While it may be tough to believe in the totality of his numbers, Villar's massive speed should never be debated and his pure hitting skills have really come along from his Astros days when you see a BB/9 rate last season of 11.6. With Villar waiting for his pitch like never before, the hits began piling up and the average went northward. Now as far as the power is concerned, yes it might be tough to buy into 19 home runs again but keep in mind last season that Villar was just starting to reach his prime at the age of 25. He won't turn 26 until this May and so Villar is now just getting into his optimum power years. Yes it would be a better idea to expect 15 home runs this season and to consider anything more than that a nice bonus but the total package of Villar is beyond impressive. We are on the side that says Villar is a legit talent who should be picked during the initial first five rounds of your draft.

2017 PROJECTION: .278 17 HR 56 RBI 90 R 54 SB

Trevor Story: Headline writers had a field day with young Colorado Rockies slugging rookie Trevor Story during his smashing debut in 2016. After all it was some "Story" as the kid took full advantage of the suspension and subsequent release of Jose Reyes to claim the starting shortstop job right out of spring training, helped by a monster performance in the exhibition season (.340/6-HR/13-RBI). The 23-year-old former first round pick then proceeded to put on a massive power display that resulted in 27 home runs and 72 RBI in only 415 at-bats; not to mention 7 steals and a decent .277 average. Just like that Story was an overnight star at the most shallow position in fantasy baseball but a torn thumb tendon finished his rookie campaign early at the start of August. One can only wonder what the numbers would have looked like if Story had gotten two more months to hit but going by his rates, 35 home runs was certainly in the cards. That is a crazy amount of power for a shortstop and basically what we have here now is Story becoming the new 2012 version of Troy Tulowitzki. About the only knock we hit Story on was his sky-high 31.3 percent K/9 rate, which if not for a very lucky .343 BABIP, would have made him more of an average liability he already was. Since Story has decent speed though, his BABIP should remain in the mid-.300 range going forward and in the process lessen any negativity from that area. With three or four more seasons to go before he reaches his prime, Story could turn into an absolute monster going forward. A second round stab here is not foolish by any means. The kid is completely legit.

2017 PROJECTION: .275 34 HR 92 RBI 88 R 10 SB

Jean Segura: The change of scenery effect was in full force when it came to Arizona Diamondbacks infielder Jean Segura in 2016. Segura was an interesting case to begin with given the fact he looked like a future star in a major breakout season back in 2013 (.294, 12-HR, 44-SB) but then followed that up with two very underwhelming offensive years for the team. Having run out of patience, the Brewers dealt Segura to the D-Backs in the winter prior to the 2016 season (for Aaron Hill and Chase Anderson) but even the team couldn't have envisioned how well their buy low acquisition would turn out. Almost as if he transformed himself back to 2013, Segura exploded at the plate in setting career-highs in batting average at .319 and home runs with 20. Showing that his speed was still very much intact, Segura also swiped 33 bags and scored 102 runs. While Jonathan Villar was the shortstop value play of the year, Segura was a close second. Turning only 27 in March, Segura is really just now moving into his prime years and that is why his power output last season was not such a shock. While Segura still doesn't walk much (5.6 BB/9), his 14.6 K/9 is excellent and shows how good a contact hitter he is. Yes his .353 BABIP means Segura will see a jump back in batting average this season but everything else seems very repeatable. Fully back in our good graces, keep in mind Segura is eligible both at shortstop and second base.

2017 PROJECTION: .295 19 HR 66 RBI 98 R 32 SB

Xander Bogaerts: Upward and onward went Boston Red Sox shortstop Xander Boagerts in 2016, with career-bests reached in 4 standard league categories (runs, RBI, HR, SB), showing how good an overall player he has developed into after turning just 24 this past October. Few hitters in baseball are more disciplined at the dish than Bogaerts (8.1 BB/9, 17.1 K/9) and he has now cemented himself as a five-category star for fantasy baseball purposes. Yes we were anti-Bogaerts prior to last season but that was due to him previously showing a mostly empty batting average. That obviously is no longer an issue as Bogaerts smacked 21 home runs and stole 13 bases, while again hitting for a very good .294 last season. Another jump in numbers is very possible for Boagerts over the next few years given that he remains in front of his prime seasons and his status as a top five fantasy baseball shortstop is very much cemented in stone now.

2017 PROJECTION: .310 23 HR 92 RBI 111 R 14 SB

Francisco Lindor: While 99 percent of the fantasy baseball community preferred Carlos Correa over his second-year counterpart Francisco Lindor in terms of 2016 drafts, the Cleveland Indians shortstop was actually the better buy given his cheaper price tag and very good offensive production. As Lindor proceeded to hit 15 home runs, steal 19 bases, and bat .301; it became crystal clear that the kid was very much a legit five-category producer. Very rarely do you see a 22-year-old go out and put up a miniscule 12.9 K/9 rate as Lindor did last season and his advanced plate approach wouldn't make it a surprise if he challenged for a batting title. While Lindor's power may not go much above where he currently resides, a 20/20/315 season in 2017 is within reason.

2017 PROJECTIONL: .314 17 HR 80 RBI 102 R 20 SB

Eduardo Nunez: The 2016 fantasy baseball season was the "Year of the Monster Shortstop Value", which was an extremely profitable class of hitter that included Jonathan Villar, Jean Segura, and veteran Eduardo Nunez. Surely no one could possibly have foreseen what Nunez accomplished last season from an offensive standpoint given the fact he bombed out with the New York Yankees due to a combination of poor batting numbers and truly comical defense in the field. Just like with Segura in Arizona, a fresh start in Minnesota seemed to be the trick to clear Nunez' mind and allow his skills to take over. Boy did they ever as Nunez hit 16 home runs, stole a monstrous 40 bases, and batted .288 in a year split between the Twins and San Francisco Giants(as per a trade deadline deal). What also seemed to be the key for Nunez last season is that he finally was granted more than 350 at-bats to show what he could do and thus get into a rhythm at the dish. Always possessing impressive speed, Nunez swiping as many bags as he did was within the realm of expectation. It was the home runs that were truly shocking given the fact Nunez' previous MLB high was just five. Again the additional at-bats helped boost him in that category as well and since Nunez has now proven he can play at a high level, another full season of plate appearances should help him stay around his 2016 numbers. Yes there is an outlier component to this to be aware of but Nunez doesn't figure to see his 2017 price tag blow up as much as you may think given the fact he was such a below-average player for so long prior to his breakout.

2017 PROJECTION: .284 14 HR 70 RBI 77 R 35 SB

Elvis Andrus: While he is still quite young at the age of 28, Texas Rangers shortstop Elvis Andrus has now become the guy you draft when all the other exciting players at the position have been scooped up. This is some fall for Andrus who not so long ago was considered a top five fantasy baseball shortstop; a designation we questioned in these pages over the years. The fact of the matter is that Andrus was overrated back then given his modest offensive output but his draft price has fallen so low recently that he now is looking like a decent value. It was a nice to see Andrus bat a career-best .302 last season and he kept up with the running in swiping 24 bases. While Andrus is no longer the 30-plus steals guy from earlier in his career, he has settled into the mid-to-late-20's there. That is no small deal since most of Andrus' value comes from that category. The rest of the Andrus package is underwhelming though as he hit just 8 home runs in 568 at-bats and we question highly whether a repeat of the .302 average is possible given the fact he was under .275 the three seasons prior. Solid but unspectacular is the name of the game here.

2017 PROJECTION: .275 7 HR 65 RBI 73 R 25 SB

Aledmys Diaz: The St. Louis Cardinals began the 2016 season by losing starting shortstop Jhonny Peralta to a broken thumb but little did they know a ready-made replacement was waiting to take off in the form of infield prospect Aledmys Diaz. Not even the Cardinals could have anticipated how Diaz would seamlessly transition to major leagues, both in the field and at the dish in a Rookie of the Year-worthy campaign. Diaz came out of the gates in March/April absolutely scorching with the stick as he hit a ridiculous .423 with 4 home runs and 18 RBI and never really let up the rest of the way (September/October was only month he didn't bat at least .275). For the season as a whole, Diaz cracked 17 home runs, collected 64 RBI, and batted an even .300. What allowed Diaz to perform as well as he did offensively was the fact he was as good as a rookie could be in terms of striking out (just a 13.0 K/9) and also drawing walks (8.9 BB/9). That is a combination which will allow any hitter to bat .300 in their sleep and so Diaz was no fluke in the average category. As far as the rest of the numbers are concerned, Diaz doesn't run much (4 steals total) which is a negative in the middle infield but 20 home runs is very much in play to offset that. While Diaz won't ever win you a league, he certainly can be a terrific plug-in-and-never-look-back fantasy baseball shortstop.

2017 PROJECTION: .302 19 HR 70 RBI 77 R 5 SB

Dansby Swanson: The prize return to the Atlanta Braves in the Shelby Miller deal, the sky is the limit in terms of the future prospects for shortstop Dansby

Swanson. Already carrying immense pedigree as the number overall 1 pick in the 2015 draft, Swanson can do it all on the field and with the bat. We got a glimpse of Swanson's ability in his 38-game debut with the Braves in 2016 as he batted .302 with 3 home runs and 3 stolen bases in 145 at-bats; a nice tease to what we could expect going forward. As impressive as that small sample size was, Swanson will turn just 23 in February, which means there are at least 3-4 more years of ceiling to go in his development. Swanson has terrific patience for a young hitter and his power/speed game should result in a 20/20 campaign as soon as this season. There are very few elite prospects such as Swanson where we will tell you to reach a round or two early to draft him but in this case, that strategy is warranted.

2017 PROJECTION: .300 22 HR 70 RBI 78 R 16 SB

Asdrubal Cabrera: When the New York Mets signed free agent shortstop Asdrubal Cabrera to a two-year deal prior to the 2016 season, the narrative around the game was that the team was bringing aboard a declining player who would suffer both in the field and with the bat. Well Cabrera certainly had other ideas as he went out and garnered some MVP talk in batting .283 with 23 home runs and 62 RBI. The 23 home runs were the second-highest total of Cabrera's career and his overall production was even more impressive when you consider he was hobbled with a very painful knee injury during the second half of the season. Still only 31, Cabrera has in fact changed a bit in terms of his offensive production. He no longer runs much anymore (just 5 steals in 2016) but Cabrera has offset that by adding some power. His advanced walk and strikeout numbers remain stable and only a slightly lucky .310 BABIP last season has to be taken into account with regards to the average likely slipping back into the .270's this season. Other than that, Cabrera seems like a rock solid buy once again.

2017 PROJECTION: .273 20 HR 66 RBI 63 R 6 SB

Didi Gregorious: Replacing a legend is always fraught with peril but New York Yankees shortstop Didi Gregorious might have written the book on how to do so based on his 2016 production. Filling the mammoth shoes of Derek Jeter was as big as it gets on that front but after some initial adjustments in 2015, Gregorious unleashed all of his skills last season in spectacular fashion in setting career-highs in ALL five standard fantasy baseball categories. Most prominently, Gregorious hit 20 home runs, drove in 70, and batted .276. While he still doesn't run as much as we originally thought was possible (7 stolen bases), Gregorious has become a power force at the plate and has really cut down on the strikeouts (13.7 K/9). While there is still not much interest being shown when it comes to walks (3.2 BB/9), Gregorious has now entered into the circle of trust as a solid daily play fantasy baseball shortstop.

2017 PROJECTION: .282 19 HR 77 RBI 75 R 5 SB

Marcus Semien: During the 2016 season, Oakland A's shortstop Marcus Semien showed himself to be the latest "tools" player in terms of hitting for power (27 home runs), stealing a few bases (10), and putting up an ugly batting average (.238). Players that fit these skill set as Semien does are often valued very differently by many when it comes to fantasy baseball. On one side of the ledger you have those who talk up the rare power that Semien brings to the shortstop position and also for the fact he seems capable of maybe adding a few more steals as well going forward. The opposing side notes how the ugly batting average (Semien has yet to hit better than .261 in his four major league seasons) take away some of the value the power brings. While both of these arguments have merit, some other things need to be noted. The first is the fact that Semien had a very unlucky .268 BABIP last season and so his .238 average should have been higher. Now how much higher is up for debate but Semien was not as bad a pure hitter as that average showed. Thus any movement upwards in Semien's average would make his power/speed game stand out even more. In addition, Semien walked a lot last season (8.2 BB/9) which portends to an average uptick as well. Yes the 22.4 K/9 is where the average issue is most stark but even a slight drop in that category would improve things there. Combined together, there are quite a few positive trends that could quickly move Semien into a much more elevated tier in fantasy baseball and that is why he should remain an upside target in drafts. Overall Semien represents a very good value play this season as the fantasy baseball community's focus on the average has made his 2017 price tag quite affordable.

2017 PROJECTION: .259 25 HR 78 RBI 77 R 11 SB

Troy Tulowitzki: Few players have earned our wrath in these pages more than Toronto Blue Jays shortstop Troy Tulowitzki and it was more than deserved given the unmatched injury risk and resulting batch of missed games going back to his Colorado Rockie days. The current version of Tulowitzki is even shakier given his ongoing (and losing battle) to injuries and now the offensive numbers are slipping sharply due to age. Tulowitzki's decline at the plate is even more noteworthy given the fact he remains in a major power park in Rogers Center and that adds validity to the 33-year-old's troubles. The speed is gone for good (1 steal all of last season) and Tulowitzki's .254 average is becoming another problem. Yes he still managed a very impressive 24 home runs but Tulowitzki is now becoming quite one-dimensional. Tulo apologists will point out that his unlucky .272 BABIP was the cause of the average drop and while that may be true, there is still an immense amount of risk here given the injuries. Another year older will only make that issue more prominent and so we remind you that investing in aging stars is almost always a losing bet.

2017 PROJECTION: .273 23 HR 77 RBI 57 R 1 SB

Orlando Arcia: The Milwaukee Brewers shipped out anything that wasn't nailed down at last year's Aug. 1 trade deadline and that means their top prospects will get a prime chance to show what they can do going forward. This group is headlined by shortstop Orlando Arica who looks to join Carlos Correa and Francisco Lindor as recent players at the position to make it big in the majors right away. While Arcia's offensive game is considered to be a level or two below Correa and Lindor, he possesses blazing speed and a burgeoning home run swing that should make him a power/speed asset real soon. Forget the .219 that Arica hit last season in his 55-game debut with the Brewers last season and instead focus on the 8 home runs and 25 steals he accumulated at Double-A in 2015 as an indication of where the kid is headed statistically. Be sure you get on the ground floor of this potential star.

2017 PROJECTION: .263 11 HR 45 RBI 65 R 19 SB

Tim Anderson: The Chicago White Sox ushered in a prime piece of both their present and future in 2016 by promoting speedy former 2013 first round pick (17th overall) Tim Anderson. While there were some expected cold spells, the young shortstop was very impressive as a rookie by hitting 9 home runs, stealing 10 bases, and batting .283 in 431 at-bats. In fact it was quite disappointing that Anderson didn't run nearly as much as expected but keep in mind this is a guy who swiped 49 bags ay Double-A as recently as 2015.   We do fully expect Anderson to run much more frequently this season and a push toward 25 steals would not be a shock. Anderson does have to do much better on the strikeout front as his 27.1 K/9 rate would have been disastrous to the average if a very lucky .375 BABIP didn't go along for the ride. He also needs to show much better patience as Anderson's 3.0 BB/9 was pathetic and again will threaten the batting average. With burgeoning power that is starting to show, there are still a bunch of tools to work with here. Just don't be surprised if Anderson's average jogs back to mediocre territory this season.

2017 PROJECTION: .266 12 HR 45 RBI 65 R 19 SB

Addison Russell: Not sure the Chicago Cubs would admit this but the progress of shortstop Addison Russell has been somewhat disappointing thus far. While Russell has shown himself to be an excellent defender, the offensive numbers leave a lot to be desired. Russell comes off a 2016 season where he batted just .238 and also struck out in 22.6 percent of his at-bats; a rough performance that got even worse in the postseason. On the other hand, Russell did hit a very impressive 21 home runs but his long stretches of hot and cold spells with the bat are frustrating from a fantasy perspective. As athletic as Russell is, he doesn't run much at all (just 5 steals in 598 at-bats last season) but the power/RBI game is one of the better combinations at shortstop out there. What it ultimately comes down to with Russell is whether or not you are willing to go with power and little speed in your middle infield or whether you want to look for a more balanced player elsewhere. What is clear with Russell is that his average is a liability and that is another negative to go with the lack of speed. We would prefer to keep on looking.

2017 PROJECTION: .255 22 HR 90 RBI 73 R 6 SB

Jung-Ho Kang: Now two full years into his major league career after coming over from Korea, Pittsburgh Pirates infielder Jung-Ho Kang has pretty much cemented his offensive profile. That profile centers on Kang being a very good power hitter (21 home runs in just 370 at-bats last season) but a non-running middle infielder (only 8 total steals in two years playing in the majors). Kang's batting .255 average a year ago was down from the .287 he hit as a rookie but part of the reason for that was due to his unlucky .273 BABIP. In fact Kang has swung the bat better than expected since he had a reputation of being a high-K guy coming over from Korea and this is seen in his very solid 21.4 K/9 rate in 2016 . We still don't know where the power upside will settle with Kang given how he missed a large chunk of last season with injury but 25 home runs is very much in play for 2017.

2017 PROJECTION: .275 24 HR 73 RBI 62 R 4 SB

Freddy Galvis: The 2016 Philadelphia Phillies roster had a slew of players who quietly put up some useful fantasy baseball numbers but with little to no fanfare attached to them. One of these players was shortstop Freddy Galvis who shockingly was a power/speed dynamo with 20 home runs and 17 stolen bases. With the Phillies in full rebuilding mode last season, they had no issue giving Galvis 624 at-bats and the veteran surely made the most of the opportunity. It was not all positives here however as Galvis batted an ugly .241 but an unlucky. 280 BABIP had something to do with that. Overall Galvis will be just 27 when the 2017 season gets underway and the Phillies have to now consider him a starting piece somewhere on the field. We say somewhere because the Phillies eventually want to promote top shortstop prospect J.P. Crawford and that should come at some point during the upcoming year. Ultimately the Crawford situation complicates things a bit for Galvis and that is why you need to tread carefully here.

2017 PROJECTION: .250 16 HR 60 R 63 RBI 14 SB

Danny Espinosa: After posting three straight ugly seasons from 2012-15, virtually no one in the fantasy baseball community had any plans to invest in Washington Nationals infielder Danny Espinosa going into last year. While Espinosa has been a chronic batting average failure, we were able to look past that negative as long as the home runs and steals were flowing as they were in 2011 (21-HR/17-SB) and 2012 (17-HR/20-SB). He did nothing but struggle across the board the following three years though and that is why what Espinosa accomplished in a comeback 2016 was so shocking. Posting career-highs in home runs with 24 and in RBI with 72, Espinosa made the grade again as a semi-useful second baseman or shortstop in fantasy baseball. Espinosa only turns 30 in April which means he has every right to be around those numbers again but we can't automatically overlook the horrid .209 average that went with his production last year. Since he qualifies again at second base and shortstop, Espinosa ideally would be a backup middle infielder on your team.

2017 PROJECTION: .233 19 HR 65 RBI 61 R 5 SB

Zack Cozart: While he never lived up to the initial hype when coming up the Cincinnati Reds minor league ladder, Zack Cozart has settled in as a solid and somewhat useful backup fantasy baseball shortstop. We say Cozart works best as a backup because he has some clear liabilities such as a career .246 batting average and a slew of injuries that have derailed a few seasons. On the positive side, Cozart has some power/speed ability as he has hit 25 home runs and stolen 7 bags the last two years combined. Having turned 31 in August, Cozart is a "what you see is what you get player" and again that makes him ideally a backup shortstop for 2017.

2017 PROJECTION: .251 15 HR 55 RBI 73 R 5 SB

Brandon Crawford: The encore to San Francisco Giants shortstop Brandon Crawford's solid 2015 breakout campaign (21 home runs, 84 RBI, .256) did not go well last season to say the least. While Crawford upped the batting average to a more useful .277, he hit just 12 home runs in a mammoth 623 at-bats (62 more than 2015). The overall package here remains limited and quite boring as Crawford doesn't run much (just 7 steals last season) and his average is never great. It also looks like the 21 home runs Crawford hit last season belong in the outlier bin as well and it also needs to be mentioned the .277 he batted was propped up by a lucky .322 BABIP. He will be 30 when the 2017 season gets underway which means there is no more upside remaining in Crawford's game. Avoid him.

2017 PROJECTION: .263 14 HR 82 RBI 65 R 5 SB

THE REST

Cesar Hernandez: Along the same lines as teammate Freddy Galvis, Philadelphia Phillies infielder Cesar Hernandez had an impactful 2016 season for those in the fantasy baseball community who took notice. Hernandez has developed into a solid contact-hitter for the Phillies, batting .294 last season while using his impressive steed to swipe 17 bags. While his power is below-average, Hernandez popped a few along the way (6 home runs in 622 at-bats) which prevented him from being a complete zero there. Hernandez draws walks at a very good clip (10.6 BB/9) and his 18.6 K/9 rate a year ago will help him maintain a nice batting average. While Hernandez doesn't quite make the grade as a daily league starter, he certainly does enough to warrant backup status.

Chris Owings: Infielder Chris Owings could make the case that he had a career-best campaign in 2016 but that is not saying much considering how poorly he had played prior to his production last season. Batting .277 with 5 home runs and 21 steals, Owings was just an NL-only or mixed league bench bat based on that modest combination of numbers. Turning 26 in August, Owings is barely holding the fantasy baseball community's attention.

Alcides Escobar: One of the more mediocre shortstops for 2017 fantasy baseball resides in Kansas City in the form of veteran Alcides Escobar. In fact Escobar has been consistently shaky over the last two years with 17 stolen bases in each campaign and his average has come in at a shaky .257 and .261 respectively. Possessing just single-digit power and for the fact he will be 30 when the 2017 season gets underway, Escobar is really just for use in AL-only formats.

Marwin Gonzalez: Former Rule 5 pick Marwin Gonzalez has become a very valuable jack-of-all-trades utility man the last few seasons for the Houston Astros, showcasing a power/speed game that resulted in 13 home runs and 12 steals in 2016. While his average is never great due to an utter avoidance of walks (4.2 BB/9), Gonzalez carries value due to being eligible all over the diamond and with his ability to contribute in the power/speed realms. Still he just works best in a backup capacity for use on light schedule days.

Ketel Marte: There was some mild fantasy baseball sleeper appeal for Seattle Mariners shortstop Ketel Marte coming into 2016 but the end result was not good as he hit just .259 with 1 home run and 11 steals in 466 at-bats. Nowhere to be seen was Marte's supposed ability to rack up the steals and be a catalyst at the top of a batting order which added to the letdown year. While he is still young at the age of 23, we need to see Marte start making progress before we get involved here again.

Alexei Ramirez: The days of Alexei Ramirez carrying even moderate fantasy baseball value appear to be over as he enters into the twilight of his career at the age of 35. A 2016 season where he hit a career-worst .241 with 6 home runs and 8 steals in 506 at-bats should spell this out for you.

J.J. Hardy: If you are a fan of J.J. Hardy, just go draft Brandon Crawford who is his younger clone. Like with Crawford, Hardy is all power and nothing else at shortstop when it comes to his hitting profile. The problem with Hardy is that he is on the edge of the career abyss at the age of 35 and with a recent spate of health trouble now added to the shaky equation. Never a good batting average guy to begin with, Hardy's power is slipping badly (9 home runs in 438 at-bats last season) and that means there is no reason to invest here anymore.

Andrelton Simmons: There are no categories in fantasy baseball for Gold Gloves or defense and that means Los Angeles Angels shortstop Andrelton Simmons should not be on a fantasy baseball roster. While still only 27, Simmons' .284 average in 2016 was very empty as he hit just 4 home runs and stole 10 bases in 483 at-bats. Players like this are reserved for the waiver wire.

Jose Iglesias: While Jose Iglesias has shown that he can hit .300 (like he did in 2013 and 2015), there is virtually nothing else in his offensive profile that makes any sort of impact in fantasy baseball. Even last season Iglesias struggled with the bat as he hit just .255 and that was a big problem since there were virtually no home runs or steals (4/7) to offset the negative there. Move right along.

Adeiny Hechavarria: Miami Marlins shortstop Adeiny Hechavarria had an empty batting average in 2015 when he hit a solid .281 but with just 5 home runs and 7 stolen bases. So when he hit just .236 last season, there was literally nothing positive to say about Hechavarria from a fantasy baseball angle as he swatted just 3 home runs and stole 1 base in 547 at-bats. All glove and no bat.

Nick Franklin: It was yet another underwhelming season for Nick Franklin in 2016 as he hit just .270 with 6 home runs in 191 at-bats for the Tampa Bay Rays. Considering that Franklin has hit UNDER .200 in two of his four major league seasons, it should be clear now how much trouble he has hitting top-of-the-line pitching. While Franklin has power and possesses decent speed, he is looking more and more like a Quad-A player every year.

Raul Mondesi Jr.: He can't hit a lick but Raul Mondesi Jr. can run like the wind. He will challenge for the starting second base job with the Kansas City Royals in spring training but for now is only shortstop-eligible. Meanwhile Mondesi comes off a horrific 2016 where he batted just .185 in 47 games with the Royals and also was suspended 80 games for a PED violation. Even in the minor leagues Mondesi was a batting average liability and you can't steal without getting on first base. It is the steals category where Mondesi will make hay in fantasy baseball but he is nothing but overall he is nothing but a guy to monitor during spring training.

THIRD BASE OVERVIEW

Wow this position is stacked. I mean it is incredible when you look at the top-end talent here as Josh Donaldson, Manny Machado, Kris Bryant, and Nolan Arenado ALL deserve to be top five picks. In fact the top six in most drafts will include that amazing foursome to go along with Mike Trout and Jose Altuve. And all four of those names are absolutely worth using a first round pick on if you choose to go first baseman in Round 3. Even if you do miss out on Bryant, Machado, Donaldson, and Arenado; there are some new high impact names on the block at this position such as 2016 value plays Hernan Perez, Jake Lamb, and Jose Ramirez. Like with shortstop, there is suddenly very good depth here that was non-existent just a few seasons ago which means there is no need to panic if you don't have a third baseman after the first few rounds of your draft.

Kris Bryant: For as many misses as there have been over the years in fantasy baseball when it comes to chasing young talent with vast upside, one slam-dunk success story has been Chicago Cubs third baseman Kris Bryant. In less than two years of major league service time, Bryant has thrust himself into mid-first round territory with his thunderous bat and overall tremendous athleticism. The numbers are already staggering here as Bryant filled up all five standard league categories in 2016 and the power was off the charts as he slammed 39 home runs, crossed the plate 121 times, and collected 102 RBI. For good measure, Bryant batted .292 with 8 stolen bases in firmly stamping himself as an unquestioned offensive monster. Want some more? How about gaining outfield eligibility in almost all leagues, while also picking up the first base tag in formats that use 5 games started as a benchmark? All of this and Bryant will be just 25 for the 2017 season. No matter where you look, there is only excellence to be found with Bryant and major credit needs to be given for the guy cutting his K/9 rate from a very ugly 30.6 mark as a rookie to an impressive 22.0 last season. There is no debating Bryant should not last past the fifth pick in all leagues this season.

2017 PROJECTION: .298 42 HR 109 RBI 123 R 10 SB

Nolan Arenado: You can make the case that Colorado Rockies third baseman Nolan Arenado is the best pure power hitter in all of baseball after he reached the hallowed 40-home run mark for the second season in a row in 2016. After smacking a monstrous 42 long balls in a spectacular breakout in 2015, Arenado went out and whacked 41 more a year ago. Perhaps even more impressive is the fact Arenado has driven in 130 and 133 runs respectively during that same span which is incredible run-scoring production. Throw in 116 runs scored and Arenado blew the doors off three categories. What really puts Arenado in a special class is that included with all that power, was the .294 average he put up last season. Keep in mind that it is very rare when a hitter can collect so many home runs and still hit above .280 as Arenado now routinely accomplishes. Yes Arenado doesn't swipe bases (2 steals in 2016) but his off-the-charts production everywhere else puts him squarely in mid-first round territory. Count on Arenado making it a 40-home run hat trick.

2017 PROJECTION: .290 42 HR 130 RBI 119 R 4 SB

Josh Donaldson: The heart-and-soul of the recent World Series-contending Toronto Blue Jays without argument has been All-Star third baseman Josh Donaldson. Since being acquired by the Oakland A's in one of the most one-sided deals in recent memory, all Donaldson has supplied the Jays in his two-season stay thus far is an MVP in 2015 and a performance last season that also netted strong consideration for the award. While he runs a tad more than Nolan Arenado (7 steals last season), Donaldson is every bit as potent with the power bat as he smacked 37 home runs and collected 99 RBI last season. Also for the second straight year, Donaldson scored exactly 122 runs. While Donaldson undoubtedly would be classified as a slugger, his advanced rates in terms of pure hitting are terrific as his K/9 last year was an impressive 17.0 and he walked at a staggering 15.6 BB/9 clip which resulted in a .284 batting average. There is nothing Donaldson can't do on the diamond and for that reason, he should be included among Arenado and Kris Bryant as mid-first round picks.

2017 PROJECTION: .286 39 HR 107 RBI 120 R 7 SB

Manny Machado: The last of the "Big Four" in terms of being classified as first round fantasy baseball third baseman, the Baltimore Orioles' Manny Machado last season completely validated his blockbuster 2015 breakout campaign. Machado made it two seasons in a row in terms of reaching the monstrous 35-home run mark by cracking 37; while he also scored 105 runs and collected 96 RBI. Machado even improved his average to a career-best .294 but he shockingly took a bagel in the steals category after going for 20 the year prior. Machado seemed to lose his speed overnight and the loss of contributions there have put him behind Kris Bryant, Nolan Arenado, and Josh Donaldson at least for now. The hope is that Machado can rediscover some running this season but even if that fails to occur, his status as a first round pick remains firm.

2017 PROJECTION: .290 35 HR 93 RBI 108 R 7 SB

Adrian Beltre: Age is just a number for perennial Texas Rangers All-Star third baseman Adrian Beltre as evidenced by his par for the course excellence at the dish in 2016. Reversing some power trends where he dipped under 20 long balls for two years running, Beltre went out and smacked 32 home runs last season with 104 RBI. Beltre also batted .300 which now makes it 4 of the last five years he has at least reached that mark. All of this from a guy who will be 38 when the 2017 season gets underway. What is really interesting about Beltre is the fact his advanced hitting numbers remain virtually unchanged from his prime years and that more than anything has allowed him to age as well as he has. A borderline Hall of Famer, Beltre is becoming one of those guys like David Ortiz that will continue to produce to the day he retires.

2017 PROJECTION: .295 25 HR 90 RBI 86 R 1 SB

Kyle Seager: There may not have been a bigger third base value in all of fantasy baseball the last four years then Seattle Mariners veteran Kyle Seager. This fact is one we have reminded you all about over and over both in these pages and on our website, as Seager continually produces terrific numbers year after year for a very moderate draft price. The reason no one ever seems to want to draft Seager is the prejudice that comes with playing your home games at Safeco Field and also for the West Coast Bias. While at least the Safeco angle is an understandable red flag, Seager has proven without a doubt that the place won't hold back the offensive numbers. Outside of cracking a career-best 30 home runs, Seager was pretty much the same guy across the board offensively last season. The average is never terrific (only once going over .270) and the steals are pretty much completely washed up (just 3 stolen bases last year) but you can write in ink 25-30 long balls. Embrace the value here.

2017 PROJECTION: .265 27 HR 95 RBI 86 R 4 SB

Jose Ramirez: After ceding the starting shortstop job in the Cleveland Indians infield to top prospect Francisco Lindor prior to the 2016 season, Jose Ramirez began the process of converting to third base in order to keep himself in the team's major league plans. While defensively there were some adjustments, Ramirez has quickly proven to be quite a force with the bat himself. Still just a pup himself as he turns 26 in January, Ramirez comes off a 2016 performance that can only be described as a breakout. What quickly stands out was Ramirez' .312 batting average and he also unveiled a power/speed game to the tune of 11 home runs and

22 steals. Throw in 84 runs scored and 76 steals and Ramirez became an overnight five-tool player last season. Now firmly set as the team's third baseman, Ramirez has to show in 2017 that his numbers the year prior were no fluke but the rate statistics show this is not an impossible chore by any means. Ramirez already is one of the best pure contact hitters in the game as his K/9 rate of 10.0 was insanely good and his 7.1 BB/9 also checked out nicely. Again some will question is there was an outlier aspect to Ramirez' 2016 but the advanced numbers stamp his performance as legit.

2017 PROJECTION: .297 12 HR 73 RBI 86 R 20 SB

Todd Frazier: Veteran third baseman Todd Frazier entered into the 2016 season in a new home locale (traded from the Cincinnati Reds to the Chicago White Sox) and came in off two tremendous offensive seasons with his power bat from 2014-15. As impressive as Frazier's 30-plus home run bat had developed into, he also supplemented that production with sneaky 10-15-steal speed. Alas Frazier's 2016 season was a bit of a mixed bag on a number of fronts. The good is that Frazier set a new career-best in home runs with 40 and in RBI with 98. He also kept on running to the tune of 15 stolen bases. The bad was that Frazier's already shaky batting average took a nosedive to a very ugly .225 as he swung at more pitches than ever before. As evidence of his increasingly hacking approach, Frazier whiffed at a very high 24.5 clip (up more than 4.0 points from 2015). That negative development bears some responsibility for the average dip but Frazier also suffered from the horrific luck that a .236 BABIP brought. In the end when you break it all down, Frazier was actually the same player he was in Cincy but just saddled with more bad luck on the batted ball than ever before. With the power exploding and the steals still part of the picture, don't over-think this too much in knocking Frazier down your ranking sheets this spring.

2017 PROJECTION: .249 38 HR 95 RBI 86 R 14 SB

Evan Longoria: Tampa Bay Rays third baseman Evan Longoria is an interesting story in fantasy baseball. The guy is still young at the age of 31 but he has run the gamut in perceived value already. Not long after he established himself with the Rays as a slugging third baseman with some speed, Longoria rocketed right into first round territory. Since losing his speed, suffering some injuries, and seeing his 30-homer past drop to the 20s, Longoria then became a guy many in the fantasy baseball community moved away from. Fast forward to 2016 and Longoria sent a firm reminder that he still has the ability to be a high-end performer as he cracked a career-best 36 home runs and collected 98 RBI. Yes Longoria still doesn't run anymore as he failed to swipe even one base but his power bat remains a force by the looks of things. The thing with Longoria now is that almost his entire fantasy baseball value rests with the power, runs, and RBI columns since his batting average has not climbed above .273 in each of the last four years. Any dip in power means that Longoria takes a decent hit in fantasy baseball so the margin of error investing here is a bit tight.

2017 PROJECTION: .270 27 HR 95 RBI 82 R 2 SB

Jake Lamb: Given the insane explosion of top tier hitting third base talent that has emerged over the last three seasons in fantasy baseball, it is easy to overlook other breakouts at the position that are bit further down the rankings ladder. A guy who fits this mold is the Arizona Diamondbacks' Jake Lamb who went nuclear with the bat in 2016 in swatting 29 home runs and collecting 91 RBI. Having had his initial two seasons in the majors interrupted with serious injuries, Lamb was never really able to hint at what was to come a year ago. We will take it however as Lamb showed some serious power and run-driving ability in the middle of the D-Backs' lineup. Now all that power came at the expense of Lamb's batting average; which at an ugly .249 was not a small problem. Striking out at a 25.9 K/9 clip will more than do the damage there and Lamb's near-neutral .294 BABIP means there was no bad luck involved. For Lamb's fantasy baseball stock to really take off, he needs to move his K/9 rate closer to 20.0. Until that happens, he will be mostly a back-end starting third base option.

2017 PROJECTION: .259 27 HR 88 RBI 84 R 5 SB

Justin Turner: From barely hanging on with the New York Mets as a utility man to developing into one of the better power/pure hitters in the game, veteran third baseman Justin Turner has really come a long way with his game. A classic late-bloomer, Turner got the high batting average down pat in 2014 when he batted .340 for the Dodgers and then the last two seasons he added the power to the tune of 27 and 23 home runs respectively. Turner checks all the tools in terms of performing as a very valuable power/average guy as he draws walks (between 7.0 and 8.5 BB/9 in his career) and keeps the strikeouts down (never going above 18.0 K/9). Other then the fact there is virtually no speed here, Turner on an annual basis is one of the very best hitting values in fantasy baseball (think Kyle Seager as a comparison). Now Turner is aging as bit as he will be 32 when the 2017 season gets underway (recent injury problems the last two years bear this out) and so just know going in there is an increased risk of a DL stint during the year.

2017 PROJECTION: .288 24 HR 86 RBI 78 R 3 SB

Alex Bregman: Boy do the Houston Astros have an insane farm system. Just a year after they unveiled monster shortstop prospect Carlos Correa, the Astros brought up the number 2 pick of the 2015 draft in third baseman Alex Bregman last summer. Considered just as much of a can't-miss as Correa, Bregman sailed through the Houston farm system with little resistance. After smacking 14 home runs in only 62 games while in Double-A, Bregman next went to town at Triple-A where he batted a scorching .333 and hit another 6 home runs in 83 at-bats. Thus it was impossible for the Astros to keep Bregman down any longer and his promotion was a "run to the waiver wire" moment. While Bregman didn't exactly light things up with the Astros (.264/8-HR/2-SB in 47 games), there is no argument to be made that he is as bright a prospect as there is in all of baseball. A hamstring injury that Bregman suffered toward the end of the year was the only negative to really speak of and so he should be on the short list as one of the most sought after fantasy baseball sleepers for 2017 drafts. We are talking about a future 30-home run masher who also can run a little and bat around .300. That is outfielder 1 territory and it is a status that Bregman will reach before too long. Do what you can to get a piece of this.

2017 PROJECTION: .279 24 HR 75 RBI 78 R 11 SB

Maikel Franco: We were big fans of Philadelphia Phillies third baseman Maikel Franco coming into the 2016 fantasy baseball season and there were more than a few reasons to justify our optimism. While in the minors and through his first foray into the major leagues in 2015, Franco showed a power bat that was also capable of hitting .300. Generally speaking, Franco yielded positive results last season for those who took our advice and drafted him. The power was very much in play as Franco bashed 25 home runs and collected 88 RBI. The batting average? Not so much as it came in at a shaky .255. But keep in mind that Franco's .255 average should have been higher as he dealt with a quite unlucky .271 BABIP. Everything else in Franco's hitting approach worked as his 16.8 K/9 was terrific and his 6.3 BB/9 was good enough. Those who choose to wait until the middle rounds to draft their third baseman and stock up elsewhere should target Franco before anyone else.

2017 PROJECTION: .280 27 HR 90 RBI 73 R 1 SB

Hernan Perez: Just when you thought the third base position in fantasy baseball couldn't get any more loaded with talent, along comes the Milwaukee Brewers' Hernan Perez who pretty much overnight became a five-tool sensation during the 2016 season. As we have seen countless times where a young player gets an extended look on a rebuilding team, Perez went wild across the board as he hit 13 home runs, batted .272, and stole 34 bases in 430 at-bats. While Perez failed to break the 60 mark in runs and RBI, a lot of that had to do with the mediocre talent around him in the Brewers' batting order. Still the kid is showing he can handle the bat as his 21.9 K/9 rate was very solid for a rookie but Perez needs to show some more patience (4.2 BB/9) so the average can shoot up higher. While there is legitimate concern regarding whether Perez was a bit of a fluke that caught opposing pitchers off guard will be determined this season and in order to protect yourself, be sure not to reach above where you think he should be picked in the draft. The speed is the most stable part of Perez' game but the average and home runs will show how high this stock goes.

2017 PROJECTION: .275 10 HR 63 RBI 65 R 27 SB

Nick Castellanos: After a few seasons of waiting and wondering if he would ever develop into the player that the team drafted in the first round back in 2010, Detroit Tigers third baseman Nick Castellanos broke through during the 2016 season on multiple levels. What stood out the most was the fact Castellanos tapped into his power as he hit 18 home runs in just 447 at-bats. Injuries interrupted his progress but Castellanos at the very least reversed the perception going into last season that he was a first round bust. While he conveyed optimism with his 2016 performance, there were still some negative signs that could not be ignored. Primarily, Castellanos' K/9 rate of 24.8 remained a negative and if not for a very lucky .345 BABIP, he would have batted much lower than .285. While he at least showed he can hang with major league pitching, Castellanos is a guy we still are hesitant to get involved with.

2017 PROJECTION: .273 19 HR 70 RBI 65 R 1 SB

Jose Reyes: The New York Mets and Jose Reyes reunited in 2016 under some ugly circumstances which certainly can't be ignored. Reyes was suspended by Major League Baseball for the first two months of the 2016 season due to his arrest for domestic violence against his wife and upon completion of the sentence, was outright released by the Colorado Rockies. Enter in the Mets who brought Reyes aboard in the ultimate buy-low after losing David Wright for the season with more back trouble. After the apology tour was given, Reyes got back to doing what he does best which is ignite lineups from the top of the batting order. Showing he was not done being an impact player, Reyes hit .267 with 8 home runs and 9 stolen bases in just 279 at-bats for the team. Reyes also picked up eligibility at third base (but lost his SS standing for the time being) as he more than ably filled in for Wright. It is tough to get a firm read on Reyes' advanced numbers (such as the fact his 17.6 K/9 was a career-worst for him) as there was quite a bit of rust to work off when he first returned. Be that as it may, Reyes is now 33 and with a long history of leg injuries. That issue is a big red flag for Reyes' value and you also need to keep in mind that his steal totals will likely never go near the 30 or above mark again. The current model of Reyes is a stripped-down version from his superstar past but he still has value nonetheless as a very affordable infield option. Reyes is expected to play a utility role for the Mets this season which means he will likely gain shortstop and maybe even second base eligibility during 2017. He can still help you.

2017 PROJECTION: .278 10 HR 67 R 46 RBI 22 SB

Miguel Sano: We spoke out against drafting Minnesota Twins 3B/OF Miguel Sano going into the 2016 fantasy baseball season, despite the fact the most of the talk centered on his chances of smacking 40 home runs for the Minnesota Twins. While there was no debating Sano's pure power, we had major reservations about his ugly K rates and damaging batting averages. Sano predictably went strikeout crazy to the tune of a pathetic 36.0 K/9 rate and that did the typical damage to his batting average as it sank to an ugly .236. The power was potent as Sano went yard 25 times in just 495 at-bats but the approach is lacking to say the least. We always advise you to stay away from pure home run-or-nothing hitters and that even goes for young ones like Sano. A tiger can't change its stripes and a hacking slugger can't stop striking out.

2017 PROJECTION: .235 27 HR 73 RBI 59 R 1 SB

Martin Prado: When there are two outs in the ninth with a man on second in a tie game, one of the guys you wouldn't want to be facing is Miami Marlins second baseman Martin Prado. While not overly flashy in the home run and steal categories, Prado has long cemented his reputation as a dogged hitter who can really put the bat on the ball. This makes him somewhat of a better real-life player then a fantasy baseball one but Prado still makes for a very good backup in our fake game. His .305 average last season was par for the course (having hit .280 or higher in 10 of his 12 years in the majors) but that number was pretty empty as Prado hit just 8 home runs and collected a tiny 2 steals in 658 at-bats. We reiterate that Prado is a good backup in mixed leagues and a bit more in NL-only but the numbers overall are just not there.

2017 PROJECTION: .295 9 HR 79 RBI 75 R 1 SB

Mike Moustakas: It was going to be a pivotal season in 2016 for Kansas City Royals third baseman Mike Moustakas on a number of fronts. The first issue centered on whether or not the by far career-best .284 batting average Moustakas put up during the 2015 season would be repeated. Considering that previously Moustakas was pretty much impossible to own given the fact he was unable to hit better than .242 the previous three years prior to that performance, which had proven to be an annual struggle that neutered any impact his intriguing power might have made. As far as his 2015 season was concerned, what was encouraging is that it appeared as though Moustakas had matured as a hitter in terms of swinging less for the fences in the interest of using the whole field. While that approach did work as he hit for that .284 average, the overall body was work was even more impressive as Moustakas cracked a high in home runs with 22. Unfortunately as the 2016 season got going, it appeared as though the old and very frustrating Moustakas was back as he hit a listless .240 with 7 home runs in 113 at-bats. Then to make matters worse, Moustakas suffered a season-ending torn ACL in his right knee. Expected to be 100 percent for the start of spring training, we are at the point now with Moustakas (having turned 28 last September) of him being what he is in terms of the ugly average and decent but not great power. In other words, Moustakas is only backup material in mixed leagues.

2017 PROJECTION: .253 19 HR 80 RBI 74 R 1 SB

Joey Gallo: Taking the whole three outcome approach to the extreme (home run, walk, strikeout) is Texas Rangers third base prospect Joey Gallo. Lauded for his Paul Bunyan power, Gallo also swings at anything in the Western Hemisphere which shows up in some truly putrid K/9 rates and batting averages. Consider that in his 36-game debut for the Rangers in 2015, Gallo put up a crazy 46.3 K/9 and a .204 average. In his 17-game cup of coffee stint last season those numbers came in even WORSE at 63.3 and .040. As powerful as Gallo is, he has the classic look of a Quad-A guy given the massive and almost historic-looking strikeout rates. Yes the first round draft pedigree (8th overall in 2012) carries weight but Gallo is not someone we suggest you go near.

2017 PROJECTION: .215 20 HR 54 RBI 48 R 2 SB

Yangervis Solarte: There are two key subject items when it comes to veteran infielder Yangervis Solarte which have held true since he made a home in the major leagues back in 2014. The guy can hit a little in a .280-ish sense, pop some home runs (mostly in the 10-15 range), and serve as a terrific fantasy baseball backup utility guy due to carrying eligibility all over the field. The same setup will hold true for 2017 as the 29-year-old Solarte is firmly in his prime years. Nothing special here to be sure but Solarte has a spot on a roster in most fantasy baseball leagues at least for another season.

2017 PROJECTION: .278 14 HR 65 RBI 55 R 2 SB

Wilmer Flores: By now the book is pretty established on New York Mets semi-regular third baseman Wilmer Flores. Receiving a bunch of playing time the last two years in replacing the perpetually injured David Wright, Flores has been incredibly consistent with his offensive numbers during that span. Consider that in 2015, Flores hit 16 home runs and batted .263 and then followed that up with 16 more home runs and a .267 average in 2016 before missing a batch of games late with a wrist injury. Overall Flores is quite ordinary as he has zero speed, his average is mediocre, and the power remains good but not great. Also you want to watch when you play Flores as he is a career .340 hitter versus lefties and only at .232 versus righties. Carrying eligibility at second base and third, Flores is a guy you want around just as a backup.

2016 PROJECTION: .265 16 HR 57 RBI 48 R 2 SB

THE REST

Yulieski Gourriel: We have another Cuban riddle on our hands in the form of Houston Astros third baseman Yulieski Gourriel. Already a late arrival at the age of 32, Gourriel came to the States this past season with a reputation of being a slugger in Cuba who also possessed the skills to hit for a good average. We have seen more than a few busts recently come from that nation however (Yasiel Puig, Alex Guerrero, Rusney Castillo) and so you are going in on blind faith with regards to investing in Gourriel for 2017. We did like the fact Gourriel struck out at a tiny 8.8 K/9 clip in his 137 at-bat test run with the Astros last season and that performance goes along with the scouting report. 3 home runs and a .262 average were not bad for a debut either as the tools seem evident enough. Again be sure to temper your enthusiasm here given the uncertainty about how Gourriel will continue to develop.

Ryon Healy: The Oakland A's have not had a lot go their way lately as some recent prospects have failed to come through with their development. They will take another shot on that front with power-hitting third baseman Ryon Healy who not only has a cool spelling to his name but who hit 13 home runs in just 283 debut at-bats last season. A firm all power and no speed third baseman, the key for Healy is maintaining a decent batting average if he wants to make hay in fantasy baseball. His .305 mark as a rookie last season was nice and his track record in the minors is impressive there (.338 at Double-A and .318 at Triple-A in 2016). Healy needs to walk more (4.2 BB/9) but he at least looks like a solid sleeper candidate to target in the late rounds of your draft.

Matt Duffy: While he was no one's definition of an impact player, third baseman Matt Duffy still opened eyes during the 2015 season when he hit .295 with 12 home runs and 12 stolen bases at the age of 24 for the San Francisco Giants. Those 12 home runs came in a massive 612 at-bats though which showed just how mediocre the power really was here. The Giants apparently realized this too as they had no issue trading him to the Tampa Bay Rays last summer; an overall campaign that was derailed by a persistent Achilles injury that shut him down for good at the beginning of September. Prior to his early finish, Duffy failed to do much at the dish as his average dropped sharply to an ugly .258 and he would hit just 5 home runs in 366 at-bats. While Duffy had some upside appeal prior to last season, 2017 drafts should see him as nothing but a very late round grab at best.

Luis Valbuena: A hamstring strain in July proved to be the 2016 undoing of Houston Astros third baseman Luis Valbuena, as he suffered a series of subsequent setbacks that resulted in August surgery. Prior to the hamstring injury, Valbuena did his usual above-average power hitting/ugly batting average bit with 13 home runs and a .260 average in 90 games. Overall Valbuena is a very shoddy .232 career hitter, which speaks to his limitations and status as more of an AL or NL-only backup bat at the hot corner. Turning 31 in November, that status won't change for 2017.

Danny Valencia: While he has a reputation of being a clubhouse jerk (just ask Billy Butler), veteran third baseman Danny Valencia has some hitting skills as he comes off a 2016 campaign where he hit .287 with 17 home runs for the Oakland A's. Valencia has been in a million different organizations in his career which perhaps speak to his troubles getting along with others but the guy can hit when given the chance. We are talking mostly backup duty here though as Valencia has no speed and never has reached the 20-home run mark.

Jeff Marte: Having already been in four different major league organizations, Los Angeles Angels third base prospect Jeff Marte had little hype attached to his name when he received a look-see from the team midway through the 2016 season. With the Angels in full rebuild, Marte certainly gave the team something to ponder as he hit 15 home runs in just 284 at-bats. Yes Marte was nothing special in any other category and his .252 average was ugly but there could be something to work with here in AL-only formats given the obvious power.

Trevor Plouffe: Given the recent massive explosion of top third baseman in fantasy baseball, mediocre veterans like Trevor Plouffe are barely even worth owning at this point. Before having his 2016 season ended early with a strained oblique, Plouffe posted his customary moderate power (12 home runs) and shaky batting average (.260). Turning 31 in June, Plouffe has no ceiling left to his name and the best we can ever ask for now is 20 home runs and a .270 average. Those statistics work enough for your backup third baseman with zero upside.

Adonis Garcia: The Atlanta Braves continue to put forth prospects to try and stake their claim at various spots around the diamond and third baseman Adonis Garcia is among this group as we head toward the 2017 season. Garcia certainly is in the picture as a piece both for the present and the future after he hit 14 home runs and batted a respectable .273 last season for the team. While Garcia is not keen on taking walks, his 16.5 K/9 rate is impressive for a guy who took a long time to make it to the majors (he turned pro back in 2007). Already turning 32 in April though, Garcia is likely already as good as he is going to get. That level of performance doesn't move him past NL-only status.

Chris Coghlan: It seems like Chris Coghlan has been around forever since he won the NL Rookie of the Year Award in 2009 but he really has had two careers in major league baseball. The first included his terrific start with the Florida Marlins and then subsequent banishment to the minor leagues after some very ugly struggles. The second included Coghlan fighting his way back to the Marlins and then eventually to the Chicago Cubs where he showed off 15/15 ability while manning the outfield and third base. Still young at 31, Coghlan's stay in the majors is being challenged again after coming off a brutal 2016 where he batted .192 with 6 home runs and 2 steals in 291 at-bats. Injuries torpedoed much of

Coghlan's year but his K/9 rate jumped by a wide margin from 2015's 18.7 to last season's 24.7 percent in a season split between the Oakland A's and Cubs. Blame some of the struggles on the injuries but Coghlan is no longer a guy who will challenge for an everyday job which means he carries next-to-no value.

David Freese: Not sure what the Pittsburgh Pirates see out of 1B/3B David Freese but it was enough in 2016 to have the team re-sign the pending free agent to a two-year extension. Freese is the definition of mediocre at the dish as he hit just 13 home runs and batted .270 in 492 at-bats. With no stolen base ability to speak of, Freese is as limited a player as you can get at positions that require power at the very least.

Yunel Escobar: It would probably surprise you to know that veteran third baseman Yunel Escobar has batted a swell .314 and .304 in each of the last two seasons. Having developed into a very good contact hitter (tiny 11.8 K/9 rate last season), Escobar unfortunately is just an empty batting average. He earns this designation for hitting just 5 home runs in 567 at-bats last season and he made no inroads in steals either in posting a bagel in that category. There is nothing even remotely worth using here.

Tyler Saladino: Serving mostly as a backup utility man on the 2016 Chicago White Sox, Tyler Saladino showed he has some offensive skills the team might want to take advantage of more. Known as a major speed demon in the minors, Saladino swiped 11 based and swatted 8 home runs in just 319 at-bats for the team in 2016. While Saladino has virtually no patience at the plate (4.1 BB/9), he batted a solid .282 as he kept the strikeouts down (19.4 K/9). On the surface it looks like Saladino will reprise his utility role for 2017 but any injury to one of the team's starters could instantly make him quite interesting.

Chase Headley: Veteran New York Yankees third baseman Chase Headley will always be known for posting one of the most obvious outlier campaigns in recent memory back in 2012 for the San Diego Padres (31-HR, 17-SB) but since then he has barely been an NL or Al-only third baseman in fantasy baseball. Despite calling the launching pad that is Yankee Stadium home, Headley managed just 14 home runs last season with a terrible .251 batting average. While he did swipe 8 bases to keep himself a bit useful there, Headley is turning 33 in May and has health red flags to go with very mediocre numbers offensively.

Travis Shaw: While he got out of the gates well (2-HR/.314 March/April), Boston Red Sox third baseman Travis Shaw got more exposed at the dish the longer he remained a starter. This was no shock as Shaw was never considered to be anything more than a moderate prospect and his 2017 outlooks is a bit dicey as he will likely have to battle it out with Pablo Sandoval for a shot at the starter's job. That is not saying much for either guy and ultimately both will cede the spot to Yoan Moncada before too long.

David Wright: By the time you read this, it could very well be possible that New York Mets third baseman David Wright has retired due to the ongoing battle he is waging against spinal stenosis. It certainly looks like a losing battle as Wright only managed to play in 37 games before he was shut down for good in late May. Even in those 37 games, Wright was downright hideous at the plate with a sky-high 33.5 percent K rate that speaks to the difficulties he is now having generating a swing with his balky back. While Wright did manage to swat 7 home runs, his all-or-nothing results and as bad as can be health, signal it is time to salute the career and move away from the guy for good.

Pablo Sandoval: By the time you read this, the Boston Red Sox could have written a check to say goodbye to veteran third baseman Pablo Sandoval. One of the biggest free-agent mistakes ever, Sandoval managed just 3 games and 7 at-bats last season before being forced to undergo season-ending shoulder surgery. With top third base prospect Yoan Moncada the favorite to win the third base job in spring training, Sandoval has no place on the Red Sox and most certainly on any fantasy baseball squad.

OUTFIELD OVERVIEW

Your format will really dictate what strategy you use here as those who play in leagues that start five outfielders will need to be more aggressive, while those who use just 3 can be a bit more deliberate. Be that as it may, you want to have a five-tool contributor from here in the first two rounds and then come back here somewhere between Round 5-7 for your second outfielder. The third outfielder should be a high upside youngster or proven veteran who specializes in home runs or stolen bases depending on what the rest of your roster looks like. What is interesting is that despite there being so many more outfielders then there are any other position besides starting pitching, the depth is not tremendous. That means be sure you have two outfielders by the end of Round 7 regardless of what format your league is.

Mike Trout: While he is getting strong heat from Boston Red Sox outfielder Mookie Betts and Houston Astros second baseman Jose Altuve, Los Angeles Angels superstar Mike Trout once again is our pick as the number 1 player for 2017 fantasy baseball. There is simply nothing that Trout can't do on the field and with a bat in his hand as he once again blew up all five standard categories last season. Now cemented in the three spot in the Angeles' lineup, Trout slammed 29 home runs, drove in 100 batters, and crossed home plate 123 times. In addition, Trout batted .315 and began running at a rate not seen since 2013 in swiping 30 bases. While Trout did lose 12 home runs from 2015, he also gained 19 steals which more than made up for the drop in power. While his overall numbers might move around a bit among the five categories, Trout is pretty much without peer in terms of the ridiculous production. Unless you are a Red Sox or Astros fan, there is no reason Trout should not be the number 1 pick in your league.

2017 PROJECTION: .311 35 HR 106 RBI 119 R 26 SB

Mookie Betts: Another season like 2016 and Boston Red Sox outfielder Mookie Betts might be able to stake his claim as the number 1 player in all of fantasy baseball. While Betts was universally praised as a burgeoning star entering into last season, his spectacular five-category production left jaws agape. I mean where do we begin? For one thing, Betts' power/speed game was epic as he hit 31 home runs and stole 26 bases batting at or near the top of the Red Sox lineup. Betts also scored 122 runs, collected 113 RBI, and batted .318. In fact Betts bettered Mike Trout in three of the five standard categories but the fact the latter has done it longer makes him the right pick for number 1 overall. Still Betts should go number 2 given what we have seen and what is really nuts is that he will be just 24 when the 2017 season gets underway. It is very rare to see such a huge offensive impact at such a young age and with incredible plate discipline as well as we just witnessed with Betts. He struck out at just a 11.0 K/9 clip last season and Betts' .322 BABIP; while somewhat lucky; was not out of this world for a speedy player. Again Betts should hear his name called second overall in almost all leagues this season and for good reason.

2017 PROJECTION: .315 29 HR 110 RBI 125 R 28 SB

Bryce Harper: Yes Bryce Harper didn't put video-game numbers last season as we all expected him to do. Yes the batting average plummeted horribly to an ugly .243. Yes Harper went from 42 home runs in 2015 to only 24 last season. I guess he stinks huh? In a performance that should change nothing about Harper's status as a top tier player in fantasy baseball regardless of position, Bryce Harper no doubt had an "off year" by his insane standards. Going into 2016, nobody should have expected Harper to repeat his 42 homers, 118 runs, 99 RBI, and .330 average. Those type of numbers come along once in a blue moon and even Harper can't be expected to maintain them. Also keep in mind that Harper goes into the 2017 season STILL just 24-years-old and with a few years of ceiling left to his name. Harper will be just fine folks so don't for a second downgrade him past the early second round at worst. Now in terms of what happened a year ago, Harper was actually just fine with his advanced numbers as he actually IMPROVED on both his K/9 and BB/9 rates. So why the average drop? Try a very unlucky .264 BABIP which haunted Harper all season. Consider that in 2015, Harper's BABIP was a sky-high .369. That is more than a 100-point drop on that front and so it is no shock Harper's average dipped. Also don't discount the fact that Daniel Murphy hitting in front of Harper got a whole bunch of fastballs that his teammate did not. With Murphy having an MVP-season himself in 2016, expect the fastballs to be more even from opposing pitchers in 2017. Finally don't overlook the fact that Harper ran like never before in setting a career-best in steals with 21. If Harper continues to run like that when his offensive numbers shoot back up this season, we are talking about top-five production. If you choose to stupidly knock Harper for his 2016 performance, we will laugh all the way to the fantasy baseball bank in snatching him up.

2017 PROJECTION: .300 36 HR 95 RBI 110 R 17 SB

Charlie Blackmon: While a bit of a late bloomer, there is no denying the massive fantasy baseball impact Colorado Rockies outfielder Charlie Blackmon has made over the last three seasons. Despite being a veteran at the age of 30, Blackmon actually reached another new height in terms of his standing in fantasy baseball in 2016. After setting career-highs in FOUR of the five standard categories (everything but steals), Blackmon has now put himself into consideration as a late first round pick for 2017 drafts. As far as those career-bests were concerned, Blackmon batted .324 with 29 home runs, 111 runs scored, and 82 RBI while batting leadoff for the Rockies. There is nothing Blackmon can't do now in terms of his offensive game and he already has legitimized himself fully given the fact the production last year was the third season in a row we have seen such great numbers here. The only thing you could possibly quibble about with Blackmon last season was the fact his steals dropped sharply from 2015's 43 all the way to 17 a year ago but that likely is a giveback to age. Even if Blackmon gives back some of his spectacular 2016 numbers, he would still remain a firm outfielder 1 in all formats. With just a 15.9 K/9 rate, buy in fully to all the numbers here.

2017 PROJECTION: .300 25 HR 77 RBI 101 R 20 SB

Ryan Braun: Having gone through the ringer (deservedly so we might add) after getting caught up in the Biogenesis mess, Milwaukee Brewers outfielder Ryan Braun has pretty much gotten himself back to outfielder 1 territory after putting forth a terrific 2016 campaign. Bringing back memories of his MVP days in terms of power and speed, Braun smashed 30 home runs, stole 16 bases, and batted .305. The 30 bombs were the most since before Braun's PED suspension and the same goes with the average. Whether one wants to question the uptick across the board last season (you would have every reason to do so), Braun makes the grade again as an outfielder 1. Keep in mind though that Braun continues to frustrate on a yearly basis with injuries; most often ending up in day-to-day situations which no doubt can be blamed on the effects of the steroids. No spring chicken anymore as Braun will be 33 when the new seasons begins, be sure to factor that in when debating an investment.

2017 PROJECTION: .290 28 HR 89 RBI 86 R 14 SB

Yoenis Cespedes: The free agency game begins again for Cuban slugger Yoenis Cespedes as he is expected to opt out of his contract with the New York Mets by the time you read this. Opt out he should as Cespedes comes off another MVP-worthy campaign in 2016 when he 31 home runs, drove in 86 runners, and batted

.280 for the team in 2016. Cespedes has changed his game since breaking in with the Oakland A's in 2012, losing all of his previous stolen base speed (3 steals last season) and upping his batting average as a result of improving both in his BB/9 and K/9 rates. While the loss of steals is an annoyance, Cespedes' four-category production warrants low-end outfielder 1 status.

2017 PROJECTION: .277 33 HR 97 RBI 83 R 5 SB

Giancarlo Stanton: The wait for 40 home runs goes on. For the third frustrating season in a row, Miami Marlins slugger Giancarlo Stanton had a large chunk of his season interrupted due to injury. This time it was a serious groin pull in mid-August that shut Stanton down for a majority of the rest of 2016 as his owners were once again left without their big home run weapon when fantasy baseball leagues were being decided. Prior to the injury, Stanton was having a somewhat rough season as his home run rate was behind his 2014 and 2015 pace and the batting average became a major liability as he finished with a shaky .240 mark. With a near-neutral BABIP of .290, no luck could save Stanton's average after he put up an insane K/9 rate of 29.8 percent and combined that with a 10.6 BB/9 that was his lowest number there since 2010. In other words, Stanton was hacking like never before and while the 27 home runs were very helpful indeed, the rest of his offensive package was not very good. Right now we have to accept that Stanton is not the first round pick that he was the last two years given the average troubles and rampant injuries. Also the brief burst of steals from 2014-15 seems gone for good as well. There is not a better pure home run hitter in all of fantasy baseball though than Stanton but he simply can't be counted on for a full year of at-bats which calls into question what you are willing to pay at the draft table this season.

2017 PROJECTION: .255 34 HR 92 RBI 88 R 1 SB

George Springer: The jury is still out on whether Houston Astros outfielder George Springer will be a superstar player or just a really good one. The former 2011 first round pick in 2011 is currently situated in the latter category as he comes off a 2016 campaign where he put up a terrific total of 29 home runs and 116 runs scored; but at the same time batted a rough .261. In addition, Springer has not run anywhere near his minor league levels, swiping just 9 bags in 162 games last season. The problems with the batting average are not unexpected as Springer's 23.9 K/9 needs to come down but there is reason for optimism a breakout can be made since he does take a bunch of walks (11.8 BB/9). Now 27-years-old,

Springer is getting very close to reaching his prime and that means what we already are seeing from him statistics-wise could very well be his best.

2017 PROJECTION: .265 27 HR 110 R 80 RBI 12 SB

Trea Turner: Meet the guy who will elicit the biggest battles at respective draft tables this spring. Outside of maybe New York Yankees catcher Gary Sanchez, there is not a more hyped and sought-after "sleeper" for 2017 fantasy baseball then sudden Washington Nationals outfield star Trea Turner. We put sleeper in quotes because it is tough to carry that label when everyone and their mother wants to own you for the upcoming season. That is understandable as Turner posted one of those overnight blockbuster fantasy baseball debut campaigns that brought back memories of Ryan Braun or with Sanchez a year ago. Turner crammed in as many glowing numbers as he could in his 73 games with the Nats as he batted a scorching .342, hit 13 home runs, and ran like Billy Hamilton in collecting 33 steals. The average and steals stand out here right off the bat but Turner is more than capable of remaining an insane contributor in both going forward. Possessing blinding speed, Turner can challenge for a stolen base crown in 2017 and his rate last season would have already won him the award. As far as the average, yes expecting Turner to hit .342 again is foolish but his low K/9 rates going back to the minors and last year (18.2) combined with the speed will make him an annual .300-plus guy. Also likely hitting at or near the top of the Washington order, 100 runs is very much in play as well. The only thing we might question was the 13 home runs in just 324 at-bats Turner hit last year, which was a rate he never approached before in the minors. In fact Turner never hit more than 6 homers at any level which means don't buy into the guy expecting 15-plus as a guarantee. Now we are not saying 15-plus homers are not possible as Turner continues to gain strength as he moves closer to his prime and keep in mind Francisco Lindor is a comparable comparison there as someone who showed little power on the farm but then ramped it up in the majors. Be that as it may, Turner is the one incredibly hyped young player we will give full permission to reach for.

2017 PROJECTION: .316 15 HR 67 RBI 99 R 48 SB

Nelson Cruz: Seattle Mariners outfielder Nelson Cruz just keeping moving along with his big-time power despite the fact he is getting up there in age at 36. His late-career home run renaissance continued onward in 2016 as he hit 43 home runs (third straight season of 40 or more) and drove in 105 batters while still calling spacious Safeco Field home. Not to be overlooked with all the power is the fact Cruz has become very durable in his later years after really struggling badly with injuries earlier in his career while with the Texas Rangers. There is little volatility to speak of here as Cruz has hit .287 and .302 the last two years; while also maintaining K/9 and BB/9 rates right along his career norms. Yes the threat of erosion grows as Cruz continues to age but as of right now, his status as a moderate outfielder 1 and power ace remains true.

2017 PROJECTION: .280 37 HR 102 RBI 91 R 2 SB

Ian Desmond: After betting on himself and losing in a very ugly manner during 2015 free agency, Ian Desmond was forced to settle for a one-year deal with the Texas Rangers for 2016 which entailed him moving from shortstop to the outfield. With all that potential negativity swirling around the guy, Desmond responded by revisiting his 20/20 past going back to his earlier Washington Nationals days by hitting 22 home runs and stealing 21 bases for the Rangers. In addition, Desmond reversed some very ugly trends with his hitting approach, slashing his K/9 rate from 2015's nasty 29.2 mark, all the way down to a respectable 23.6 last season. That development allowed Desmond to bat .285; an average that was his highest since 2012. Throw in 107 runs scored and 86 RBI and Desmond was back to being a five-stool stud in fantasy baseball while carrying eligibility at shortstop and in the outfield. Of course the shortstop eligibility is gone for now but Desmond could gain it back depending on how things shake out in free agency. The best move for Desmond would be to return to Texas and keep himself in a prime hitter's park but it was very encouraging to see him go back to his old Washington roots with his batting approach. Having reached the 20/20 mark in four of the last five years, Desmond is back to being a trusted commodity.

2017 PROJECTION: .273 20 HR 88 RBI 98 R 22 SB

Mark Trumbo: Just like A.J. Pollock was our sleeper pick of the year for 2015 fantasy baseball, it was Baltimore Orioles outfielder/DH Mark Trumbo who claimed that title for 2016. What was ironic about us recommending Trumbo so strongly prior to last season was the fact that we previously had no use for the guy during his years with the Seattle Mariners and Arizona Diamondbacks. While we always appreciated Trumbo's power, his habitually ugly batting averages, penchant for injury, and pricey draft price left us wanting more. What we always stay true to however is that EVERY player is worth drafting if their price falls far enough and that is what Trumbo presented leading into 2016. Adding to the intrigue was the fact Trumbo was acquired by the Baltimore Orioles during the Hot Stove Season as the move put the slugger back into a prime power ballpark after languishing the previous year in spacious Safeco Field with the Seattle Mariners. Instantly Trumbo made us look very smart by putting forth a ridiculous March/April (6 home runs and a .337 average) which set the stage for a truly dominant season with the bat. Trumbo would lead all of baseball in home runs with 47 and he also would light things up as well in runs (94) and RBI (108). The average remained an issue at .256 but that should not have been a shock considering Trumbo strikes out a ton (25.5 percent) which has been a career-long problem. Having timed his offensive bonanza perfectly with free agency on tap, Trumbo's 2017 value will depend greatly on where he ends up during the winter. As long as Trumbo avoids another Safeco Field-like ballpark, he should be good for at least 35 home runs and 100 RBI. With the draft price now trending upwards off such a big 2016 however, we likely have reached a point where passing on Trumbo is the right away to go as you never want to buy players coming off a career-year.

2017 PROJECTION: .251 35 HR 98 RBI 88 R 1 SB

Lorenzo Cain: After graduating into a borderline outfielder 1 in fantasy baseball terms during a terrific career-year campaign in 2015 (when he hit .307 with 16 home runs and 28 stolen bases), Lorenzo Cain saw his numbers decline across the board last season as he finished the year on IR due to a serious wrist injury. Prior to the wrist going bad, Cain continued to do his power/speed thing with 9 home runs and 16 steals in 434 at-bats (which were rates that were not much below his 2015 pace in those categories) but the counting numbers in runs and RBI sank as the K.C. lineup struggled around him. In addition, Cain struck out a bit more (19.4 percent compared to 16.2 in 2015) which caused the average to slide some to .287 but nothing too drastic. Still it really was the wrist that literally hurt Cain more than anything and he will be back to full health for the start of 2016 with a slightly lowered draft price. Flat in his prime at the age of 30, Cain represents a very safe investment for your outfield and he could easily come close to replicating his big 2015 numbers if the health cooperates.

2017 PROJECTION: .300 15 HR 92 R 65 RBI 26 SB

Starling Marte: Considering the recent offensive decline of Andrew McCutchen, you can safely argue that the multi-talented Starling Marte is the best outfielder on the Pittsburgh Pirates. Now fully into his prime at the age of 27, Marte has cemented himself as one of the best outfielders in all of baseball as well and his skills across all five categories make him a gem to own in fantasy. Blessed with speed to burn, Marte ran wild in 2016 as he set a career-high in steals with 47 and he would have topped 50 if not for missing almost all of September with a stubborn bout of back soreness. Marte also put up a career-best .311 average as he continued to smooth out the edges on a swing that was prone to striking out when he first arrived in Pittsburgh. Consider that during each of his first three years in the majors, Marte's K/9 rate was 24 percent or higher. The last two seasons though Marte has lowered that mark to 19.4 and 19.7 percent respectively and that is why the .311 he hit last year is legit. Now there were some minor negatives worth pointing out in terms of Marte's 2016 numbers, with the most obvious being his mediocre 46 RBI and only 9 home runs. The drop in home runs was particularly disappointing as Marte seemed set to cross the 20 mark after he clubbed 19 just the year prior. Perhaps the back problems that ruined the end of Marte's 2016 played a role but we can consider the 9 home runs an outlier since he reached double-digits in every one of his three previous seasons. What we might have to do is to keep the home run projection closer to 20 instead of anticipating a jump up any higher but that is a small giveback considering the five-tool ability. We reiterate that Marte is only now getting settled into his prime years and so we can safely grade him out as a prime outfielder 1 for 2017 fantasy baseball for at least a few more years. While Marte is not Mike Trout, he should still go no later than the third round in drafts this spring.

2017 PROJECTION: .295 15 HR 65 RBI 88 R 38 SB

Christian Yelich: There are few swings that are as natural and free-flowing as Miami Marlins burgeoning star outfielder Christian Yelich and the fantasy baseball community began to understand this when watching him swing the bat during the 2016 season. The former 2010 first round pick of the team took a few years to find his comfort zone at the major league level but last season showed that Yelich can be a high-end guy for years. While Yelich didn't light the world on fire in any one area, he did contribute to all five standard categories in batting .298 with 21 home runs and 98 RBI. Add in 78 runs scored and 9 steals and Yelich seems primed to push into the outfielder 1 range for 2017. In fact some comparisons can be made to Mookie Betts in terms of a young outfielder on the cusp of greatness as the Red Sox outfielder appeared on the verge of in 2015. We then saw Betts go nuts last season and that sort of jump is very much in play for Yelich. While you want to see the stolen bases jog back upwards into the double-digit range, everything else seems set to take off this season.

2017 PROJECTION: .308 25 HR 100 RBI 86 R 15 SB

A.J. Pollock: Well that encore didn't go according to plan. We were never more proud then when we tabbed Arizona Diamondbacks developing outfielder A.J. Pollock as one of our most hyped fantasy baseball sleepers for the 2015 season and then sat back and watched him put up a monster five-category superstar campaign. Operating mostly out of the leadoff or number 2 spot in the Arizona order, Pollock batted .315 with 20 home runs, and 39 stolen bases. Pollock also put up a huge tally in runs with 111 and even chipped in with 76 RBI ,which is a tremendous number considering the batting spot. No matter how you looked at him, Pollock's 2015 haul was that of a top tier fantasy baseball outfielder and so it was no shock when he sailed into second round territory for 2016 drafts. It was then where fate intervened as Pollock fractured his elbow in spring training which landed him on the disabled list to begin the year and even threatened his season in general. Pollock's injury was about as huge a blow as could be felt given the high draft cost and the fact Pollock didn't even take a swing that counted. Still for those who kept him stashed on their roster, Pollock fought his way back to the team in late August where he flashed his 2015 power/speed game by cracking 2 home runs and stealing 4 bases in 41 at-bats. Alas a very bad situation somehow got worse when Pollock suffered a mid-September groin injury that finished his season early. So in the end Pollock's owners got only those 41 at-bats and his season served as a firm reminder that disaster can strike any player at any time. So in terms of what you do with Pollock moving forward, the obvious call is to completely throw out his 2016 and give him a giant mulligan since there is still a ton of ability here. Keep in mind Pollock is still only 29-years-old and the fractured elbow was a fluke-type injury that does not in any way earn him a health risk designation. 2015 is very repeatable given the remaining youth and home ballpark and again on paper would put Pollock close to the top tier outfielder realm. The best part in all this though is that since many were burned by Pollock last season, his 2017 draft price will come down by a sizable margin and that means he could turn into a huge value once again like he did in 2015. Count us among those who are big fans of Pollock and who suggest you put last season totally out of your mind and draft him with aggressive confidence this spring.

2017 PROJECTION: .300 17 HR 67 RBI 92 R 34 SB

Jackie Bradley Jr.: Boy is the Boston Red Sox outfield the envy of every other team in baseball outside of maybe the Pittsburgh Pirates. Not only do the Red Sox possess a monster in Mookie Betts, they also saw former 2011 first round pick Jackie Bradley Jr. fully develop into a high-end performer in 2016. Yes it did take

Bradley a couple of years to figure out major league pitching but his performance last season was phenomenal. The biggest surprise was the power as Bradley smacked 26 home runs and drove in 87 batters; rates he never approached coming up the minor league ladder. He also scored 94 runs and picked up 9 steals to help almost everywhere. We say almost everywhere as Bradley's .267 average was shaky but that would be splitting hairs when evaluating the entire product. Bradley draws walks at a high rate (9.9 BB/9) which should help remedy the average in due time and that will only make his case for low-end outfielder 1 inclusion more viable. Upwards we go.

2017 PROJECTION: .274 24 HR 88 RBI 97 R 12 SB

Adam Jones: There may not be a more consistent prime-time fantasy baseball hitter in the entire game than Baltimore Orioles outfielder Adam Jones based on what we have seen out of the guy since he developed into a solid outfielder 1. While Jones is no longer the base-stealer he was earlier in his career, the rest of his offensive numbers can pretty much be written in ink. Consider that over the last three seasons, Jones' home run total have come in as follows: 29, 27, and 29. You also etch in stone a .280 average to go with 80-90 runs as well. With Jones' BB/9 and K/9 rates very stable, there is little to no volatility in the numbers. Instead the only issue we would have here is the fact Jones is becoming more injury prone by year as he is now into his 30's. As long as you take that into account, Jones is about as safe a player to invest in as there is.

2017 PROJECTION: .280 28 HR 88 RBI 86 R 2 SB

J.D. Martinez: It was a bit of a tough year for Detroit Tigers slugging outfielder J.D. Martinez in 2016 as he missed 7 weeks with a fractured elbow of all things. Once back on the field though, Martinez was his customary power-hitting self as he put up 22 home runs in just 517 at-bats. Martinez also reaffirmed his status as a very valuable home run/average combo hitter; a standing that has him on the border of outfielder 1 status in fantasy baseball. Over the last three seasons, Martinez has batted .315, .282, and .307 and that is despite routinely putting up K/9 rates that are above 24.0. For some reason or another, Martinez is that rare hitter who routinely beats the BABIP curve by quite a lot (.319 or more in each of the last four years). This is strange since Martinez doesn't have the pure speed that most often correlates to staying ahead there but we will take it nonetheless. Putting it all together, Martinez carries a nice price tag for 2017 fantasy baseball as his name doesn't seem to make anyone run out to get him. The production says you should re-think that mindset however.

2017 PROJECTION: .300 33 HR 107 RBI 90 R 2 SB

Stephen Piscotty: We told you in these pages last season to choose Stephen Piscotty over Randal Grichuk when it came to the upstart St. Louis Cardinals outfielders. The reason we sided with Piscotty was due to the fact he was a better pure hitter than Grichuk and also had developing power that stood a good chance of emerging soon. The former 2012 first round pick wound up with 22 home runs , 86 runs scored, and 85 RBI last season; putting himself into high-end outfielder 2 territory. Piscotty even ran a bit with 7 steals but his .273 average came in a bit below expectations. An uptick there should start occurring as soon as 2017 though as Piscotty had a very solid 20.5 K/9 rate last season and at the age of 26 for 2017, some upside remains.

2017 PROJECTION: .286 24 HR 90 RBI 88 R 8 SB

Carlos Gonzalez: Along the same lines as Matt Kemp, Colorado Rockies outfielder Carlos Gonzalez has successfully changed the dynamics of his game in terms of contributing numbers for fantasy baseball. Knowing full well his speed had vanished, the former 20/20 first round dynamo began to go all-out in swinging for the fences. The result was a monster 2015 campaign where Gonzalez went yard 40 times in transforming himself overnight into one of the best power hitters in the game. We told you leading into last season however that Gonzalez' 40 home runs reeked of being an outlier and that was proven true as his number there settled back into the mid-20's at 25. Despite the unsurprising drop, Gonzalez collected 100 RBI and scored 87 runs while batting a respectable .271. That placed him in firm outfielder 2 range and that is where Gonzalez will reside for the time being. As we said earlier, the speed is gone here and so there will be no more steals to be had. That has actually helped Gonzalez stay healthy the last couple of seasons after he went through a number of years with leg and hand injuries attempting to steal. Also with Gonzalez swinging for the fences like never before, his batting average will no longer approach the .300 mark as well. Yes the flash has dimmed some but Gonzalez still offers enough to help you.

2017 PROJECTION: .273 27 HR 99 RBI 90 R 2 SB

Michael Brantley: Considered one of the better pure hitters in all of baseball, Cleveland Indians outfielder Michael Brantley had a season to forget in 2016 due to a series of shoulder injuries that eventually led to surgery. In between Brantley amassed just 43 at-bats in 11 games for a season total of 0 home runs, 1 stolen base, and a .231 average. It has now been two full seasons since Brantley went 20/20 with 20 home runs and 23 stolen bases in 2014; numbers that were considered an outlier compared to his regular per game career rates. That was proven to be a fact the following season when Brantley sank to 15 home runs and 15 steals but he remained solid across all five standard categories. Still young at the age of 29, Brantley will enter the new year with full health and stands a very good chance of reprising his 2015 numbers. While we correctly told you all not pay the sticker price on Brantley two seasons ago, the reduced 2017 draft price has us going the other way now given the prospects for him being a solid value play. What has made Brantley such a good hitter is the fact his K/9 rates are habitually in the single-digits and he also draws a high number of walks. As a result, Brantley should be able to hit .300 in his sleep and again contribute around a 15/15 ratio with his home runs and steals. Good comeback potential.

2017 PROJECTION: .315 16 HR 88 RBI 86 R 16 SB

Gregory Polanco: The Pittsburgh Pirates now have three multi-talented outfielders in their starting lineup after Gregory Polanco took a sizable leap in his development during the 2016 season. Clearly growing into his power, Polanco set a new career-best in home runs with 22 and also kept it up on the bases with 17 steals. There are still some limitations here, such as a batting average that came in at .258 last season (after setting .235 and .256 marks his first two years in the league). Polanco did have a slightly unlucky .291 BABIP however and with his K/9 rate coming in at a very good 20.3, an uptick is almost a given going forward. So far Polanco's development is mirroring that of teammate Starling Marte in terms of gaining power as he goes along and he needs to get back to the 27 steals he had in 2015 so he can maximize his fantasy baseball impact. While he is not knocking on the outfielder 1 door yet, Polanco's remaining upside and already solid play make him a potentially good sleeper pick again.

2017 PROJECTION: .267 23 HR 88 RBI 79 R 20 SB

Andrew McCutchen: Wow that was a rough season for former Pittsburgh Pirates outfielder Andrew McCutchen in 2016. McCutchen's customary slow start in April never really turned around for the better and there were a slew of statistical red flags that are concerning. Start with the stolen bases as McCutchen picked up just 6 steals last season and that total marked the fourth straight year he saw a decline there. Then there is the batting average as McCutchen hit a woeful. 256 which ended up being a career-low for the veteran. McCutchen also posted a K/9 rate in the 20's for the first time in his career at 21.2. Yes there were some health problems that hampered McCutchen but his erosion in steals alone downgrades him from five-category classification. Now firmly in his prime at the age of 30, McCutchen no longer carries the flash he once did and he presents more risk than ever before. This could go either way in 2017 but the trends point to McCutchen being a step or two below his past first round value.

2017 PROJECTION: .288 23 HR 89 RBI 90 R 9 SB

Odubel Herrera: We challenge you to find another publication that touted Philadelphia Phillies emerging outfielder Odubel Herrera the way we did in these pages last year. Recognizing the power/speed game that was just starting to show up in 2015, Herrera was one of our favorite sleeper picks for 2016 fantasy baseball. Generally speaking, Herrera made good on our tout in hitting 15 home runs, stealing 25 bases, and batting .286. Throw in the 87 runs scored and Herrera was golden in four of the five standard categories (just 49 RBI was the one negative). Only 25-years-old by the time the 2017 season gets underway, we are doubling down on recommending Herrera again as a guy who could very well take that next step into outfielder 1 territory. Even if that doesn't occur, Herrera is skilled enough across the board that he should at the very least be a firm outfielder 2. Get on board here.

2017 PROJECTION: .293 17 HR 57 RBI 93 R 28 SB

Justin Upton: The extreme hold and cold spells at the plate for Detroit Tigers outfielder Justin Upton are becoming more pronounced by the year and that is obviously not a good thing. Upton certainly didn't make a good first impression with his new team after signing a ridiculous six-year deal worth a whopping $132.8 million; coming out cold as ice with the bat in enduring a .233 first half with just 9 home runs. Upton got going in the second half by upping those numbers to .260 and a very locked-in 22 home runs that saved his season but the damage was already done leading up to that point in the eyes of his owners. The former number 1 overall pick in the 2005 draft has become a very polarizing figure in fantasy baseball as he has never lived up to the "can't miss" label that many originally placed on him. Instead Upton has developed into a very good but quite flawed player, with the biggest issue centering on his annually terrible K/9 rates. Upton was in prime form there last season as his 28.6 K/9 was downright pathetic and his .246 average came in very shoddy as well. Yes we certainly can't argue with 31 home runs from anybody and Upton also went north of 80 both in runs and

RBI. Still the batting average is a big problem now and Upton has also seen his stolen bases slide into the single-digit in moving closer to the age of 30. As long as you know Upton will help you just in three categories, be serviceable in one other, and then destroy you in the last, feel free to check him out. Just be clear to yourself that Upton will drive you nuts along the way given the drastic and wild swings in production.

2017 PROJECTION: .253 30 HR 89 RBI 86 R 12 SB

Billy Hamilton: Few players have been more polarizing in all of fantasy baseball the last few seasons than Cincinnati Reds outfield burner Billy Hamilton. After Hamilton put up video game-like stolen base totals while in the minor leagues for the Reds, the hype machine went into overdrive when he finally made it up to the majors as prospective owners began picturing what it would be like to own a player who could top 100 in that category. The only problem was that Hamilton needed to get on first base first in order to begin collecting steals and that initially proved to be a big problem for him as he batted a pathetic .250 and .226 his first two years in the bigs. Despite the batting issues, Hamilton was STILL able to run wild to the tune of 56 and 57 stolen bases respectively in those two seasons which showed just how much of a difference he could make there. Still as 2016 fantasy baseball drafts got underway, most Hamilton owners went in accepting that he was a one-category specialist and that whatever else they got would be gravy. Much to their pleasant surprise, Hamilton did take some nice strides forward with his hitting as he pushed his batting average up to an respectable .260, while also once again running non-stop in collecting 58 steals. In fact Hamilton would have easily sailed into the 60's in stolen bases if not for an oblique injury that he suffered toward the end of last August which finished his season early. Having turned 26 in September, Hamilton is not going to improve much more going forward and he remains a very limited player who will help only in steals and somewhat in runs. In fact he somehow managed to accumulate all of 17 RBI last season in 460 at-bats which is almost impossible to believe. Also despite the uptick to .260 with his batting average, Hamilton saw his K/9 rate jump to a high 20.2 mark (up from 2015's 16.5). A .329 BABIP helped save Hamilton from another year of average negatives but the point is not to assume he will be able to repeat that .260 mark going forward. Once again draft Hamilton just for steals and be grateful for whatever else you may get.

2017 PROJECTION: .255 4 HR 26 RBI 75 R 63 SB

114

Matt Kemp: As he continues to move along the backstretch of his career, Atlanta Braves outfielder Matt Kemp has successfully reinvented himself on the fly in fantasy baseball terms. A former power/speed monster with the Los Angeles Dodgers, Kemp is now more or less a pure home run hitter after his speed vanished a few years ago. Kemp certainly did the job on the run-producing part as he mashed 35 home runs , collected 108 RBI, and scored 89 runs. Those are the only three categories Kemp can help you in since his speed is completely shot (1 stolen base all of last year) and his .262 average was the second year in a row coming in under .270. Kemp seems to know hitting home runs are now his calling card as he is hacking more than ever (career-low 5.4 BB/9 in 2016) and the batting average will continue to take a hit because of this approach. As long as you grade Kemp on his current level of production and not live in the past, he can work nicely as a moderate outfielder 2.

2017 PROJECTION: .262 30 HR 100 RBI 88 R 4 SB

David Dahl: Young former first round pick who plays in one of the best hitter's parks in the game and who can hit for power and steal bases? Yes please. Already we are extremely intrigued by Colorado Rockies outfielder David Dahl who has the classic look of possibly being the next big five-category star. Having been called up midway through the 2016 season to make his MLB debut, Dahl showed what all the fuss was about as he hit 7 home runs, stole 5 bases, and batted .315 in just 63 games with the club. Having been drafted 10th overall in 2012, Dahl has the pedigree and the skill set to be a huge talent. Some work needs to be done before Dahl reaches that stage; specifically a K/9 rate that is elevated (24.9 with Colorado, 25.6 at Double-A last season). The Rockies only played Dahl on a semi-regular basis so as not to not overwhelm him and as a prospective owner, it would be a nice idea to temper expectations some as well. While the ceiling goes very high, there will be bumps along the way.

2017 PROJECTION: .289 19 HR 65 RBI 67 R 15 SB

Andrew Benintendi: Already loaded with young outfield talent led by Mookie Betts and Jackie Bradley Jr., the Boston Red Sox added to their riches at that position when they promoted top prospect Andrew Benintendi at the start of August. Having made a rapid ascent to the majors after being selected in the first round (7th overall) in 2015, Benintendi looked right at the home in the major leagues by hitting .295 with two home runs and a steal in just 118 at-bats. While it was no doubt a cup of coffee debut for Benintendi, he should be in the Red Sox' plans as a starting outfielder for 2017. The upside here is massive as Benintendi has five-tool ability which he showed by hitting .295 with 8 home runs and 8 steals in his brief 63-game stay at Double-A before his promotion last season; skills that fit him in nicely with Betts and Bradley. With Benintendi not being up with the Red Sox for long, the fact he was not able to blow things up with his bat will help keep the fantasy baseball community more at bay some. Bid aggressively.

2017 PROJECTION: .288 17 HR 65 RBI 78 R 19 SB

Yasmani Tomas: For all the recent and well-deserved criticism of Cuban hitting busts (Alex Guerrero, Rusney Castillo, Yasiel Puig). a point must be made to respect the development thus far of Arizona Diamondbacks outfielder Yasmani Tomas. After a so-so rookie debut in 2015 (9 home runs, .273 average), Tomas really found his comfort zone last season as he went crazy with the power. Tomas' 31 home runs was among the most affordable power displays in fantasy baseball in 2016 and his 83 RBI were not too shabby either. In fact Tomas was one of the few things that went right for the D-Backs last season and at the age of just 26 when 2017 gets underway, the future looks profitable here. Keep in mind that Tomas is a slugger all the way; right on down to his high 24.2 K/9 rate that will make hitting above .275 a challenge. Also there is little speed her as well (just 7 total steals through two seasons) and that puts Tomas squarely into the pure power-hitting specialist tier.

2017 PROJECTION: .274 30 HR 86 RBI 73 R 4 SB

Adam Eaton: While he has not completely lived up to the initial hype that followed multi-talented outfielder Adam Eaton while he was coming up the Arizona D-Backs system, the guy has turned into a very useful player for the Chicago White Sox the last couple of seasons. Eaton is one of those classically undervalued players in fantasy baseball who can help in all five standard categories but without lighting up any. It is these type of players that most often appear on winning fantasy baseball rosters as the value can be sizable and Eaton has that look after batting .284, cracking 14 home runs, and stealing 14 bases last season. Eaton gets it done in the advanced world as well since both his 16.3 K/9 and 8.9 BB/9 are in the positive ranges and the fact he will still only be 28 when the new season gets underway is also attractive. We can't think of many better outfielder 3 options for 2017.

2017 PROJECTION: .286 14 HR 57 RBI 95 R 15 SB

Nomar Mazara: The Texas Rangers had to be giddy by what they saw in the spectacular 2016 rookie debut of outfielder Nomar Mazara. At the age of just 21, Mazara came out of the gates with a red-hot bat (.333 Mar/April) and also hinted at some big future power. While Mazara tailed off in the second half of the year due to a likely bout of fatigue given the fact it was his first season of playing such a long schedule, his final total of 20 home runs and a .266 average are just scratching the surface of what he can do. With a K/9 rate of just 19.7 last season, Mazara only has to work on his low walk rate (6.69 BB/9) which will likely come with further development. When that happens, Mazara will be a slam dunk .300 hitter with power that could reach 30 home runs before you know it. The only issue with Mazara is the fact he has zero speed which was quite clear by the fact he didn't swipe a single base last season. The kid is the real deal.

2017 PROJECTION: .288 23 HR 79 RBI 73 R 1 SB

Marcell Ozuna: Things are back on track now with Miami Marlins outfielder Marcell Ozuna as he comes off a solid 2016 campaign where his bat did the talking and any previous immaturity became a non-factor. While Ozuna is no superstar, the power bat is impactful and he was a help in three standard categories last season (runs, RBI, home runs). Ozuna has now hit 23 home runs in two of the last three years and that seems to be around his ceiling going forward. A .266 average needs improving but Ozuna has done work to help there by lowering his K.9 rate under 20.0 in 2016 to a much better 18.9. Still young at the age of 26 when the 2017 season gets underway, there could be a smidge of upside left for Ozuna. Ultimately he should be priced only in the outfielder 3 range as he carries negatives in average and stolen bases.

2017 PROJECTION: .270 25 HR 79 RBI 77 R 1 SB

Carlos Beltran: If only we could age as nicely as Carlos Beltran has. Despite playing in his age 39-season, Beltran reinforced his Hall of Fame worthiness as he hit 29 home runs (his most since 2012), drove in 93 runs, and batted .295 in a year split between the New York Yankees and Texas Rangers in 2016. It was outfielder 2 production out of Beltran for the price of a late round pick and it makes you wonder what else he has up his sleeve as he turns 40 in April. Of course we remind you that Beltran is as brittle as they come health-wise and upticks in production that come out of nowhere for a hitter over the age of 35 always have to be treated as a last-gasp output. In other words, continue to draft Beltran in the late rounds and don't sweat it if someone else reaches for him.

2017 PROJECTION: .276 22 HR 80 RBI 67 R 1 SB

Melvin Upton Jr.: Who knew that it would be Melvin and not Justin who became the more valuable fantasy baseball outfielder in 2016. Back from the fantasy baseball dead, Melvin Upton Jr. saved his career by posting a shockingly good comeback season in hitting 20 home runs and stealing 27 bags in a year split between the San Diego Padres and Toronto Blue Jays. It wasn't all perfect as Upton Jr. kept up with his career-long struggle in the batting average department by hitting only .238 (due to a 28.8 K/9 rate) but he now gets to take aim at the friendly outfield dimensions of Rogers center from the jump. Despite the fact Upton Jr. will be 32 when the new season gets under way, he showed a year ago that the power and speed are still in good working order.

2017 PROJECTION: .235 17 HR 75 R 67 RBI 24 SB

Jay Bruce: Nothing has really changed when it comes to the fantasy baseball outlook for veteran New York Mets slugger Jay Bruce. Other than his new home of course after the Reds dealt Bruce to the Mets at the Aug. 1 deadline. While Bruce really struggled in his two-month stint with the Mets, his overall 33 home runs and .250 batting average were par for the course statistically. That means a high number of home runs and RBI, plus a decent dent in runs. The average will always remain ugly and Bruce is now down to a stolen base total you can count on one hand. We have never been big boosters of Bruce given the average issues and that won't change now.

2017 PROJECTION: .259 30 HR 95 RBI 70 R 5 SB

Khris Davis: One of the more unexpected outlets of major power production in 2016 fantasy baseball came from the bat of veteran slugger Khris Davis. While the holes in Davis' swing remained gaping (27.2 K/9 and .247 average), he still connected enough to swat 42 home runs and drive in 108 batters for the Oakland A's. Davis has now pretty much established himself as an all-or-nothing batter since he doesn't run (1 total steal in 2016) but he can hit the baseball hard upon contact. For all the home runs you are buying though, a horrid batting average comes along for the ride to offset the positives there. Use just as an outfielder 3 or more ideally as a bench guy.

2017 PROJECTION: .245 33 HR 93 RBI 82 R 2 SB

Hunter Pence: Age remains undefeated when it comes dragging down the numbers of all pitchers and hitters at some point in the latter stages of their careers and this is something that former ultra-durable outfielder Hunter Pence can attest to. For the second year in a row in 2016, Pence missed extensive time with injury as he got into just 106 games for the San Francisco Giants. When he as active, Pence still played relatively well as he hit 13 home runs, collected 57 RBI, and batted .289. Pence turns 34 in April however and that means his injury risk will remain high into the 2017 season. A former fantasy baseball outfielder 1 going back to his Houston Astro days, Pence is now nothing more than a back-end starter. While Pence is capable of still hitting 20 home runs, his five-tool days are over as he has just five steals over the last two years.

2017 PROJECTION: .286 17 HR 82 RBI 80 R 5 SB

Adam Duvall: The 2016 Cincinnati Reds were another team who began ushering in a rebuild and that allowed them to take a long look at power-hitting outfielder Adam Duvall. Duvall was coming off a 2015 performance at Triple-A where he hit 26 home runs in just 437 at-bats and so they Reds gave him a starting spot in the outfield to begin the new year as a sort of audition. Well at least for the first half of the season, Duvall delivered as he slammed 23 home runs and collected 61 RBI. Unfortunately the fun didn't last as Duvall's high-K rate approach got exposed the more he played and his second half numbers (10-HR, .231 average) nosedived. For the season as a whole, 33 home runs and 103 RBI looked very nice but not so much the .241 average. The problem here is that opposing pitchers now have a firm scouting report on Duvall and that means more struggles to begin 2017 is very possible. While not a Quad-A guy per se, Duvall's strikeout-prone ways make him susceptible to being sent back to the minors at any time given the expected dry spells that come with such an approach. Admire the home runs from last season but move right along in terms of drafting Duvall this spring.

2017 PROJECTIONL: .235 25 HR 86 RBI 75 R 3 SB

Joc Pederson: Any early enthusiasm we had for Los Angeles Dodgers outfielder Joc Pederson just prior to his debut with the team has pretty much completely evaporated in the two years since. That is what happens when you post horrid batting averages of .210 and .246 during your first two seasons with the Dodgers, while also going above the 27.0 K/9 mark on both occasions as well. In addition, Pederson's former 30-stolen base minor league speed has been completely MIA since coming to the majors, with just 10 total steals in 2015 and 2016 combined. The plate disciplined is non-existent as Pederson swings for the fences almost every time up and he certainly has the strikeouts to prove it. The power is very good without a doubt as Pederson swatted 26 long balls as a rookie and then followed that up with another 25 last season but that is pretty much the only positive thing you can say about the guy thus far. However with an average that can only hurt you and with the expected steals not anywhere near a part of Pederson's statistical show, we can't recommend him as anything more than an outfielder 3 with severe limitations.

2017 PROJECTION: .249 27 HR 72 RBI 67 R 8 SB

Aaron Judge: While former 40-homer slugger Adam Dunn has been retired for a few years now, his game might have very well been reincarnated in the form of New York Yankees outfield prospect Aaron Judge. Standing a hulking 6-7 and 275 pounds, Judge looks more like a football player than a Major League outfielder as it is. The 24-year-old former 2013 number 1 pick of the Yankees (32nd overall), Judge earned a reputation coming up the minor league ladder as having immense pure power that drew comparisons to Dunn and Giancarlo Stanton. Upon his promotion last summer, the parallels seemed to fit right on down to the high strikeout rates that all three guys put up or have put up in the majors. In fact Judge was ridiculous in that category last season as he somehow recorded a 44.2 K/9 which is almost hard to believe and is the main reason he hit a terrible .179. Clearly Judge is raw and has a decent learning curve to make for 2017 but the power is easy and very impressive. In fact Judge could put up 30 home runs in 2017 and nobody would be surprised but the average could struggle to go over .240 which is a big problem. The strikeout rates will likely stay over 30.0 percent this season and that means the hit to your team average will offset some of the home run and RBI value Judge brings to the table. We don't recommend chasing Judge in drafts given his obvious shortcomings and the Yankee tag figures to make him quite overrated as well. Now we are not suggesting Judge won't be a star someday but that doesn't figure to happen this coming season given the swing issues he has.

2017 PROJECTION: .248 27 HR 83 RBI 70 R 4 SB

Michael Conforto: The sophomore jinx was in full effect for New York Mets outfield prospect Michael Conforto last year, as the 2015 darling was nothing but a colossal bust once April was in the books. Having spent next-to-no-time in the minors after being selected by the Mets in the first round of the 2014 draft, the lack of seasoning on the farm became evident last season as opposing pitchers began to exploit the apparent holes in his swing. As a result, Conforto began to press like crazy and saw his K/9 rate skyrocket to a shoddy 25.6. A demotion to the minors soon ensued during the early summer and the season was pretty much a disaster despite being called back up in September. A .220 cumulative batting average was the end result for Conforto and now he has to try and push the bad memories of last season behind him. As far as 2017 is concerned, Conforto remains highly regarded in and around baseball due to his powerful swing and good patience at the dish. That will eventually translate to 20-plus home runs and a decent average but you have to wonder if the scars from 2016 will linger a bit into this season. Remember that Conforto doesn't turn 24 until March and that means his vastly depressed draft price could make him a huge post-hype sleeper candidate.

2017 PROJECTION: .266 16 HR 63 RBI 56 R 2 SB

Randal Grichuk: Admittedly we were not big fans of St. Louis Cardinals slugging outfield prospect Randal Grichuk prior to the start of the 2016 season; instead preferring teammate and fellow farmhand Stephen Piscotty. The issue we had….and it was a big one….was Grichuk's penchant for striking out a ton and thus the expected damage his average would bring. It always needs to be remembered that high-K sluggers like Grichuk can supply an exciting amount of home runs but the ugly averages they bring take away a lot of spice from that power. Grichuk went right along with that scouting report last season as he hit an impressive 24 home runs in 478 at-bats but also supplied a nasty .240 average. His 29.5 K/9 was a joke and even though he remains young at the age of 25, Grichuk can't possibly be anything more than an outfielder 3 with his current approach.

2017 PROJECTION: .245 26 HR 74 RBI 71 R 4 SB

Matt Holliday: Age doesn't discriminate as it claimed another victim in veteran outfielder Matt Holliday during the 2016 season. Universally considered one of the better pure hitters in all of baseball over the last 15 years, Holliday completely entered into the late phase of his career last season where he swung for the fences like never before as his bat speed slowed down to the point he became a batting average liability. Before a fractured right thumb ended his season in mid-August, Holliday was hitting a by far career-low .242. Once again taking aim at the outfield fences like never before, Holliday also posted a BB/9 walk that was under 10.0 (8.3 percent) for the first time in his career. The 19 home runs in 424 at-bats was still a very good ratio at the age of 36 but Holliday was pretty much a one-category producer only as his speed left the station back in 2009. As of press time it was not a given the St. Louis Cardinals would pick up Holliday's $17 million option and even if he plays elsewhere, the writing is clearly on the wall that he is now nothing more than a bench bat at best.

2017 PROJECTION: .259 19 HR 75 RBI 74 R 1 SB

Rajai Davis: Since he already has made a career out of supplying terrific numbers relative to annually cheap draft costs, it shouldn't come as a shock that Rajai Davis once again provided a very useful 2016 campaign for his owners. Despite having reached his mid-30's, Davis has shown no signs of slippage in his always potent speed game by swiping 43 bags (his most since 2013) and he also posted a career-bests both in home runs (12) and runs (74). Getting a 12/43 season from ANYONE is big and Davis achieved those totals while not even having been drafted in many leagues prior to the year's start. One of the best base stealers during this current era, Davis needs to keep on running as his .249 average last season did reveal at least some slippage. With a K/9 that is now over 20 at 21.4, Davis is likely chasing more to overcome a decline in bat speed. Be that as it may, no one will likely make an effort to target Davis in 2017 drafts and that means another nice profit can be made even if the steals drop some.

2017 PROJECTION: .257 9 HR 45 RBI 65 R 30 SB

Curtis Granderson: In one of the more strange statistical developments of the 2016 fantasy baseball season, New York Mets outfielder Curtis Granderson put forth a terrific power campaign by slugging 30 home runs for the NL wild card winners. You would think with all that power, Granderson would have been around at least 80 RBI as well. Didn't happen as the utter lack of protection in the injury-ravaged Met lineup prevented Granderson from collecting more than his 59 RBI. It was a staggering combination of numbers to say the least but Granderson did show that his home run swing is still in fine working order. In fact what Granderson did on the power front was doubly-impressive when you consider he operates in spacious Citi Field and had little protection around him in the lineup. Be that as it may, Granderson is pretty much just a home run asset at this late stage of his career (36 for 2017) and his .237 average last season is par for the course now on that front. Also Granderson's days of being a very good steals guy has been a thing of the past for awhile, with just 4 steals in 633 at-bats bearing this out. The home runs alone make Granderson an outfielder 3 for another year but backup status would be a better idea.

2017 PROJECTION: .243 25 HR 75 RBI 86 R 3 SB

Dexter Fowler: Having saved himself with a last-minute decision to pull out of going to the Baltimore Orioles as a fourth outfielder, Dexter Fowler made the most of another chance to bat leadoff for the Chicago Cubs in 2016. While Fowler never turned into the star many made him out to be during his early Colorado Rockie days, he still had reached the level of being a firm outfielder 3 who could help in multiple categories. Over the last two years, Fowler has posted 17/20 and 13/13 splits in his power/speed game and that is a fantasy-friendly combination to say the least. The batting average is the epitome of mediocre as Fowler's .276 mark last season pretty much represents a best-case scenario there and he is no spring chicken anymore in turning 31 this March. Nothing much changing in this offensive profile.

2017 PROJECTION: .271 14 HR 46 RBI 88 R 15 SB

Max Kepler: The Minnesota Twins are hoping their prospects can help get the team back to respectability and leading that charge will be talented outfield Max Kepler. After a 9 home run/18 stolen base season in 2015 at Double-A stamped Kepler as a decent prospect, the Twins gave him a look-see during their comically poor 2016 season. Generally speaking, Kepler did well as he showed big power in hitting 17 home runs in just 447 at-bats and he also added in 6 steals. A .235 average was ugly on the surface but don't buy into it since Kepler suffered from the horrid luck a .261 BABIP brought forth. Having always drawn a high number of walks, Kepler kooks like a very good upside player who will be quite cheap at the draft table this spring.

2017 PROJECTION: .265 19 HR 73 RBI 61 R 9 SB

Leonys Martin: When you have been doing this for as long as we have, you come across some quirky stuff that defies explanation. Take the fact that it took Leonys Martin leaving one of the best hitting parks in the game in Texas and then moving to one of the worst in Safeco Field in Seattle for him to finally unleash his offensive ability. There is no other way to state that Martin was a huge failure in Texas as he face-planted so badly in 2015 that the team sent him a back to the minors and it was no shock that the team wound up giving up on him after that horrific performance. Enter the fresh start scenario for Martin in Seattle and what happened next was impossible to figure out. Showing power he never hinted at before, Martin hit 15 home runs which was an eye-opening feat in and of itself considering his history. Martin also kept at it with the speed part of his game in swiping 24 bases and scoring 72 runs. A 15/24 ratio in the power/speed categories is a terrific set of numbers in fantasy baseball and that helped to overlook the ugly

.247 average Martin put up last season. What seemed to happen here in our estimation is that once he began hitting home runs early in the year, Martin started swinging for the fences like never before. The evidence came in the form of Martin's career-worst 25.9 K/9 rate and that helped knock the average way down. Now a veteran who will turn 29 in April, Martin has zero ceiling left to his name and is more apt to slightly jog back from his numbers last season then improve on them. There is some fluke aspect in terms of those numbers and so for that reason, be sure you draft Martin only as an outfielder 3 this season.

2017 PROJECTION: .255 11 HR 53 RBI 71 R 25 SB

Cameron Maybin: Back with the Detroit Tigers after a winter trade from the Atlanta Braves, the encore for outfielder Cameron Maybin in the Motor City was a bit rough in 2016. With injuries allowing Maybin to only take part in 94 games, the counting numbers were not very impressive. In actuality though, Maybin performed well both with the bat and with his legs for the season year in a row as he batted .315 and collected 15 stolen bases. The major reason that Maybin had made a tour around the majors (Detroit, Miami, San Diego, Atlanta) was because of some horrid plate discipline and strikeout rates that derailed his early prospect hype. The light bulb seemed to go on for Maybin with the Braves in 2015 however as he posted a 10/23 split with his power/speed game and that solid play last season seemed to legitimize his semi-breakthrough. Turning just 30 in April, Maybin looks like a solid power/speed guy you can pick up late in your draft for your outfielder 3 slot.

2017 PROJECTION: .267 11 HR 57 RBI 63 R 19 SB

Ender Inciarte: Having been traded out of a very crowded outfield situation with the Arizona Diamondbacks to the Atlanta Braves the previous winter, it certainly looked on the surface that speedy leadoff man Ender Inciarte had a prime breakout opportunity. Some early injuries and a cold initial performance with the bat stunted the initial impact for Inciarte but he fought back with a good second half to salvage things. Overall Inciarte did the leadoff thing pretty well by hitting a very solid .291, scored 85 runs, and swiping 16 bases. While Inciarte is strictly just a three-category asset in fantasy baseball, there is also some remaining upside here as he turns just 26 in April. Inciarte has terrific pure hitting skills which can be seen in his very low 11.8 K/9 and decent enough 7.8 BB/9 last season. That makes him perfectly suited for the leadoff spot and with the Braves having a much better lineup to begin 2017, Inciarte will likely see a boost in his runs and steals to go with an average that will be a help. Go back to the well here.

2017 PROJECTION: .302 5 HR 40 RBI 92 R 24 SB

Byron Buxton: The post-hype sleeper tag certainly applies to Minnesota Twins outfielder Byron Buxton as 2017 fantasy baseball draws near. The former ultra-hyped 2012 first round pick (second overall) has had nothing but extreme struggles at the dish during his first two stints in the majors in 2015 and 2016, hitting a woeful .209 and .225 respectively. What has held Buxton back from permanently sticking in the major leagues are horrific contact struggles, as his K/9 rates of 31.9 and 35.6 the last two seasons with the Twins are a complete disgrace. Underneath all of those strikeouts however are very intriguing power/speed tools that Buxton began showing in last year by cracking 10 home runs and swiping 10 bags in just 331 at-bats. The consensus scouting report on Buxton has been that of a future 25/25 monster and that remains in play given the fact he will be just 23 when the 2017 season gets underway. Buxton ultimately looks like a classic case of being rushed to the majors by the Twins and that actually has delayed his growth given all the confidence-shattering struggles he has had at such a young age. The hype is still permeating around Buxton so don't think you can be a major buy low here but at the same time, his draft price won't be insane either. Still very well worth a look given the potential that remains in Buxton's game.

2017 PROJECTION: .248 17 HR 56 RBI 65 R 23 SB

Josh Reddick: It is an old habit when it comes to pushing outfielder Josh Reddick as a very affordable and impactful fantasy baseball commodity in these pages. While no one ever seems to want to own the guy, Reddick routinely goes out there and threatens a 15/15 ratio with his power and speed, while also posting useful batting averages. While he missed a slew of games last season with injury, Reddick did the job when on the field as he hit 10 home runs, stole 8 bases, and batted .281 for the Oakland A's and Los Angeles Dodgers. A former hacker who went often went over the 20.0 K/9 mark, Reddick got that number down to just 12.8 last season and he also drew walks at a solid 8.9 BB/9 rate. There is once again sneaky value here so be sure to keep a late round pick handy for this annually profitable player.

2017 PROJECTION: .278 19 HR 75 RBI 73 R 7 SB

Yasiel Puig: It has become nothing short of a comical joke the career direction Los Angeles Dodgers outfielder Yasiel Puig has taken the last few seasons. Plagued by injuries, ridiculous immaturity, and a bat that has been nowhere near as potent as it first seemed, Puig is simply not worth the trouble in almost all fantasy baseball leagues for 2017. While he is still just 25, Puig needs to get his head on straight before he can even be looked at for possible usage. Still there are continued glimpses of ability here as Puig hit 11 home runs and stole 5 bases in just 368 at-bats last season but his .263 average was the second year in a row he has been under .270. The draft price has come down severely here which could actually make Puig a decent and extreme buy low but again there are too many red flags here to count.

2017 PROJECTION: .267 17 HR 61 RBI 65 R 9 SB

Kevin Kiermaier: Last season Sports Illustrated did a piece on Tampa Bay Rays outfielder Kevin Kiermaier by saying he was quite possibly the most underrated player in all of baseball. That could be somewhat true when you factor in Kiermaier's incredible outfield defense but his offensive numbers tend to leave one wanting. That mostly centers around Kiermaier's annually poor batting averages, which was an issue that didn't get any better in 2016 as he hit .246. But in actuality, Kiermaier was pretty darn good overall last season as he set career-bests both in home runs with 12 and in stolen bases with 21. Also as far as that ugly average was concerned, Kiermaier should have had a better result there as his .278 BABIP was quite unlucky and his advanced rates in K/9 (17.9) and walks (9.7 BB/9) were both terrific. As a result, investing in Kiermaier for 2017 fantasy baseball is actually a pretty good idea given the 12/21 ratio with his power/speed game and for an average which will rise this season. We are sold.

2017 PROJECTION: .259 12 HR 48 RBI 62 R 20 SB

Jacoby Ellsbury: We are into some really ugly years now for rapidly fading New York Yankees outfielder and leadoff man Jacoby Ellsbury. Already with a well-earned reputation for being more brittle than glass, Ellsbury's previously potent offensive game is now in major decline. A former perennial stolen base title contender, Ellsbury managed just 20 steals in 626 at-bats last season, with him barely even attempting to run from August through the end of the year. Since most of Ellsbury's value comes in his stolen bases, there is pretty much nothing else worth talking about here in terms of numbers helping you in fantasy baseball. Along with the steals erosion, Ellsbury's average has been shaky since 2011, which of course was his epic outlier season when he hit 32 home runs and batted

.321. Since that all-time fluke campaign, Ellsbury has hit .271, .271, .257, and .263. With his power only residing in the single-digits, we strongly suggest avoiding Ellsbury altogether this season.

2017 PROJECTION: .270 8 HR 53 RBI 75 R 22 SB

Michael Saunders: Location, location, location. Having escaped from spacious Safeco Field in Seattle to the launching pad that is Rogers Center in Toronto, multi-talented outfielder Michael Saunders finally began to put forth consistent offensive numbers for the first time in his career. Having already given glimpses of power/speed ability in the past (12-HR/13-SB with Mariners in 2013), Saunders changed the narrative a bit in 2016 but still with overall solid results. Specifically speaking, Saunders set career-highs in home runs with 24 and runs scored with 70 in becoming a locked-in member of the Blue Jays' potent batting lineup. While the power was terrific, Saunders stopped his running game dead in its tracks as he swiped just one bag. In addition, Saunders showed no improvement in terms of past strikeout and batting average struggles. Posting a crazy 28.1 K/9 rate, Saunders only managed a .253 average that was a clear liability to his owners. With his past stolen base game nowhere to be found, the average hit took a lot of impact away from the home runs. Since he will be 30 when the 2017 season gets underway, you have to wonder if Saunders will ever get back the steals. If not, then Saunders only can be an outfielder 3 at best given his one-dimensional approach.

2017 PROJECTION: .257 20 HR 55 RBI 65 R 5 SB

Shin-Soo Choo: Pretty much if something could have gone wrong, it did for Texas Rangers outfielder Shin-Soo Choo in 2016. Injuries were the main storyline here as Choo was only able to get into 44 games before a fractured forearm finished him for good in mid-August. Now an aging 34, Choo was nonetheless still productive in his 44 games as he hit 7 home runs and picked up 6 steals. The steals were interesting in particular as it looked like Choo was finished swiping bags. However the holes are getting bigger in Choo's swing as he has been above 22 percent in his K/9 each of the last three seasons and he is impossible to depend on given all the injuries he has gone through during that span. Still worthy of being an outfielder 3 on the odd times he is healthy, Choo can be ignored until the very late rounds of your draft as no one will be fighting you for him anymore.

2017 PROJECTION: .266 15 HR 82 R 73 RBI 10 SB

Tyler Naquin: The loss of All-Star outfielder Michael Brantley for pretty much the entire 2016 season could have been a big setback for the Cleveland Indians if not for the eye-opening rookie debut of former 2012 first round pick Tyler Naquin. Having been thrown into the fire in replacing Brantley on an everyday basis, Naquin was terrific as he hit 14 home runs, stole 6 bases, and batted .296. Naquin was not over-matched in the least against Major League pitching given the surface numbers but keep in mind there also was a sizable fluke aspect to his performance. For one thing, Naquin got ridiculous BABIP luck to the tune of a .411 mark. When you consider that .300 is neutral, it is easy to see how Naquin's average was royally propped up. That means for 2017, you must dial back average expectations for Naquin into the .270 range and that doesn't make him look as attractive on that front. Also Naquin struck out at an insane 30.7 K/9 rate last season which is another major issue for his batting average. While the power/speed tools look decent, Naquin is more apt to disappoint and take a step back this season then to help you.

2017 PROJECTION: .271 16 HR 57 RBI 65 R 10 SB

Mallex Smith: Speed, speed, and more speed defines the game of Atlanta Braves outfielder prospect Mallex Smith. The 23-year-old dynamo began showing the major leagues how potent his skills are on that front during his rookie debut in 2016, picking up 16 stolen bases in just 215 at-bats. Unfortunately for Smith, a hit-by-pitch fractured his left thumb in June and the slow recovery of the bruise surrounding the digit kept him from returning to the team for the rest of the season. Despite that mini-setback, Smith will be a key part of the rebuilding phase that is currently underway as the Braves open up a new ballpark in 2017. A starting outfield spot is Smith's to lose, not to mention hitting near the top of the lineup as well given his top-notch speed. While he only hit .238 last season, Smith batted at least .280 at every spot in the minors from 2014 through 2016, which means there is plenty of room for improvement in that category. With a great 9.3 walk rate that will surely go up as he gets more acclimated to major league pitching and with speed to burn, Smith could top 30 steals in 2017 if he stays healthy. A terrific later-round steals play.

2017 PROJECTION: .271 5 HR 52 RBI 78 R 26 SB

Gerardo Parra: What a bust this guy was. My goodness it was ugly for Colorado Rockies outfielder Gerardo Parra during the 2016 season as he came nowhere closer to living up to his solid sleeper hype after signing into one of the best hitting parks in the game during free agency. Coming off a breakout season in 2015, Parra somehow managed just 7 home runs, 6 steals, and a pathetic .253 average while calling Coors Field home. A serious ankle injury clearly derailed Parra's season as he only got into 102 games but now his 2015 performance is starting to look a bit like an outlier. If you want to try a buy low here given the fact Parra is back with the Rockies and the advantages the ballpark brings for 2017, feel free to do so. Ultimately he is barely holding onto low-end outfielder 3 value.

2017 PROJECTION: .278 9 HR 45 RBI 74 R 14 SB

Carlos Gomez: At the age of 31, it is beginning to look like Carlos Gomez is becoming a journeyman right before our eyes. A fantasy baseball first round pick as recently as just prior to the 2015 season, Gomez has been besieged with injuries that look like they have taken a firm toll on his offensive numbers. 2016 was just nasty for Gomez and his owners as a .210 average and just 5 home runs in 295 at-bats got him a pink slip from the Houston Astros midway through the year. The Texas Rangers signed Gomez soon after his release and had to be pleased when he turned things around to the tune of hitting .284 with 8 home runs and 5 steals in just 116 at-bats. We are in murky times now though with Gomez whose health has never been worse and his numbers have been all over the map the last two seasons. As a result, interest in Gomez is at an all-time low which could make him an actual value play for 2017 fantasy baseball. We are not saying that Gomez' very ugly performance last season should be ignored but instead are pointing out the fact he is still relatively young and by the looks of his good work with the Rangers, also capable of putting up decent numbers. Since the consensus in the fantasy baseball community is that Gomez is finished, you won't have to pay much to see if a comeback campaign is possible.

2017 PROJECTION: .277 16 HR 58 RBI 74 R 17 SB

Jason Heyward: Already it looks like the Chicago Cubs gave out the single worst free agent contract in history when they signed outfielder Jason Heyward to an 8-year deal worth an insane $180 million. Just one year into the deal, Heyward couldn't even be trusted to start Game 1 of the World Series given how listless his offensive game was for the NL Central champions. In fact Heyward was downright pathetic last season as he hit just 7 home runs, stole 11 bases, and batted .230. The Cubs always make a point in saying they also paid Heyward for his excellent defense but give us a break. The guy is an utter disaster and shouldn't be bothered with in 2017 fantasy baseball.

2017 PROJECTION: .255 9 HR 59 RBI 73 R 14 SB

Melky Cabrera: Chicago White Sox outfielder Melky Cabrera is a guy you probably couldn't give away in your league as he carries little-to-no pop in fantasy baseball and that is understandable when you look at his non-PED numbers. 2016 was a decent year for him though as Cabrera batted .296, hit 14 home runs, and collected 86 RBI. Nothing earth-shattering but Cabrera's haul made the outfielder 3 grade. Now 33 as the 2017 season gets underway, Cabrera can only repeat what he accomplished last year and a slip at his age is also not something to be ignored. If you want him, it won't take much to do so.

2017 PROJECTION: .288 12 HR 74 RBI 70 R 4 SB

Angel Pagan: A free agent at press time, veteran outfielder Angel Pagan should find another starting spot for at least one more year despite the fact he will be 35 when the 2017 season gets underway. Speed-oriented players like Pagan usually don't age well though and we saw decent slippage last season when he stole just 15 bases in 543 at-bats. Gone are the days where Pagan swiped 25-plus bases and even 20 could be a reach at this late stage of his career. What was a nice development for Pagan's value is that he was able to swat a career-high 12 home runs last season. While no doubt a mediocre total, home runs from Pagan help offset the erosion in his stolen bases. Be that as it may, we are just talking about an outfielder 3 and a low-end one at best.

2017 PROJECTION: .267 8 HR 53 RBI 65 R 14 SB

Brett Gardner: New York Yankees veteran outfielder Brett Gardner is becoming quite a shaky fantasy baseball investment as he moves into his late 30's and this is a fact based on the sliding numbers he put up during the 2016 season. Once a 40-stolen base speed gem, over the last five seasons Gardner has seen his totals in that category drop sharply all the way down to just 16 last season in 634 at-bats. Since most of Gardner's value comes from steals, this is a major problem for his value going forward. Even the two-season uptick in power Gardner showed from 2014-15 (17 and 16 home runs in each year respectively) seemed a thing of the past as well since he dropped to only 7 in that category last season. Having posted nothing but mediocre batting averages throughout his career, Gardner has almost nothing left to give his prospective owners in terms of helpful numbers in fantasy baseball. Turning 34 in August, that doesn't figure to change for 2017.

2017 PROJECTION: .262 10 HR 46 RBI 83 R 19 SB

Nick Markakis: Many are still trying to figure out why on the earth the Atlanta Braves thought it was a good idea to sign Nick Markakis to a four-year deal during the heart of a team teardown just prior to the 2015 season. Markakis was predictably boring and underwhelming with his numbers in the two years since, with 2016 having little in the way of positives to talk about. He contributed a bit in the power categories with 13 home runs and 89 RBI but even that was not so impressive when you consider it took him an insane 684 at-bats to do so. With zero steals and a mediocre .269 average, Markakis really is now just for those involved in NL-only leagues.

2017 PROJECTION: .277 11 HR 80 RBI 65 R 1 SB

Jayson Werth: Now entering into the last year of the much-panned mammoth 7-year contract that Jayson Werth originally signed with the Washington Nationals, one can say the guy has not at least earned back a large portion of the dough. Even at the age of 37 last season, Werth put forth a good accounting of himself as he hit 21 home runs for the NL East winners. Alas Werth was mostly just a two-category help (also putting forth a nice 84-run scored campaign) as his average of .244 was very ugly (following a .221 performance in 2015) and there is no more speed left in this well. While Werth still draws walks (11.7 BB/9), he is moving past the useful stage.

2017 PROJECTION: .236 17 HR 65 RBI 74 R 2 SB

Alex Gordon: At one time considered a top outfielder 2 in fantasy baseball due to possessing an ability to hit for power and steal bases, the current version of the Kansas City Royals' Alex Gordon is quite ugly. While Gordon managed to post some semblance of a power/speed game by hitting 17 home runs and stealing 8 bags, a .220 batting average shows the slippage in his game. Always a bit heavy on strikeouts, Gordon has gone out of the universe now as his ridiculous 29.2 K/9 last season showed. With a lot of injuries in the past likely robbing from Gordon's bat potency and overall athleticism, he can be nothing more than an outfielder 3 at this stage of his career.

2017 PROJECTION: .254 16 HR 56 RBI 67 R 7 SB

Corey Dickerson: Add Tampa Bay Rays outfielder Corey Dickerson to the Vinny Castilla-Dante Bichette grouping of hitters who were MVP candidates while calling Coors Field home but then who became nothing but mediocre players when playing their local games at a different ballpark. Lauded as a possible future batting title winner to go with expected 25-30 home run power, Dickerson proved how the thin air in Colorado helped inflate his numbers into a very fluky realm. The evidence is striking here as Dickerson hit just .245 for the Rays last season; an average that was way down from the .304 and .312 he hit for the Rockies from 2014-15. While the 24 home runs Dickerson swatted with the Rays is a very solid total, you can forget about any visions of 30 long balls or 90-plus RBI which would have been in play if he stayed in Colorado. With Dickerson's strikeout rate coming in at an ugly 24.5 K/9 and with him also not showing good patience at the dish (6.0 BB/9), there is little reason to think a bounce back can occur this season. Avoid.

2017 PROJECTION: .256 23 HR 68 RBI 59 R 0 SB

Brandon Drury: The loss of All-Star outfielder A.J. Pollock for almost the entire season in 2016 presented an opportunity for prospect Brandon Drury to show the team what he could do. A big start surely opened eyes (8 home runs total from March through the end of May) and put Drury on the fantasy baseball map. What really went unnoticed was the fact that even though Drury's power dried up the last four months of the year (just 8 total homers), he batted .296 in the second half which showed that he could fight against the adjustment pitchers were trying to make against him. The 20.0 K/9 rate was impressive for any rookie hitter but Drury's .282 average was helped along by a lucky .327 BABIP. As far as the total product here is concerned, Drury is strictly a power guy who won't help you in stolen bases at all. That could work in Chase Field as an outfielder 3 but Drury is far from a proven commodity.

2017 PROJECTION: .273 17 HR 63 RBI 60 R 2 SB

Keon Broxton: When the Milwaukee Brewers began cleaning house midway through the 2016 season, opportunity presented itself to speedy outfielder Keon Broxton to make good on his somewhat faded potential. A former third round pick in 2009, Broxton made his way through the Arizona and Pittsburgh systems before finding his way to Milwaukee for 2016. After flashing interesting power/speed numbers at Triple-A where he hit 8 home runs, stole 18 bags, and batted .287 in between stints with the Brewers, Broxton began playing regularly during the summer. The big speed that has always been the calling card for Broxton was immediately impactful as he swiped 22 bags in only 242 at-bats. Even more impressive and surprising as well was the fact Broxton also added 9 home runs. A 9/22 ratio in the power/speed categories is an impressive haul and that alone put Broxton quickly on the fantasy baseball map in August. There were negatives though such as a .238 average and a very nasty 36.4 K/9 rate. Clearly Broxton has to get his strikeouts under control to realize his full potential but the fact he was able to make such a nice contribution in the home run/steal categories with such a terrible contact rate is very impressive. The damper here was a season-ending fractured wrist suffered in September but Broxton no doubt has earned a chance to be a regular in 2017. A name to stash away as a late round sleeper with not a lot of fanfare attached.

2017 PROJECTION: .255 14 HR 52 RBI 62 R 27 SB

Jarrod Dyson: For the fifth season in a row, Kansas City Royals veteran Jarrod Dyson perfected his ability to be a contributor both in real and in fantasy baseball despite not getting a full allotment of at-bats. In just 337 at-bats in 2016, Dyson stole a potent 30 bases and batted a solid .278. The 30 steals were the fourth time in the last five years Dyson went for at least that many and all without more than the 337 at-bats he had last season. While we would love to see how many steals Dyson could net with a full-time starting gig, at the age of 32 he is not likely going to get that shot now. If it were to happen however, Dyson would be a monster steals guy on a daily basis.

2017 PROJECTION: .275 1 HR 27 RBI 48 R 28 SB

Kevin Pillar: It was a minor step back in production for Toronto Blue Jays outfielder Kevin Pillar in 2016, as the speedster saw declines almost across the board offensively compared to his 2015 production that first put him on the fantasy baseball map. Still Pillar wasn't terrible as a he posted a 7/14 split in his power/speed game but a .266 average was a sizable drop from the .278 he hit the year prior. The Blue Jays seem to like trotting Pillar out there on a daily basis however and in mixed formats that carries some backup outfielder status.

2017 PROJECTION: .270 8 HR 54 RBI 59 R 15 SB

Steven Souza Jr.: For the second season in a row, Tampa Bay Rays outfielder Steven Souza Jr. caught some fantasy baseball attention with modest power/speed numbers (17-HR/6-SB) but his average remained a huge problem at .247. What is really telling about the holes in Souza's swing though is that the .247 he batted last season was a decent improvement over the simply brutal .225 mark he posted in 2015. Souza has made Mark Reynolds proud the last two years by posting insane K/9 marks of 33.8 and 34.0 which contributes directly to his horrific batting average problems. Making matters more concerning in terms of Souza's immediate future, he was forced to undergo season-ending hip surgery last September. The red flag there is that hip surgery is a procedure that often leads to diminished power the following year. Since Souza only had moderate power to begin with, this is no small matter. Turning 28 in April, Souza is pretty much now into his prime years as well which means he won't likely do much better than what he already is producing at the dish. We hate investing in batting average liability guys and only make exceptions if there is immense power/speed ability. These are skills Souza doesn't possess.

THE REST

Travis Janjowski: Having quickly cleaned house after back-to-back disappointing seasons, the San Diego Padres will now be a prime spot for young prospects to make their mark. One of these prospects is 2012 first round pick Travis Jankowski whose big-time stolen base ability makes him a possible late round pick in fantasy baseball. Jankowski gave a glimpse of this speed in 2016 when he swiped 30 bases in just 131 games with the team during his rookie debut. While the steals are clearly bountiful, Jankowski is strictly just a one-dimensional play as he hit .245 with the Padres and struck out at an ugly 26.1 K/9 clip. Throw in the fact Jankowski has little-to-no-power and he should be relegated to deeper mixed leagues and NL-only formats.

Ben Revere: This peanut stand has always respected the game of speedy outfielder Ben Revere; mostly due to his very good annual contributions in steals, average, and runs. Unfortunately none of that was in play in 2016 as Revere endured a truly brutal season for the Washington Nationals that included a .217 average, 44 runs scored, and all of 14 steals. Of course Revere spent a large portion of the year on the DL due to an oblique injury but even when on the field, he was a complete joke offensively. Revere's year was so bad that he may not be guaranteed a starting outfield spot for 2017. Until he shows signs of life again at the dish, Revere can be ignored.

Paulo Orlando: Longtime minor league speed demon Paulo Orlando finally got an extended look from the Kansas City Royals in 2016 due to the rampant spate of injuries that decimated the team's outfield. A pronounced stolen base guy in the minor leagues, Orlando showed that skill in his 128-game stint by swiping 14 bags and batting a very impressive .302. Orlando also has some pop in his bat as well (5 home runs) but this is purely a speed buy all the way. With the Royals coming back with a healthy squad to begin the new season, Orlando is destined for backup duty at the major league level or maybe a demotion back to the minors. Only worth a look if injuries open up time for him again.

Hyun Soo Kim: Signed over from Korea for the 2016 season, the Baltimore Orioles mostly used outfielder Hyun Soo Kim as a backup or semi-starter throughout the year. Accruing just 346 at-bats, Kim made the most of them by hitting 6 home runs and posting a .302 average. While a small sample size no doubt, Kim showed a nice approach at the dish with his K/9 (14.7) and walk rate (10.4 BB/9). Right now it is unknown if Kim's role will change for 2017 but he is a person of interest if any more playing time opens up.

Trayce Thompson: While he can't shoot a basketball as good as his brother, Los Angeles Dodgers outfielder Trayce Thompson can surely smack a baseball at a higher level than Klay. After stalling in the Chicago White Sox system, Thompson took advantage of a chance to stick in the Dodgers' outfield early in the 2016 season by smacking a combined 11 home runs in May and June. The former 2009 second-round pick was known for possessing decent power while in the minor leagues so his performance there was not a total shock but the rest of the package left a lot to be desired. For one thing, Thompson struck out in 25.2 percent of his at-bats which went a long way toward his tough to stomach .225 average. Yes there was some bad BABIP luck involved (.255) but Thompson was too much an all-or-nothing hitter last season before he succumbed to a July shoulder injury that never allowed him to return to the field. As far as his 2017 outlook is concerned, Thompson is in no way is a lock to be a starting member of the Dodgers' outfield and his fantasy baseball outlook is even more shaky given the holes in his swing.

Avisail Garcia: The Chicago White Sox can't be happy with the lack of progress made by outfielder Avisail Garcia as he went backwards in almost every offensive category in 2016. While he was considered a decent prospect while coming up the Detroit Tigers organization, Garcia sank to just 12 home runs, 4 steals, and a shoddy .245 average last season. With a K/9 that is getting out of control at 25.4, Garcia doesn't seem to be worth our time anymore.

Domingo Santana: The Milwaukee Brewers gave outfielder Domingo Santana the plush leadoff spot entering into the 2016 season but injuries and overall mediocre play with the bat made him just another waiver guy. Santana was a joke with his K/9 rate of 32.4 and he is lucky to have gotten extreme BABIP luck (.359) or else his .256 average would have been a whole lot worse. 11 home runs in 281 at-bats was impressive but Santana should be kept on the wire this season.

Michael Taylor: More of an athlete then a hitter, Washington Nationals outfielder Michael Taylor looks more and more like a young Chris Young. While his pure hitting can be atrocious at times (32.5 K/9 rate in 2016), Taylor has the power to collect home runs and the speed to pile up steals. He would go 7/14 in the power/speed categories last season in just 237 at-bats for the Nats but Taylor seems destined for more fourth outfielder duty at the start of the 2017 season. That limits any upside he might retain and so there is no reason to look in his direction unless injuries open up a starting spot.

David Peralta: 2016 was a complete abomination for Arizona Diamondbacks outfielder David Peralta as he missed almost the entire year with an injured wrist that required eventual surgery. We had recommended Peralta as a late round sleeper prior to 2016 given the fact he hinted at some power/speed/average ability the year prior but now he is starting all over for the upcoming season.

Scott Schebler: The Cincinnati Reds will likely look to continue bringing in young players to play for the team in 2016 and outfielder Scott Schebler could be a part of the mix. A former 26th round pick of the Los Angeles Dodgers, Schebler has put forth decent power/speed numbers in the minor leagues that make him a bit intriguing. Even in his debut with the Reds last season, Schebler did well enough in hitting 9 home runs in 282 at-bats to open some eyes. He is older than you think at 26 but Schebler is worth a look as a very late round pick given the power/speed tools.

Mitch Haniger: Former 2012 first round pick (7th overall) Mitch Haniger will be a big part of the Arizona Diamondbacks' future before too long. Between stops at Double-A, Triple-A, and with the D-Backs, Haniger hit a total of 30 home runs and stole 12 bases. Haniger has also hit for good batting averages in the minors and so he needs to be a person of interest as a late round pick.

Adam Frazier: Yet another Pittsburgh Pirates outfielder of note is the speedy Adam Frazier but right now he is blocked at the major league level and even behind top prospect Adam Meadows. Having hit .301 with 2 home runs and 4 stolen bases in his 66-game debut with the team in 2016, Frazier would be an interesting steals grab if he somehow found consistent time with the team.

Colby Rasmus: When the biggest news you make during the past season centers on being the rare MLB player to accept the $15.8 million qualifying offer and not what you did on the diamond, you got some problems. That was the 2016 experience of vastly overpaid Houston Astros outfielder Colby Rasmus who took his perennial batting average struggles to a new low in hitting just .206 and striking out in 29.0 percent of his at-bats. A rare St. Louis Cardinals failed prospect, Rasmus has proven himself to be nothing more than a power specialist and even there he disappointed last season in swatting just 15 home runs in 417 at-bats. If Rasmus is not hitting home runs, he is almost completely useless to you since he has zero speed and no plate discipline. Let the guy rot on the wire.

Seth Smith: The career story of Seth Smith being a very effective hitter against lefties and a bust against righties remains true as 2017 fantasy baseball approaches. Smith has done well in that role for the Seattle Mariners, hitting 16 home runs in just 438 at-bats played mostly against lefties last season. That has value just in AL-only formats though so don't go chasing Smith in drafts this spring.

Jorge Soler: There has been a recent run of Cuban hitting busts the last few seasons; a group that includes Alex Guerrero, Yasiel Puig, Rusney Castillo, and the Chicago Cubs' Jorge Soler. Through three MLB seasons, Soler has failed to reprise his impressive minor league numbers and now he is nothing but a backup outfielder on the Cubs getting squeezed for at-bats. A .238 average and 12 home runs is all Soler could muster in 264 at-bats last season and with no opening for a starting spot, his fantasy baseball outlook is grim.

Billy Burns: One of the more head-scratching flameouts in 2016 fantasy baseball was the brutal performance put forth by speedy outfielder Billy Burns. A breakout sensation in 2015 when he went out and swiped 26 bases with a .294 average for the Oakland A's, Burns was so hideous at the dish last season (.234 with 14 steals) that he was sent back to the minors. The A's then took things further by dealing Burns to the Kansas City Royals at the Aug. 1 deadline. On the surface it looked like a cheap buy-low for the Royals but Burns didn't fare much better when they gave him a late-season look (.243, 3 stolen bases). As 2017 approaches, Burns will challenge for a starting outfield spot on the Royals but there are plenty of other stolen bases options you can check out late in your draft which are more stable.

Steve Pearce: Well on the back nine of his career at the age of 33, INF/OF Steve Pearce was pretty solid when he played in 2016. After starting the year with the Tampa Bay Rays and then finding his way back to the Baltimore Orioles at the

August 1 trade deadline, Pearce hit 13 home runs in 302 at-bats and collected 35 RBI. A career journeyman whose 2014 season went down as a sizable outlier (21 HR/.392 average), Pearce may have to settle for a backup role to begin 2017. He is also coming off surgery to repair tendons in his right forearm which required a 4-6 month recovery. With recent ill health being combined with age, there really is no reason to draft Pearce this season.

Chris Young: Signed by the Boston Red Sox to primarily start versus lefties, Chris Young did his thing at a decent level in 2016 when he batted .276 and swatted 9 home runs in just 227 at-bats. Long on years (33) and having become a complete liability versus righties, Young should not be drafted.

Brandon Guyer: Another late bloomer at the age of 31, Guyer is quickly becoming a journeyman backup outfielder after splitting his 2016 between the Tampa Bay Rays and Cleveland Indians. While he can run a bit and crack the odd home run, Guyer is barely worth owning even in AL-only leagues.

Logan Morrison: It was yet another underwhelming season for outfielder Logan Morrison in 2016 as he batted a listless .238 with 14 home runs and 4 stolen bases in 398 at-bats. While the power was decent, Morrison has now hit under .240 for two straight seasons and injuries remain a big problem as his year was cut short early in September due to needing surgery to fix a tendon sheath issue in his wrist. Having turned 29 in August, Morrison is no longer a guy who carries any upside and his one-dimensional power game doesn't require him to be drafted.

Franklin Gutierrez: One of the nicest stories of 2015 fantasy baseball was the comeback of Seattle Mariners outfielder Franklin Gutierrez from missing all of 2014 with illness that threatened to never allow him to play again. Gutierrez stuck with it though and wound up hitting 15 home runs with a .292 average in just 59 games in his return to Seattle that year. Alas the good times only somewhat kept on rolling last season as Gutierrez did hit 15 home runs but only with an ugly .246 average. A 30.0 K/9 was a huge problem that showed up in the average and now at the age of 34 in February, Gutierrez already seems like old news.

Tommy Pham: The St. Louis Cardinals are well-stocked with young outfield talent and that means Tommy Pham faces a tough time initially finding consistent at-bats with the big club. There are evident tools here as Pham hit 9 home runs in his 183 at-bats last season but only an injury to one of the team's starters will make him relevant.

Nori Aoki: Still being able to hit .283 for the Seattle Mariners at the age of 34 in 2016 was a nice accomplishment for veteran outfielder Nori Aoki but a 4/7 split in his home run/stolen base categories in 467 at-bats speak to the sharp limitations we now have here. While we always loved the very good bang for the buck you got in drafting Aoki, that doesn't apply any longer given the empty average he carries at this stage.

Ichiro Suzuki: Now that he got 3,000 hits out of the way, one would think Ichiro Suzuki would go off into retirement at the age of 43. Well not when you were able to bat .291 in 365 at-bats for the Miami Marlins as a backup sparkplug. Even if he does return, Suzuki is just an empty average now as he managed just 10 steals and he never had power to begin with.

Coco Crisp: The very underrated career of outfielder Coco Crisp came full circle in 2016 as he ended up back with the Cleveland Indians who he debuted with way back in 2002. Always getting a boost from these pages due to extreme speed and quiet five-category production during his heyday, the end is close by for Crisp as he will enter into the 2017 season at the age of 37. Having hit just .231 and stolen just 10 bases, Crisp is on statistical fumes at this late stage of his career. It was a good career nonetheless.

Eddie Rosario: After catching some attention as a rookie in 2015 when he hit 13 home runs, stole 11 bases, and batted .267, Minnesota Twins outfielder Eddie Rosario was pretty much right on par with those numbers last season. Spending a decent chuck of the year at Triple-A, Rosario amassed just 354 at-bats with the Twins where he hit 10 home runs, stole 5 bases, and hit .269. While his ugly 25.7 percent K/9 rate damages the batting average, Rosario does possess some power/speed ability that could allow him to squeeze out OF 3 status if he gained enough at-bats. Rosario is not guaranteed a starting outfield spot for 2017 however which means he is nothing but a guy to monitor early on in the season.

Abraham Almonte: An early PED bust pretty much took away any slight sleeper hype Cleveland Indians outfielder Abraham Almonte had for 2016. Still there are some tools here as Almonte has speed to burn and can also hit the odd home run. Abraham's average has been a problem every time he has gotten a shot to stick in the majors though and at the age of 28 in June and with a PED stain on his resume, look elsewhere for late-round upside.

Matt Joyce: While he could grab hold of a minor league deal prior to spring training, there is pretty much nothing positive to speak of in terms of veteran outfielder Matt Joyce. A guy you used to pick up during his inevitable hot start, Joyce can still hit some home runs. Really though there is no reason to even think of investing in Joyce under any circumstance this season.

Robbie Grossman: A journeyman player who is now in his fourth major league organization, outfielder Robbie Grossman has yet to cement a job in the major leagues yet. He received his most at-bats ever in 2016 when he hit 11 home runs in 389 at-bats but nothing is guaranteed moving into the new season. While the .280 average was nice, Grossman struck out at a 24.7 K/9 clip and he looks nothing more than a part-time player for 2017. Part-time work means no fantasy baseball value.

Ryan Rua: Filling a utility/spot-starting role for the Texas Rangers in 2016, outfielder Ryan Rua made the most of his time by posting a 8/9 ratio with his home runs and steals in a total of just 269 at-bats. Rua is destined for the same role in 2017 if he makes the team but that is not even a given since there are clear limitations here. Those include a whiff-happy approach (28.3 K/9) that serves as a sizable impediment to Rua's batting average (.258). Only worth looking into in Al-only formats if some consistent starts get put together.

Mikie Mahtook: An older prospect at the age of 26, Tampa Bay Rays outfielder Mikie Mahtook failed to show much of anything in his 65-game run with the team in 2016. Batting just .195 with 3 home runs, Mahtook looks like a Quad-A player right now.

Michael Bourn: Another example on how players whose value depends almost entirely on stolen bases don't age well can be seen in veteran outfielder Michael Bourn. While still young enough at the age of 33, Bourn is down to accepting minor league deals to try and stick in the majors as he barely qualifies as backup material. Just 15 stolen bases in 413 games and a poor .264 average bears out how Bourn is a complete non-story in fantasy baseball this season.

Danny Santana: After two ugly seasons in a row, it has become quite clear that Minnesota Twins outfielder Danny Santana's 2014 "breakout" (.310/7 HR/20 SB) was a gigantic fluke. After batting a woeful .215 as a colossal bust the following season (a performance that got Santana sent back to the minors), he was not much better in 2016 after an initial hot start. Before suffering a season-ending Grade 2 shoulder sprain, Santana hit just .240 with 2 home runs and 12 steals in 248 at-bats. Stop chasing potential that is just not there.

Josh Hamilton: The sad back-end career of Josh Hamilton took another ugly step downward as he missed the entire 2016 season with a series of knee injuries that included two surgeries covering arterial/meniscus damage and an ACL reconstruction. The Texas Rangers placed Hamilton on release waivers last August and at 36, there is no telling what the next chapter will be for the oft-injured and troubled Hamilton. While his short MVP Mickey Mantle impersonation days were a sight to be seen, Hamilton is fading with a whimper as he has zero fantasy baseball value and is not guaranteed of even being on a team in 2017.

UTILITY

Victor Martinez: Having posted one of the all-time outlier campaigns in 2014 when he hit .335 with 32 home runs and 103 RBI, there was nowhere to go but down for Detroit Tigers 1B/DH Victor Martinez for the 2015 season. We were right up in front of the line telling you to avoid Martinez at all costs and thus were not shocked in the least when he had a complete disaster of a year , hitting only 11 home runs with a .245 average in a year filled with injury setbacks. It certainly looked like Martinez had reached his "cliff season" where he tumbled over into fantasy baseball irrelevancy but the guy apparently still had some more tricks up his sleeve. With a draft price that went to the end of standard league rounds, Martinez showed he was far from done in reclaiming his slugging name by hitting 27 home runs, collecting 86 RBI, and posting a .289 average at the age of 37. Almost completely a DH at this stage of his career, the lessening of wear-and-tear on Martinez gives him a better chance to ward off the knee troubles that have interrupted some of his previous seasons but we again have to warn you off a drop in numbers for 2017 due to a number of reasons. The age factor is most prominent as Martinez will be 38 when the new season gets underway and asking him to replicate 27 home runs is quite foolish. Also counting on Martinez to stay full healthy for a second year in a row is also asking a ton and so those are two huge strikes against him right out of the gate. Like with most other older veterans though, it won't cost a lot to take that risk which means Martinez can be your UTIL or CI bat once again this season.

2017 PROJECTION: .288 23 HR 88 RBI 67 R 0 SB

Kendrys Morales: Those who have been long-time readers of ours know how we always have had a soft spot for veteran first baseman Kendrys Morales. Maybe it stems from the fact we were in on the ground level with Morales before he made it big with the Los Angeles Angels but we also stuck with the guy through his grueling two-season recovery from the devastating broken leg he suffered in a home plate pile-up after swatting a game-winning bomb. While Morales had never come close to the 34 homers he hit in 2009 for the Angels in his pre-broken leg days, what he had accomplished was to settle into being a very good value play first baseman in fantasy baseball who could hit 20-25 long balls with decent RBI numbers. That is until 2016 when Morales seemed to turn back the clock to his Los Angeles days as he reached the 30-home run mark for the first time since the broken leg (finishing right at that number for the Kansas City Royals) and in turn wound up being a terrific value yet again. Having also supplied 93 RBI, Morales did his job in terms of pure power. In digging into the numbers a bit more, Morales is becoming more and more a pure slugger as his K/9 rate of 19.4 last season was his highest in 5 years and his .263 average is down more than a little from his earlier days around .290-.300. Age has something to do with that as Morales will turn 34 in June but he has been very durable in his career outside of the broken leg. Also Morales gets a bit of a boost in moving into the launching pad that is Rogers Center after coming to an agreement on a three-year deal with the Toronto Blue Jays in free agency. That makes it more likely Morales can duplicate the 30 home run uptick he put forth last season. When you break it down, those who make an investment here are getting very good contributions in two categories (RBI, HR) and that goes well enough in your UTIL or CI spot.

2017 PROJECTION: .266 26 HR 90 RBI 65 R 1 SB

STARTING PITCHING OVERVIEW

While it is true that home runs in the 2016 season were at their highest levels since the steroid years, we remain firmly entrenched in the pitching era. Nowhere is this more clear then when one takes a look at how ridiculously deep the starting pitching fraternity goes and that once again is the case for 2017 fantasy baseball. As a result of this trend, we remain true to our firm strategy of not drafting a pitcher until Round 5 at the earliest and you can even go a round or two past that mark if you wish. In fact during this era of pitching dominance, each season we have seen a deep batch of new arms show up on the scene and perform like above-average starters which drives our point home. 2016 was no different and so while we all would love to own Clayton Kershaw or Max Scherzer, the easy call to make here is to start assembling your staff in the early middle rounds and then come back here every third round or so from that point onward. Even if you wait until the end of the draft to start taking pitchers, the depth is so great that you can still field a competitive staff. Going with the hitters early is still the way to begin your draft.

Clayton Kershaw: Even the very best are not immune from injury. Such was the case for Los Angeles Dodgers ace and consensus number 1 fantasy baseball starting pitcher Clayton Kershaw in 2016. Coming off a ridiculous 2015 campaign where Kershaw reached the hallowed 300-K plateau (301 in 232.1 innings) with a 2.13 ERA, a herniated disk in his back sent the multiple-Cy Young winner to the DL for more than two months. Kershaw's absence was monstrous considering all those lost potential ace-like numbers and his 28-inning return in September/October was too little/too late for many of his owners. While we are not talking about any elbow or shoulder trouble here, a back injury can also be a big problem for any athlete and flare-ups happen often as well. On skills alone, Kershaw has no peer in the game and his insane dominance (ERA under 2.00 three of last four years/double-digit K/9 three straight) makes him the only pitcher we would endorse in Round 1. Still young as he turns just 29 in March, Kershaw remains the standard against whom every other pitcher is judged. While he carries a bit of risk now for the first time in his career, Kershaw once again should be the first pitcher off the board in all leagues without there being any debate.

2017 PROJECTION: 19-4 1.96 ERA 0.88 WHIP 241 K

Max Scherzer: After tossing not one but TWO no-hitters in a spectacular 2015 campaign for the Washington Nationals, it was tough to imagine that Max Scherzer could top such a dominant season. Well Scherzer unveiled some new tricks in 2016 as he reached a new high with his already insane K/9 rate (11.19) and that led to another new career-best in strikeouts with 284. While Scherzer has been widely considered the number 2 starting pitcher in fantasy baseball behind Clayton Kershaw for a few years now, the argument can be made that he passed his Los Angeles Dodgers counterpart based on possessing much better durability. While Kershaw missed half of last season with a herniated disk in his back, Scherzer pitched over 200 innings for the fourth year in a row. So far all of those innings have not hurt Scherzer but he did see a spike in his HR/9 (1.22) that was more of an issue the first half of the year. On the plus side, Scherzer has maintained terrific control with all of those strikeouts and his win total will remain very impressive considering he pitches for one of the best teams in baseball. There is simply nothing to say here that is remotely negative regarding Scherzer's makeup and he is as safe an early round investment as one can make at this volatile position.

2017 PROJECTION: 20-4 2.75 ERA 0.99 WHIP 272 K

Madison Bumgarner: The legend of Madison Bumgarner continues to grow. Already considered a slam-dunk top five fantasy baseball starter coming into the 2016 season, the San Francisco Giants ace somehow pitched even BETTER during the year as he posted a career-best 2.74 ERA and 9.97 K/9 (252 strikeouts in only 226.2 innings) . All this from a guy who redefined what it was to be a postseason megastar during his and the Giants' run toward becoming World Series champions in 2014. Considered to have the most renowned rubber arm in the game, the 27-year-old Bumgarner is as close to a lock as it gets in terms of being a top tier fantasy baseball starter. Bumgarner checks all of the boxes in that in addition to his excellence in ERA and strikeouts, he also possesses impeccable control and keeps the ball in the park. In fact one can make the argument that Bumgarner has passed Clayton Kershaw for the title of number 1 starter in all of baseball since he had the by far better health last season. With Kershaw missing half of 2016 with a back injury, Bumgarner's ultra-durability is a prime asset which shouldn't be overlooked.

2017 PROJECTION: 19-5 2.62 ERA 1.02 WHIP 241 K

Chris Sale: Where at one time Chicago White Sox ace Chris Sale was considered one of the biggest injury risk pitchers in the game, the guy has put that fear to rest over the last two seasons as he tossed 208.2 and 226.2 innings respectively. Now a clear veteran as he turns 28 in March, the threat of Tommy John surgery has lessened for Sale and instead it now becomes more about the numbers than ever before. Those numbers remain excellent but his last two years have in fact seen Sale's ERA move into the mid-3.00 range after a four-year run where he posted marks in that category of 3.07 or lower. Sale admitted last spring training that he was focusing more than ever on pitching to contact so as not to exhaust his elbow and run his pitch count up. This bore itself out in Sale's K/9 rate which at last season's 9.25 was a big drop from the 11.82 he put up in 2015. Still the guy was able to stretch his 200-plus strikeout totals to four straight seasons in 2016 with 233. Whether the dip in K/9 was a one-year anomaly or not remains to be seen but Sale's ERA of 3.41 and 3.34 the last two seasons are where he should be graded on now. With as good control as there is in all of baseball (1.79 BB/9) and a solid home run rate (1.07), there are very few ways with which to score runs against Sale. We have said in this space repeatedly there is not a pitcher who engineers more eye-popping box scores then Chris Sale and his status as a top five ace remains firm.

2017 PROJECTION: 16-7 3.25 ERA 1.05 WHIP 228 K

David Price: While those who were interested in drafting David Price for the 2017 fantasy baseball season couldn't have been happy with his decision to sign back into the AL East as a free agent with the Boston Red Sox, there may not have been a pitcher more equipped to excel there then the former Cy Young winner. Having already put up ace numbers in the division with the Tampa Bay Rays and Toronto Blue Jays, Price was a guy we made an exception for in terms of our stated desire never to invest in an AL East pitcher. At least early on in the 2016 season however, even Price seemed to be succumbing to the massive amount of offensive bats in the division as he posted horrible ERA's both in March/April (5.76) and May (4.62). Still throughout his rough first half, we told anyone who would listen to buy low on Price given his track record and for the fact he was the victim of some awful BABIP luck. Price did rally in the second half (3.58 ERA) but the totality of his season was disappointing to say the least. Ultimately though, Price was an interesting case in that while his composite 3.99 ERA was well below his past ace standards, his .310 BABIP finished in the unlucky range. Corrected from the luck, Price's FIP (3.60) and XFIP (3.52) ERA's were a bit better. In addition, Price was actually a strikeout monster throughout the year as he punched out 228 batters in 230 innings for a K/9 of 8.92. Averaging nearly a K per inning as Price did last season is doubly impressive in the American League and that is especially true when in the AL East. His control remained excellent as always (1.96 BB/9) as well which then would make you wonder why Price struggled on the surface for the stretches that he did. The answer is somewhat found in the fact that Price's 1.17 HR/9 rate was his career-high by a wide margin and that again can be blamed on the division and calling Fenway Park home. We have heard for awhile now that Price's incredible ability to always be around the strike zone also leaves him susceptible to the long ball and his 2016 numbers back up this premise. Even more than bad BABIP luck, nothing can distort numbers more sharply than a home run issue. Unfortunately giving up more home runs is the literal "Price" that the guy has to pay for operating in such a tough pitcher's environment. So in terms of 2017 fantasy baseball, Price should really be graded now as more of a 3.00-plus ERA guy then the mid-2.00 stud he was with the Rays. Price is still as good a strikeout artist as there is in the game and that keep him in the ace realm once again for 2017. Just a lower-rated ace than the top five pitcher he once was.

2017 PROJECTION: 19-9 3.33 ERA 1.19 WHIP 227 K

Jake Arrieta: For those who had planned to draft Chicago Cubs ace Jake Arrieta for the 2016 season, the understanding going in had to be that there was no way he was going to replicate what was a truly insane campaign the year prior when the veteran put up numbers that were in the "had to see it, to believe it" realm. After all this is what happens when you register a 1.77 ERA, 0.86 WHIP, and punch out 236 batters in 229 innings. We sounded the alarm on Arrieta prior to last season though for that obvious reason and others, such as his struggles in the 2015 postseason and for the career-high in innings that the formerly health-troubled righty put forth. Typically pitchers see their numbers decline across the board after such an intense workload (254 total frames including the playoffs) and Arrieta fell right in line there as his 2016 ERA jumped to 3.10 and his WHIP to 1.08. In addition, Arrieta leaked strikeouts as his K/9 of 8.67 was a decent drop from 2015's 9.28. Still you can't argue with the overall numbers as Arrieta still made the fantasy baseball grade in also winning 18 games but it is a reminder that he will be 31 in March and has pitched a ridiculous amount of innings the last two years for a guy who battled some terrible injuries earlier in his career. In the end it is a much safer and more accurate bet to expect last season's numbers when drafting Arrieta as opposed to his outlier 2015 and also accept that he carries more risk than other fantasy baseball aces that surround him in the starting pitcher rankings.

2017 PROJECTION: 18-8 3.15 ERA 1.07 WHIP 197 K

Noah Syndegaard: Virtually no one would have put their money on Noah Syndegaard to be the last ace standing out of the New York Mets rotation in 2016. It was in fact Syndegaard who was the only member of the vaunted "Big Five" of Jacob DeGrom, Matt Harvey, Steven Matz, and Zach Wheeler, who wound up pitching through the season. The reason many would doubt Syndegaard's health is for the fact that if you were to draw up what a classic Tommy John elbow victim would like it, Thor would be it. Syndegaard checks all the red flag boxes such as being under the age of 27, having the ability to throw extremely hard (average fastball velocity of 98), and for taking a jump in innings from one year to the next. While Syndegaard did have a few scares along the way (and developed a bone spur that did not require removal), he was able to throw 183.2 innings in the regular season, while posting ace numbers. Syndegaard is about as pure a power pitcher as you can get as his 10.68 K/9 rate and 218 strikeouts could attest. Posting a dominant 2.60 ERA, Syndegaard is also the extremely rare young flamethrower who possesses excellent control (2.11 BB/9). That makes it virtually impossible for opposing hitters to get much to hit off of Syndegaard and again only health can derail him. As we look toward 2017, Syndegaard is an easy top ten fantasy baseball ace but his health is an issue that won't go away. When you make an investment in Syndegaard, you are clearly crossing your fingers and hoping things don't go wrong with his health. Let's see how lucky you are.

2017 PROJECTION: 16-8 2.52 ERA 1.14 WHIP 223 K

Corey Kluber: When talk begins to center on who the best starting pitchers in the game are today, you often find that Cleveland Indians ace Corey Kluber gets left out of the conversation. This would be a mistake due to the fact that Kluber is every bit an ace and has proven that with some excellent pitching the last three seasons. While the month of April has never been kind to Kluber (career 4.00 ERA/1.24 WHIP), he has posted ERA's of 2.44, 3.49, and 3.14 the last three years. In addition, Kluber is one of the best strikeout artists in the game today as he has punched out 269, 245, and 227 batters in that same time frame. 2016 just reinforced what we already now know about Kluber, which is that he is every bit a fantasy baseball ace who can certainly qualify as an anchor for your rotation. We can quibble a bit with his lucky .271 BABIP but otherwise Kluber is a pretty safe investment for this season.

2017 PROJECTION: 15-7 3.21 ERA 1.07 WHIP 234 K

Johnny Cueto: Location means everything. This theme certainly applied to San Francisco Giants ace starter Johnny Cueto who smartly signed back into the National League with the team as a free agent last winter after struggling in his cameo with the Kansas City Royals in the American League in late 2015. Having firmly established himself as a fantasy baseball ace during his tenure with the Cincinnati Reds, Cueto was quietly as dominant as any arm in the game in posting ERA's under 3.00 four straight years from 2011 through 2014. He was on his way to making it five straight in 2015 when he took his 2.62 ERA with the Reds to the Royals at the July 31 trade deadline. From that point through the remaining last two months of the season though, Cueto struggled against the tougher and deeper American League lineups. The numbers didn't lie as Cueto posted an ugly 4.76 ERA and 1.45 WHIP in his 13 starts with the Royals and that is why it was so key for him agree to a deal with the Giants that winter, placing him back into the easier NL and one of the best pitching parks in the game. As a result, Cueto quickly turned back into his ace self as his ERA went back under 3.00 at 2.79 and his K/9 sailed back up to an impressive 8.11. What also makes Cueto so tough is that he doesn't beat himself, excelling with his control (1.84 BB/9) and home run rates (0.61 HR/9) After winning 18 games in the process, the righty remains a very safe investment for 2017 as he still sits firmly in his prime in turning only 31 in February. That means Cueto has a few seasons left of ace production barring any more injuries. Coming in as one of the more cheaper fantasy baseball ace starters, Cueto is as good as any pitcher to anchor your rotation.

2017 PROJECTION: 19-5 2.62 ERA 1.05 WHIP 192 K

Jon Lester: It is very rare when an already well-regarded starting pitcher puts forth a career-year at the advancing age of 32 but that is exactly what the Chicago Cubs' Jon Lester achieved during the 2016 season. While the Cubs caught a ton of flak for the massive contract they gave Lester prior to 2015, the results have made that money well spent. Lester in fact took things to another level last season in winning 19 games for the best team in the majors, while posting career-bests in ERA (2.44) and WHIP (1.02). Lester also just missed running his string of 200-plus strikeout seasons to three in a row by finishing with 197 (good for a K/9 of 8.75). After a mid-career dip with the Boston Red Sox, Lester's second wind as he entered into his 30's has been beyond impressive. Being able to operate in the easier National League has also eliminated some of the shaky WHIP's Lester put up in his Boston days and his arm can be included in the "rubber" class. Now Lester did get some decent BABIP help (a lucky .256) which when adjusted sent both his FIP and XFIP ERA above 3.40 but again nothing major in terms of possible red flags. About the only thing we might have to concern ourselves with when it comes to investing in Lester for 2017 is that he has thrown a massive amount of innings over the last five years and eventually he is going to have to pay the piper for that. We can't ever predict when that might occur so continue drafting Lester as a more moderately priced ace for your fantasy baseball pitching staff.

2017 PROJECTION: 18-8 3.34 ERA 1.08 WHIP 191 K

Stephen Strasburg: When it comes to Washington Nationals ace starting pitcher Stephen Strasburg, the narrative for his career has remained the same since the day he debuted in terms of fantasy baseball. On talent alone, the power arsenal of Strasburg put him in top five territory among all pitchers. However an annual problem for Strasburg that undermines his value has been a penchant for elbow/arm injuries. When drafting Strasburg, one always has to factor in at least one DL stint given that history and he already has had a Tommy John surgery in his past. 2016 was no different as Strasburg hit the DL after coming down with elbow soreness in August after a horrid three-start stretch. Things would only get worse as Strasburg lasted just 2.1 innings in his first start off the DL with renewed elbow trouble that resulted in a regular season-ending flexor strain. The line of demarcation when it came to how the elbow negatively impacted Strasburg last season was clearly evident when you viewed his dominant first half of the year (2.62 ERA/1.01 WHIP/132 K in 106.2 IP), which was then followed by that terrible three-start stretch when the pain surfaced after the break (6.15 ERA/1.34 WHIP/51 K in 41 IP). Strasburg actually posted a career-best K/9 rate of 11.15 last season, which shows you how massively good his stuff remains but the injury risk doesn't go any higher when it comes to fantasy baseball ace starters at the draft table.

2017 PROJECTION: 14-5 3.15 ERA 1.11 WHIP 188 K

Cole Hamels: A longtime favorite in these pages and one of the more underappreciated ace starters in fantasy baseball, Cole Hamels actually was a guy who we told you to avoid for the 2016 season. While he was still in his prime years, the reason we knocked Hamels was simply due to his move from the NL to the AL which began at the 2015 trade deadline after the Philadelphia Phillies moved him to the Texas Rangers. We don't have to explain to you how pitchers typically see their numbers rise in ERA and WHIP, while also losing strikeouts when making the jump from the NL to the AL and Hamels did see this trend occur during his initial two month stint with the Rangers that year. Compared to his first four months of 2015 with the Phillies, Hamels saw his K/9 drop and his .BAA jump with the Rangers. While we still expected Hamels to be a very good pitcher going into last season, we downgraded him from ace territory to more of an SP 2. Well Hamels proved us and many other publications wrong as he once again performed like a true number 1 starter last in posting a 3.32 ERA and striking out 200 batters in 200.2 innings. That is not to say Hamels still didn't experience some erosion in his new league as his 1.31 WHIP could attest. When you consider that Hamels' previous high in WHIP was the 1.29 he posted in 2009 with the Phillies, you can then understand how the tougher batting orders in the American League had something to do with the rise there. Hamels also fought his control like never before as his 3.45 BB/9 was almost a full free pass over his 2.63 number in 2015. Be that as it may, Hamels still has the stuff to be a top-end guy but he also turns 33 in December which should give one some pause when grading him out again as an ace. On the other hand, Hamels has always come cheaper than he should in yearly drafts given the excellent numbers which means we will sign off on drafting him as your staff anchor again.

2017 PROJECTION: 15-7 3.39 ERA 1.27 WHIP 198 K

Danny Salazar: If one were to formulate a list of the best young power pitchers in the game today, you can make the case that the Cleveland Indians' Danny Salazar belongs at or near the top of this group. Turning only 27 in January, Salazar has put up K/9 rates of at least 9.4 or more in all four of his major league seasons. With a fastball that can touch triple digits being augmented by knee-buckling offspeed stuff, Salazar is about as tough a pitcher in the game to get a hit off of. Last season saw Salazar take things to a whole new level in his development as he finished the first half of the year with a dominant 2.75 ERA and struck out a monstrous 118 batters in 104.2 IP. Trouble began to brew though in late July as Salazar started complaining of soreness in his elbow which necessitated a trip to the disabled list in a month that saw him post a troubling 6.14 ERA. Upon returning from the DL, Salazar was hit very hard to the tune of a 12.41 ERA in his 12.1 August frames and then September saw him suffer some renewed pain in the elbow that led to an MRI. The MRI revealed a flexor strain and thankfully no structural damage but Salazar was officially finished for the remainder of the regular season. Overall Salazar finished the year with a 3.87 ERA but that number is a bit of a fluke as a good amount of that was caused when the elbow began to go bad. Focus in on the 10.55 K/9 in appreciating the immense talent that Salazar is and pray that the elbow holds up for 2017. Outside of health, Salazar has to really go back to work on his control which completely betrayed him last season. His BB/9 was unacceptable at 4.13 and that in turn led to an ugly 1.34 WHIP. Consider that in 2015 Salazar was able to post a 2.58 BB/9 and it shows you that he is capable of getting back on track there. If this does happen, Salazar could win the Cy Young.

2017 PROJECTION: 14-5 3.24 ERA 1.25 WHIP 192 K

Carlos Martinez: We advised our readers to be very careful when weighing a 2016 investment in St. Louis Cardinals fireballing righty Carlos Martinez. Already the ace of the staff despite just making his full-season debut in 2014, Martinez was one big red flag going into last season after being shut down the previous September with shoulder soreness. Shoulder injuries are often the surest way to derail or even ruin a pitcher's career and so Martinez was radioactive to us when it came to 2016 drafts. While it wasn't a completely smooth ride (Martinez again had a shoulder scare in the middle of the year), he still logged 195 innings and his 3.04 ERA was almost identical to the 3.01 mark he put up in that category the year before. A few things to note however is that Martinez lost more than one strikeout per nine compared to 2015 (9.22 to 8.02) and you have to wonder if the previous shoulder injuries have taken a slight bit of bite from his stuff. Martinez also pitched a bit over his head as his .286 BABIP was in the lucky realm. When the luck was adjusted, Martinez was less impressive with a FIP ERA of 3.60 and an XFIP of 3.81. Finally, Martinez has not solved his control issues one bit as his 3.23 BB/9 last year was the third season in a row that number went above 3.15. There are quite a few caveats here with Martinez and of course the threat is real for some more shoulder trouble. We again advise you to be careful here and only try to snag Martinez as an SP 3 if possible.

2017 PROJECTION: 14-8 3.39 ERA 1.23 WHIP 175 K

Kyle Hendricks: On a Chicago Cubs starting pitching staff that includes top tier names Jon Lester and Jake Arrieta, who knew that it would be Kyle Hendricks who had the most dominant season from this group in 2016. Coming off a 2015 campaign where he pitched to a good but not great 3.95 ERA, Hendricks blew all of his projections out of the water by a mile. Winning 16 games while posting an ERA of 2.13 and a WHIP of 0.98, Hendricks was arguably the best fantasy baseball pitching value of the year considering his original modest draft cost. What is really interesting though is that Hendricks' 2016 advanced numbers nearly matched what he did the year prior. In fact Hendricks' 8.05 K/9 rate in 2016 was LOWER than his 2015 mark of 8.35. Also his walk and home run rates were both only slightly below what he put up the season before as well. So in situations like this, some good BABIP luck has to be a prominent factor and it certainly was for Hendricks at .250 which was one of the most fortunate numbers there in all of baseball. In fact when you correct the luck involved, Hendricks' FIP (3.20) and XFIP (3.59) ERA's are not anywhere near the composite 2.13 he posted last season. As a result, Hendricks is likely to be quite overpriced for 2017 as many will judge him on his 2016 numbers. This would be a big mistake given the fact that a good amount of luck on the batted ball helped Hendricks post those gaudy digits and the expected correction for this season will make the ratios rise by more than a little. We won't be drafting Hendricks due to the sticker price and neither should you.

2017 PROJECTION: 15-10 3.24 ERA 1.07 WHIP 175 K

Carlos Carrasco: For those who cut the check at the draft table for Cleveland Indians hard-throwing lefty Carlos Carrasco, it was a bit of a disappointing year in 2016. An early-season hamstring strain sent Carrasco to the DL for all of May and then a comebacker fractured his hand during a mid-September outing which ended things prematurely. Despite these two setbacks, Carrasco pitched well in posting a 3.32 ERA, 1.14 WHIP, and 9.23 K/9. All impressive ratios no doubt but the sum totals did not live up to what was expected by his owners. When you dig into the numbers, Carrasco made it three straight seasons where he posted a K/9 over 9.00 and he has now firmly solved his early career control woes by putting up a personal best 2.11 BB/9. Carrasco still gives up too many home runs as his 1.29 HR/9 shows but the guy has dominant stuff and comes at a decent price at the draft table as the injuries kept the counting numbers down a bit. We are still big boosters of Carrasco and suggest going back to the well here since he had no arm/shoulder trouble in 2016.

2017 PROJECTION: 14-8 3.38 ERA 1.15 WHIP 182 K

Jacob DeGrom: If you needed any more evidence that young pitchers are extremely prone to injury the season following a sizable jump in innings, look no further than the New York Mets rotation in 2016. Matt Harvey succumbed to season-ending thoracic shoulder surgery, Steven Matz and Noah Syndegaard both developed bone spurs in their elbows, and ace Jacob DeGrom battled velocity issues all year and eventually went under the knife himself for an ulnar nerve problem. As far as DeGrom was concerned, he had quite a bit of hype attached to his name entering into last season as he came off a Cy Young-worthy 2015 where he posted a 2.54 ERA, a 0.98 WHIP, and a tiny .210 BAA. DeGrom also cemented his fantasy baseball ace status by striking out 215 batters in only 191 innings. That comes out to a dominant 9.66 K/9 and sent DeGrom's draft stock soaring for 2016. With the Mets reaching the World Series though, DeGrom would up throwing a very high 223 innings at a still young age of 27. In fact since DeGrom was drafted originally as a shortstop, that major jump in innings was double trouble for him given the youth of his pitching elbow. Well as so often happens in these situations, DeGrom experienced major trouble last season, beginning in spring training when his fastball velocity was down in the 91-93 range from the previous year's average of 95-97. Still DeGrom was able to pitch through the velocity dip and quite well I might add as he went into the All-Star break with a 2.61 ERA, 1.11 WHIP, and 91 K's in 93 innings. In other words, ace-like DeGrom. Unfortunately the wheels began to come off during the second half, with the biggest alarms sounding when DeGrom was battered in three straight starts in late August and into the start of September. That September 1st outing would be DeGrom's last as he was soon shut down for good with irritation in the ulnar collateral ligament in his elbow which required surgery. No structural damage was found however which means DeGrom will be good to go for spring training but his risk went up a whole bunch for 2017 in terms of fantasy baseball. Even before he went out with the elbow, DeGrom was struggling during the second half for the second season in a row. As great as his overall numbers were in 2015, DeGrom was on fumes by the time the postseason began and so we have to wonder if there is some Dan Haren in him in terms of fading when the innings pile up. The extra rest should do DeGrom good in terms of his 2017 prospects but he should be drafted now not as an ace but as a SP 2 with decent risk.

2017 PROJECTION: 14-7 3.22 ERA 1.14 WHIP 181 K

Yu Darvish: A solid buy low opportunity presented itself for 2016 fantasy baseball in the form of Texas Rangers ace Yu Darvish as they veteran Japanese fireballer was making his way back from Tommy John elbow surgery. After all it was Darvish who struck out a ridiculous 277 batters in just 209.2 innings back in 2013 and since then was considered the best power arm in the game in terms of K's. All of those seasons of very heavy inning usage in Japan came back to bite Darvish in the States though as an injury-marred 2014 then morphed into a Tommy John diagnosis the following spring training. Be that as it may, Darvish still represented an attractive value play during 2016 drafts given his overpowering stuff and drastically reduced sticker price. He would return in late May but Darvish would last just three starts before he went right back on the DL with neck/shoulder pain. At that point Darvish was looking like a bust already but the guy fought back to return to the team in July where he began to look like his old self once finally healthy. While his composite 3.41 ERA was a bit higher than his career norms, the biggest positive here was that Darvish's K/9 rate of 11.84 was a career-best and showed that his stuff is once again overpowering hitters. In addition, Darvish showed his best control in his 100.1 innings last season, with his 2.78 BB/9 rate serving as the first time he went under 3.00 in that category. In terms of 2017 fantasy baseball, on stuff alone Darvish is a number 1 starter but his health remains a huge red flag. The history of Japanese pitchers flaming out early after just a handful of seasons in the majors is stark (Daisuke Matsuzaka, Hideo Nomo) and so Darvish needs to be handled carefully at the draft table in terms of cost.

2017 PROJECTION: 14-7 3.22 ERA 1.28 WHIP 205 K

Justin Verlander: Wow that was an unexpected comeback. Admittedly, we ripped Justin Verlander to pieces both in our draft guide last season and throughout both 2014 and 2015 as he seemed like a pitcher on the verge of a major crash. After a series of insane workloads from 2009 through 2013, Verlander began to show dips with his velocity and in a related development, increased control problems. The former Cy Young winner struggled terribly in 2104 as he posted a 4.54 ERA and saw his K//9 drop all the way down to a below-average 6.95. The K/9 fall was staggering as Verlander was at 8.96 just the season prior but it showed how all of a sudden he was declining in a major way due to the drop in velocity. 2015 was better as Verlander rebounded with a solid 3.38 ERA but the K/9 did not rise up much as it stayed at a mediocre 7.63. With two years in a row of underwhelming numbers now in the books, there was no way anyone could have foreseen what Verlander was about to put forth during the 2016 season. Almost like he went into a time machine back to 2012, Verlander became that power pitching monster again as he struck out 254 batters in 227.2 innings (10.04 K/9), while showing big-time bite on his stuff as he posted a glowing 3.04 ERA. With his control as good as ever at a 2.25 BB/9, Verlander checked all the boxes in terms of pitching like a fantasy baseball ace despite being drafted in the SP 4 range. When we look toward 2017, it is tough to say if Verlander can repeat such an explosion of numbers as he turns 34 in February. Remember Verlander almost has no peer when it comes to his workload going back to 2006 and so a falloff again would not be a surprise. Try and draft Verlander as an SP 3 in order to play it safe.

2017 PROJECTION: 15-9 3.34 ERA 1.07 WHIP 219 K

Chris Archer: In the sport of horse racing, the term "bounce" is one that is used to describe a thoroughbred that follows up a career-best running effort with a dud. That term can also pertain to fantasy baseball when it comes to young starting pitchers. The premise centers on a pitcher under the age of 27 who makes a sizable jump in innings thrown and then the next season struggles with his stuff due to an arm that does not come back all the way to top strength as a result of fatigue from the previous year's workload. That certainly applied to the Tampa Bay Rays' Chris Archer in 2016 as the righthander was downright horrific the first half of the year when he pitched to a 4.66 ERA and .1.44 WHIP. Archer gave up 18 home runs in 110 first half innings and he also walked the ballpark (3.93 BB/9). In short, Archer looked about as opposite as can be from his monster 2015 breakout when he struck out 252 batters and posted a tiny 3.01 ERA. Based on his ugly 2016 first half, many openly questioned if Archer's performance the year before was a fluke. Well Archer answered that question during the second half of last season as the dominance returned (3.25 ERA and 1.87 BB/9). By the end of the season, Archer cleared the 230-K mark once again with a total of 233 and his overall 4.02 ERA was good considering the tough start. Putting it all together, Archer has now strung back-to-back seasons together where his K/9 has been above the 10.00 mark and that is Max Scherzer or Chris Sale territory. While Archer still gives up too many home runs and battles control issues from time-to-time, there are few arms in baseball that can deliver such impressive heat. Finally, the 4.02 ERA will act as somewhat of a cover in keeping Archer's draft price low enough to where you could make a major value score. Buy in heavily.

2017 PROJECTION: 12-9 3.52 ERA 1.15 WHIP 230 K

Michael Fulmer: Not since the Boston Red Sox traded a young Hanley Ramirez to the Florida Marlins for Josh Beckett has a trade between two teams benefitted both sides so tremendously. That was the end result at the 2015 trade deadline when the New York Mets dealt one of their top pitching prospects in Michael Fulmer to the Detroit Tigers for Yoenis Cespedes. While Cespedes went out and hit 17 home runs in two months to help the Mets reach the World Series and then had a monster 2016 as well, Fulmer went out and challenged for the AL Cy Young as a rookie in 2016. After struggling his first two starts after being promoted in late April, Fulmer dominated the rest of the way as he compiled a composite 3.06 ERA, 1.12 WHIP, and 132 strikeouts in 159 innings. All at the age of 23 and while operating in the rough American League might we add. While Fulmer's 7.47 K/9 rate didn't wow anyone, his control was impeccable (2.38 BB/9) and he kept the ball in the park (0.91 HR/9). We do have to point out though that Fulmer's BABIP was way in the luck range at .268 and when adjusted, his FIP (3.75) and XFIP (3.95) were not as impressive. Considering the mediocre K rate, Fulmer is likely going to see a bit of a regression in his overall numbers this season and that is something to be aware of as he figures to be an expensive commodity for 2017. No Fulmer is not a fantasy baseball ace but he still looks like a darn good pitcher who is still improving.

2017 PROJECTION: 15-7 3.32 ERA 1.14 WHIP 158 K

Kenta Maeda: While projecting how Japanese pitching imports will perform in Major League Baseball is never an exact science, Kenta Maeda proved to be the real deal during his 2016 rookie debut with the Los Angeles Dodgers. Maeda left no doubt that he had the stuff to excel against the best hitters in the world as he roared out of the gates with a 1.41 ERA in March/April. What became easy to see with Maeda was the fact that his control was tremendous and he kept the ball in the park which are the two big keys for a pitcher adjusting quickly to the majors. What was a surprise when it came to Maeda though was his 9.17 K/9 rate since he was not a big strikeout guy in Japan. The unfamiliarity aspect of Maeda likely helped get that number as high as it went but Maeda overall was very good. Like most Japanese pitchers in their first go-round in the States, the long grind of the season took its toll as his ERA came in at an elevated 4.25 in the second half. Other than some BABIP luck though (.283 which resulted in a 3.50 FIP and 3.70 XFIP ERA), Maeda's number were very impressive. It stands to reason that with a full year of experience under his belt, Maeda can improve on his composite 3.48 ERA as a rookie but the flip side is that the K/9 might come down a bit since that number was in outlier territory when looking at his whole professional career. There may not be a better SP 3 out there and in fact, Maeda has the stuff to make the SP 2 grade going forward into this season.

2017 PROJECTION: 15-7 3.32 ERA 1.11 WHIP 182 K

Aaron Sanchez: The conversion from reliever to starting pitcher went about as well as could be expected for the Toronto Blue Jays' Aaron Sanchez in 2016. A selection to the All-Star Game and an AL-leading 3.00 ERA at the age of 24 instantly put Sanchez among the elite arms in fantasy baseball and set him up as a highly-sought after pitcher for the upcoming season. No one could have seen this type of performance coming though, especially since Sanchez showed terrible control the year prior when he walked batters at a 4.29 clip. There were no such struggles last season however as Sanchez lowered his BB/9 mark to a much more palatable 2.95 and more importantly considering the offensive potency of the AL East, kept the ball in the park (0.70 HR/9). Now for the bad news and yes there is quite a bit. Sanchez was not a big strikeout guy in achieving that sparkling ERA as his 7.55 K/9 was right on the average line and that could lead to future issues considering how tough the division always is. In addition, Sanchez' .267 BABIP was well into the fortunate zone and things become even more frightening when you look at his adjusted FIP (4.61) and XIP (4.27) ERA's which are not very pretty. Finally, Sanchez is your classic injury risk for 2017 given his youth and the fact his innings jumped from 102 innings in 2015 to a ridiculous 192 in the 2016 regular season. Almost every time such a combination is put together, injury trouble ensues. Given the BABIP luck and the extreme risk Sanchez' health presents, try and avoid him if you can.

2017 PROJECTION: 14-8 3.84 ERA 1.22 WHIP 163 K

Masahiro Tanaka: Masahiro Tanaka's Elbow: 2, Skeptical Fantasy Baseball Community: 0. Despite pitching with a slight tear in his UCL, the New York Yankees' ace made is through a second full season in 2016 without having to undergo the Tommy John knife. Well almost made it all the way through as Tanaka was shut down the last week of the season after developing a minor flexor strain down by his wrist and not in the elbow. Prior to the shutdown, Tanaka was downright tremendous at times as he won 14 games, put up a 3.07 ERA, and a 1.08 WHIP. The 199.2 innings were uninterrupted until the end and so it seems like Tanaka has figured out how to pitch at a high level with the tear. Now the UCL issue has had some impact though on Tanaka's results which can be found in his declining K/9 rate. Consider that prior to suffering the tear midway through his 2014 rookie season, Tanaka was a strikeout artist as shown by his very high 9.31 K/9. After the diagnosis has been a different story as that number dropped to 8.12 in 2015, and then a very mediocre 7.44 last season. Unable to generate the heat he once did with his fastball and admittedly not throwing the four-seamer as much anymore due to the stress it causes on his elbow, Tanaka is a different pitcher than he was when first bursting onto the scene. Despite all this, Tanaka can be a very good SP 2 in fantasy baseball even with the declining fastball. His control remains impeccable (1.62 BB/9) and he made tremendous strides with the long ball in lowering his HR/9 to a career-best 0.99. A .270 BABIP was slightly lucky (3.50 adjusted FIP ERA) but other than that, Tanaka is getting the job done for his owners now on a yearly basis. Of course any one pitch can send Tanaka right to the operating table which has to be weighed before an investment and that is why we suggest drafting him as your SP 3 instead of as an SP 2 given the risk he brings carries.

2017 PROJECTION: 14-7 3.37 ERA 1.07 WHIP 162 K

Zack Greinke: While they certainly made a supreme effort to buy their way into contention for the 2016 baseball season, pretty much nothing went right for the Arizona Diamondbacks. Right at the top of the setback list was the at times ghastly performance of ace starting pitcher Zack Greinke. The same Grienke whom the D-Backs earned a whole bunch of ridicule for after signing him to a ridiculous six-year contract worth $206.5 million. Instead of purchasing a pitcher they believed could front their rotation and help them reach the postseason, the D-Backs instead got a 4.37 ERA, 1.27 WHIP, and a year pockmarked by injury setbacks. Greinke never looked comfortable for an extended stretch in his first go round in the desert and his season as a whole was disturbing on a number of levels. For starters, Greinke had THREE months where his ERA was 5.50!!!! or above and he also missed the whole month of July with a left oblique strain. Putting a topper on the whole mess, Greinke was not able to finish out the month of September after developing shoulder soreness. All of this from the same pitcher who was arguably the most dominant starter in all of baseball the year prior when he registered a 1.66 ERA, 0.84 WHIP, and 200 strikeouts. So how could things go from one extreme to the other in just one year? Well when digging into the numbers, some ugly truths emerge. Let us first start out by saying that 2016 marked the fourth straight season where Greinke saw his average fastball velocity decrease. Once a 97-mph dynamo with the heater while with the Kansas City Royals, Greinke is now barely in the 90-91 range. We are talking Jered Weaver or C.C. Sabathia here in terms of fastball decline and that alone has made Greinke so much more hittable that ever before. In addition, Greinke went from one extreme to the other when it came to home ballpark. Dodger Stadium has for years been one of the best pitcher parks in the game, while Chase Field in Arizona has been known as a home run haven. Chase Field is a bad marriage for a pitcher whose fastball is betraying him and who even in his best days, gave up home runs are a high rate. Thus it was no shock to see Greinke's HR/9 rate soar to 1.30 and his hit rate jump up as well. Also while Greinke's control was solid, his BB/9 rate went from 2015's 1.62 to 2016's 2.33 which added some more base runners for him to deal with. Finally, the erosion of Greinke's fastball has cut down his margin of error in that he no longer can escape trouble as often with the strikeout. After putting up a dominant 9.21 K/9 rate in 2014 with the Dodgers, the last two years have seen that number dip dramatically. In 2015 Greinke lost more than ONE K/9 as he posted an 8.08 mark there and last season was even worse at a very mediocre 7.60. With the league average around 7.50, Greinke is nothing more than a middling K pitcher right now and that further adds to all the trouble. In fact it is staggering how badly things have turned here and almost completely across the board in all categories. Add in the ugly recent health and Greinke is a guy I wouldn't go near for 2017 fantasy baseball. That should be obvious.

2017 PROJECTION: 13-10 3.80 ERA 1.25 WHIP 160 K

Gerrit Cole: The Pittsburgh Pirates did the only sensible thing they could do with ace SP Gerrit Cole when they shut him down for good in mid-September after a series of disturbing elbow problems. The premature ending to his season was the topper on what was a truly rough campaign for Cole coming off of his dominant 2015 when he registered a 2.60 ERA, collected 202 strikeouts, and won 19 games for the Pirates. It appeared as though the arm trouble that plagued Cole while coming up the Pittsburgh minor league system was a thing of the past and so it was no shock that he was drafted to be a fantasy baseball ace for 2016. Well from the beginning Cole looked nothing like he did just the year prior, with the first indication of trouble showing up in a lowered K/9 from April onward. Consider that in 2015 Cole's K/9 was an impressive 8.74 and just a year later, he would finish at a more mediocre 7.60. The fastball velocity was also down a bit which again showed up in the lowered K rate. Soon the injuries began to show up as Cole started feeling pain in both his elbow and forearm. This was a very scary thing as often pain in these areas can lead to Tommy John surgery. That worst-case scenario was avoided but Cole was a complete injury mess the second half of the season as he hit the disabled list twice. The ultimate result was an ERA of 3.88 that jumped more than a full run compared to 2015 and a very cloudy outlook. As we look toward 2017, the only choice that can be made with Cole from our vantage point is to ignore him completely when it comes to the draft. There is major injury risk here and the ongoing elbow problems portend to more trouble ahead. Tommy John surgery can result at any time and so there is no need to invest here given the risk. Take Cole completely off your cheat sheets.

2017 PROJECTION: 12-8 3.48 ERA 1.22 WHIP 162 K

Felix Hernandez: 2016 was set up to be a very crucial and at the same time telling year for longtime Seattle Mariners ace Felix Hernandez. The reason for the scrutiny was due to the fact that Hernandez was coming off a troubling 2015 campaign where he showed major chinks in his pitching armor for the first time in his stellar career. Leading into 2015, we had already begun mentioning all the massive inning totals Hernandez had accumulated since arriving in the majors at the age of 20 and how eventually that would come back to bite him through diminished stuff. It was only a matter of time before Hernandez' arm began to be negatively affected by all those innings and 2015 certainly looked like it was beginning to take hold. While Hernandez got off to a good start that year, his second half was very ugly as he pitched to a 4.48 ERA and a 1.34 WHIP. His composite 3.53 ERA was his highest since 2008 and that season saw his fastball velocity decline for the third straight year. Even more troubling, Hernandez' 8.52 K/9 was the third season in a row he saw a drop there as well which further called into question his future as an ace pitcher. So as the 2016 season approached, we sounded the alarms regarding Hernandez and how we felt he was one to avoid in drafts given all of the negative trends that were developing. As it turned out, our words of caution were prudent as Hernandez added to the concern about his stuff as his 3.82 ERA was even worse than the year prior and his K/9 dropped for the fourth year in a row to a now mediocre 7.16. This from a guy who was an annual visitor to the 200-K club but who now is seeing his fastball dip to the low 90's as the hits really begin to pile up. Also as we see in many cases of pitchers who begin losing strikeouts, the control falls by the wayside as well since the approach has to change. Hernandez has not responded well to this as his 3.82 BB/9 rate was insanely elevated by his previously lofty standards (his previous high was just 2.58) and his 1.12 HR/9 was itself a career-worst as opposing hitters can now get around on his fastball like never before. Finally, Hernandez hit the DL for a large portion of 2016 with a serious calf injury and so now we also have to worry about his health going forward. By now it is quite clear that Hernandez is a vastly declining fantasy baseball stock who needs to be avoided in all formats.

2017 PROJECTION: 12-11 3.86 ERA 1.26 WHIP 161 K

Carlos Rodon: Hard-throwing Chicago White Sox lefty Carlos Rodon was another one of the young "light bulb went on" prospects during the second half of the 2016 season. After pitching terribly in the first half of the season with a 4.50 ERA and 1.53 WHIP, Rodon was a completely different performer after the All-Star Break as he lowered those ratios to 3.45 and 1.22 respectively. The key to the breakthrough was Rodon finally harnessing his stuff and not walking the ballpark, which was a major problem up to that point as a professional. By the end of the season, Rodon's 2.95 BB/9 was an encouraging development and any further improvement there could quickly move him toward ace status. The reason such a giant leap is possible is because Rodon has some of the most overpowering stuff in baseball. His 9.16 K/9 points him toward being a future 200-strikeout monster and that could come as early as 2017. His 1.25 HR/9 also needs work but all signs are heading in the right direction. Reach a round or two early to be sure you get a piece of this.

2017 PROJECTION: 14-10 3.61 ERA 1.33 WHIP 178 K

Lance McCullers: Like with almost every young and hard-throwing pitcher in 2016, the Houston Astros' Lance McCullers dealt with injuries that stole chunks of his season and left his fantasy baseball owners frustrated by his lost statistics. A power pitcher personified with his near 100-mph fastball, McCullers started the year on the disabled list due to a scary bout of shoulder soreness. While no structural issues were found, it was not until May when McCullers first debuted and things didn't go well as he registered a 4.76 ERA for the month amid 16 walks in 20.2 innings. For as awesome a strikeout pitcher as McCullers has been (above 10.0 K/9 each season in the minors and a 9.24 as a rookie in 2015), walks have always been a big negative. Both trends were as stark as can be throughout the course of last season as McCullers finished with a dominant 11.78 K/9 but his BB/9 was disgusting at an unfathomable 5.00. In addition to the early shoulder trouble, McCullers hit the DL for a second time in August with a sprain of his right elbow. Clearly there are some red flags here centering on the walks and ill health. McCullers is a full effort pitcher whose delivery is a bit rough and that adds stress/strain to his right arm. As a result, McCullers is a tremendous risk for 2017 given what we have seen thus far. Yes the attraction is obvious here as McCullers could easily soar past 200 strikeouts if he can stay on the mound but his health is just not allowing that to happen. The epidemic of young pitchers getting injured now makes investing in guys such as McCullers more risky than ever before and possibly not worth your time or effort.

2017 PROJECTION: 12-6 3.17 ERA 1.29 WHIP 155 K

Jose Quintana: It has always been baffling to us why Chicago White Sox pitcher Jose Quintana doesn't get much love in the fantasy baseball community. After all the lefty has pitched under a 3.80 ERA in all five of his major league seasons and that drops under 3.40 each of the last three years. Want more glowing numbers?

How about the fact Quintana has excellent control (BB/9 rates of 1.92 and 2.16 the last two years) and he keeps the ball in the park on a consistent basis. Finally, Quintana is as dependable as they come health-wise which is no small thing considering how often pitchers get hurt. You always know what you are going to get when you invest in Quintana and that is one of the best SP 3's in the game.

2017 PROJECTION: 14-10 3.32 ERA 1.14 WHIP 182 K

Alex Reyes: The St. Louis Cardinals know how to develop prospects, as they annually are lauded for having one of the best farm systems in the game of baseball. They bolstered that assessment in 2016 when they unveiled top pitching prospect Alex Reyes to spectacular results. In the heat of a pennant race, Reyes looked like an ace starter as he struck out batters at a 10.17 K/9 clip and posted a dominant 1.57 ERA in 46 innings. An extreme groundball pitcher, Reyes's home run rate was ridiculous at 0.20. Of course the requisite control problems went along for the ride (4.50 BB/9) like it does for most young power arms but Reyes looks like he fits with Julio Urias as quite possibly the best pitching sleeper for 2017 fantasy baseball. We are making it a point to get Reyes on all of our teams this season and so should you.

2017 PROJECTION: 12-6 3.33 ERA 1.15 WHIP 170 K

Joe Ross: While he didn't it nearly as bad as his brother Tyson when it came to injuries, the Washington Nationals' Joe Ross had a very difficult 2016 season as he was only able to toss 105 innings due to spending a large chunk of the year on the disabled list. Ross missed 10 weeks with a shoulder injury which is always a big deal but he fought back to make a September return and at least for now quiet concerns about his health moving toward the 2017 season. The 25th overall pick in the 2011 draft, Ross has recorded ERA's of 3.64 and 3.43 his first two years in the majors but he is not his brother when it comes to strikeouts. Still Ross is not a total zero there either as his 8.10 and 7.97 marks with the K/9 are a bit above-average and his control is as good as it gets for a young pitcher. Throw in the fact that Ross keeps the ball in the park and there is still a good deal to work with here despite the injury issues. Draft him as an SP 4 with the strong possibility Ross could be more than that if he stays away from health woes.

2017 PROJECTION: 14-8 3.37 ERA 1.21 WHIP 155 K

Steven Matz: For a guy that is only 25, New York Mets lefty Steven Matz has certainly ran the gamut when it comes to arm/shoulder trouble in his young career.

After going under the Tommy John knife soon after getting picked in the second round of the 2009 draft, Matz hit the DL twice in his debut with the Mets in 2015. Despite all the setbacks, Matz had shown ace-level ability in dominating at the minor league level and then during his 2015 rookie campaign (2.27 ERA/1.23 WHIP/34 K's in 35.2 regular season innings). As a result, the Mets were counting heavily on Matz entering into 2016 but the year turned out to be more of the same on the injury front. Prior to the injuries, Matz was dominant out of the gates as he pitched to a 3.86 ERA in April and then followed that up with an unhittable 1.31 mark in May while averaging a K/IP. By the start of June however, Matz was diagnosed with a bone spur on his elbow which immediately began a string of rough outings that saw him post a horrific 5.74 ERA in June as questions began to circulate that he would have to go under the knife. Matz continued to pitch through the ailment but he eventually hit the disabled list in August with rotator cuff irritation that turned into a shoulder impingement. That proved to be the end-all for Matz as he finished with only 132.1 innings but with solid overall numbers when he was on the hill (3.40 ERA/1.21 WHIP/129 K). While surgery to remove the bone spur takes care of that one issue but the bottom line with Matz is he remains one big injury mess waiting to happen given how many ailments he already has dealt with. While the stuff is ace-level, you can't even count on 150 innings from Matz when you cut the check at the draft table and that makes him one of the biggest boom or bust pitchers out there. Sometimes a guy is too much of a headache to be worth the effort no matter how talented he is and that looks to now be the case with Matz.

2017 PROJECTION: 12-7 3.19 ERA 1.19 WHIP 157 K

Tanner Roark: When the Washington Nationals are not stupidly trying out Tanner Roark in the bullpen as they did with disastrous results at the start of the 2015 season, they have on their hands a very good overachieving pitcher who fits in perfectly behind aces Stephen Strasburg and Max Scherzer. We say overachiever because Roark was originally a 25th round draft pick and it is not often you see a guy selected this low win 16 games with an ERA of 2.83 as Roark accomplished in 2016. When you throw out the skewed numbers from 2015 due to the bullpen stint, Roark has pitched to last year's 2.83 ERA and 2013's 2.85 mark in the Washington rotation. This is more than enough of a sample size to conclude that in fantasy baseball, Roark works as a very good SP 3. You can't project Roark's value to go any higher than that however due to the fact he is limited in the strikeout department (7.37 K/9 last year), to go with some shaky control (3.13

BB/9). Also Roark did in fact post a lucky .269 BABIP, which when adjusted comes out to a more shaky 3.79 FIP and 4.17 XFIP ERA. On a terrific team like the Nationals, Roark should challenge 15 wins again with useful ratios but keep the overall price somewhat in check despite the sparkling ERA last season.

2017 PROJECTION: 15-8 3.41 ERA 1.19 WHIP 163 K

Julio Teheran: It was a very successful comeback season for the Atlanta Braves' Julio Teheran in 2016 to say the least. While it appeared as though the Braves had a star pitcher on their hands when he posted a glowing 2.89 ERA during the 2014 season, the follow up to that performance in 2015 was very ugly at times. While Teheran rallied with a good second half that lowered his ERA that season to a good enough 4.04, sharp rises in walks and home run given up were big red flags that stuck to him during 2016 drafts. Those who kept the faith in Teheran were rewarded though as he was back to his near-ace self in registering a 3.21 ERA. Everything else fell back into place as Teheran's 1.96 BB/9 was exceptional and he kept the ball in the park with a 1.05 HR/9. While it seems like he has been around forever, Teheran is only going to be 26 in January which means there is actually a bit of upside remaining. The Braves figure to be a more competitive team in this year as well since they will be opening up their new ballpark and that should lead to some more wins. We are back on the bandwagon here.

2017 PROJECTION: 14-9 3.17 ERA 1.04 WHIP 173 K

Jon Gray: Location, location, location. The Colorado Rockies fully unleashed top pitching prospect Jon Gray in 2016 and the former 2013 first round pick (third overall) didn't disappoint as he struck out 185 batters in just 168 innings (9.91 K/9). This being Colorado though, Gray's 4.61 ERA and 1.26 WHIP were elevated but there is more to these surface ratios then meets the eye. One would expect that Gray's home numbers would be worse than his road performance given the dry air of Coors Field but the exact OPPOSITE happened. Shockingly, Gray's home ERA of 4.20 was better than the 4.91 mark he put up in away starts. Instead Gray's slightly unlucky .308 BABIP did more damage to his ERA than Coors Field and that is where some optimism lay as his FIP (3.60) and XFIP (3.61) were much more in line with the potent K rate. Having turned only 25 in November, Gray has every right to improve on his decent 2016 numbers but it is tough projecting him anywhere above the SP 3 range given the home ballpark. In those league that cap innings though, Gray's power approach works nicely.

2017 PROJECTION: 12-11 3.84 ERA 1.24 WHIP 195 K

Julio Urias: The future is bright when it comes to the Los Angeles Dodgers pitching rotation and much of that optimism is centered on 20-year-old power lefty prospect Julio Urias. After proving to be virtually unhittable in the minors, the Dodgers promoted Urias to the big club in May. Urias' first stint with the team was marred by nerves and some ugly control but his second run beginning in late July went much better. Flashing the power stuff that made him such a talked-about commodity in the first place, Urias struck out major league hitters at a massive 9.82 K/9 clip in his 77 innings. Like almost every single young power arm though, control was fleeting as Urias' 3.62 BB/9 shows a lot of room for improvement. However the kid keeps the ball in the park with his groundball-heavy approach and the swinging strike percentage is already impressive. Also no one can argue with a 3.39 ERA when pitching half the season at the age of 19 at the major league level. If you could target only one sleeper pitcher this season, make sure it is Urias. Meet the next Felix Hernandez.

2017 PROJECTION: 13-6 3.20 ERA 1.16 WHIP 163 K

Jeff Samardzjia: It was a season to forget for veteran starting pitcher Jeff Samardzjia in 2015 as his one and only season with the Chicago White Sox was nothing short of a disaster. With his strikeout stuff not playing as well in the DH-league, Samardzjia was a big liability the whole year as he finished with a 4.96 ERA and a 1.29 WHIP. Things were so bad that Samardzjia was cast aside to waiver wires in most leagues, marking a major fall from grace for a guy who in 2014 struck out 202 batters and put up a sterling 2.99 ERA. Sensing a buy low opportunity, the always smart San Francisco Giant front office signed Samardzjia as a free agent and it was at that point where we began discussing him as a good bounce back fantasy baseball starter for 2016. While there were some rocky moments, Samardzjia performed well as he sent his ERA back down under 4.00 at 3.89 and won 12 games in 203.1 innings. Now 32-years-old, Samardzjia has in fact changed as a pitcher due to age. For one thing, Samardzjia is not a fireballer anymore like he was when he first arrived with the Chicago Cubs. His 7.39 K/9 rate was pretty much average last season but Samardzjia was good both with his control (2.39 BB/9) and his home runs against (1.06). The light doesn't shine as brightly as it once did but Samardzjia remains in a prime pitcher's park which makes him a rock solid SP 3/4.

2017 PROJECTION: 13-8 3.78 ERA 1.21 WHIP 165 K

Robbie Ray: Sometimes strikeouts show up in unexpected places and one of those locales was the left arm of the Arizona Diamondbacks' Robbie Ray in 2016.

Never considered a top prospect as a former 12th round pick, Ray made it through the Washington Nationals and Detroit Tigers organizations before he found his major league footing in Arizona. Even during his full season debut in 2015, Ray was well off the fantasy baseball radar despite hinting at the power to come in posting a 3.52 ERA and 8.39 K/9. 2016 was a whole different story though as Ray exploded in the strikeout department as he punched out 218 batters in just 174 innings. That ratio came out to an 11.25 K/9 rate which is Clayton Kershaw territory. Ray can get the fastball up to the upper 90's but it was the development of his secondary pitches that really allowed his power stuff to take off. What was puzzling though is that for all of those strikeouts, Ray's season ERA was terrible at 4.90. That ERA made no sense and when you dug under the statistical hood, you found out what was really going on. Specifically speaking, Ray's .352 BABIP was as unlucky a number as any starting pitcher had last season and his adjusted FIP (3.76) and XFIP (3.46) showed a much more realistic ERA based on the K's. Having turned just 25 last October, Ray still has room to improve on his 2016 numbers and the key will be smoothing out his poor control which is always a common occurrence for young pitchers. Highly recommend.

2017 PROJECTION: 12-12 3.75 ERA 1.15 WHIP 215 K

Tyler Glasnow: It was not the rookie debut that top Pittsburgh Pirates pitching prospect Tyler Glasnow would have imagined after he was promoted by the team at the beginning of July. Glasnow would only make two starts before he was sent to the disabled list with soreness in his pitching shoulder and he would not return until the middle of September where the Pirates then placed him in the bullpen. He would get a few starts by the end of the month but altogether Glasnow pitched in only 23.1 innings for the Pirates which pretty much made 2016 a lost year. On talent alone Glasnow is as respected as any pitching prospect in the game but his penchant for injuries is a big problem for his development. In addition, Glasnow has some major control issues that need to be ironed out which means we are talking about two big red flag that need to be weighed before making an investment. On the positive side, Glasnow has been a monster strikeout pitcher at every level (including his debut with the Pirates as he posted a 9.26 K/9 rate) and his ceiling remains very high. The chatter surrounding Glasnow has been muted somewhat off such a rough year but that should only help you at the draft table. Boom or bust.

2017 PROJECTION: 10-5 3.77 ERA 1.33 WHIP 137 K

Marco Estrada: Sometimes in fantasy baseball you get pitchers who just seem to have a knack toward beating the BABIP curve. With an average BABIP for a pitcher somewhere around the .300 mark, any swing north or south of that number one year usually means a correction the following season. A rare bucking of that trend has been seen in the Toronto Blue Jays' Marco Estrada who just a year after posting a ridiculously lucky .216 BABIP in 2015, somehow stayed in that fortunate region in 2016 in posting a .234 mark in that category. That is a crazy amount of good luck and it means Estrada is a guy to be a bit leery of for 2017 fantasy baseball with regards to maintaining his 3.48 ERA from last season. Aging a bit at the age of 33, Estrada does help himself with a decent strikeout rate (8.44 K/9) but his control suddenly vanished in 2016 as shown by his ugly 3.32 BB/9. Consider that one of the main strengths of Estrada in going back to his Milwaukee Brewers days was his impeccable control and this is not a good development when you call Rogers Center home. Again looking at the last two seasons, Estrada's FIP and XIP in both campaigns is over 4.00 despite composite ERA's that finished below that during that span. The idea of Estrada again beating the BABIP curve like he has the last two years is something we can't get behind.

2017 PROJECTION: 14-9 3.77 ERA 1.16 WHIP 161 K

Jered Eickhoff: The Philadelphia Phillies have a bright future that includes a revamped pitching staff which is filled with potent young arms. A prominent member of that youth movement is righthander Jerad Eickhoff who hinted at some big-time ability in 2016 by pitching to a 3.65 ERA, 1.16 WHIP, and 7.62 K/9. Eickhoff has a vast four-pitch arsenal that is highlighted by some of the best control we have seen in years from a young pitcher (1.92 BB/9) and hints at more good numbers to come. A .278 BABIP was in the lucky zone which is something to be aware of (4.15 FIP/4.19 XFIP) but the biggest issue Eickhoff has to get under control is his penchant for home runs. That could be a big problem for Eickhoff as his home ballpark is one of the best power locales in the game. If Eickhoff can just cut into his 1.37 HR/9 rate by even a little, he could easily take the next step forward in his development.

2017 PROJECTION: 14-11 3.57 ERA 1.15 WHIP 173 K

John Lackey: Despite entering into his late 30's, crafty Chicago Cubs veteran righty John Lackey keeps trucking along as a very solid innings-eater in 2016. Lackey certainly did his part for the majors' best team as he posted a 3.35 ERA and struck out his most batters (180) since 2006. The 8.60 K/9 rate was an unexpected surprise but Lackey continued to excel in not issuing walks (2.53

BB/9) and keeping hitters off balance with his vast array of pitches. Possessing one of the better rubber arms in the game, Lackey is fully capable of being a solid SP 4 again this season, as he is guaranteed to win a bunch of games at the very least. While we are not banking on 2016's strikeout numbers returning, everything else seems repeatable for at least one more season.

2017 PROJECTION: 14-8 3.66 ERA 1.16 WHIP 167 K

Kevin Gausman: There has been another graduation to upper-level status among the starting pitching fraternity this season, especially over the last month of the 2016 fantasy baseball campaign. What kind of graduation am I referring to? The graduation of a starting pitcher from a green and unready kid to an upper-level arm that yields good to great numbers for his owners. Such a scenario has now unfolded with the Baltimore Orioles' Kevin Gausman who put up big numbers a year ago in pitching to a 3.61 ERA while calling the ultra-tough AL East home. Now a maturing 25-year-old, the former 2012 first round pick (4th overall) seems to have reached a level that jived with his status as a hyped prospect in the Baltimore system. Taking a quick trip down memory lane, Gausman was a guy who lit up the minor leagues soon after getting drafted, putting up sparkling ERA's and good K rates on the farm that got him on the fast track to the majors. Gausman would make his debut for 47.2 innings a year later in 2013 but he quickly showed he was not ready by posting an ugly 5.66 ERA and 1.34 WHIP. Things started to turn a year later as Gausman lowered his ERA to a solid 3.57 but the WHIP remained high at 1.31 as walks were a problem. Even more concerning was the fact Gausman's K rate plummeted to a horrid 6.99. Combined together, this was not the first round future star many were waiting to see. Still Gausman was about ready to start working out the kinks and in the process, put himself on the path toward taking that next step in his development. Of course it the 2016 season where everything came together for Gausman after he came back from early season injury issues. We already noted the ERA and WHIP but the biggest thing that has launched Gausman's fantasy baseball stock are the strikeouts. After posting a much improved 8.25 K/9 in 2015, Gausman pushed that number to an even higher 8.72 mark last year. Overall Gausman punched out 174 batters in 179.2 innings and the hit rate also trended downward. Using his fastball in conjunction with improving offspeed stuff that was a work in progress earlier in his career, opposing hitters are more off-balance than ever facing Gausman. A 2.35 BB/9 is a glowing number for Gausman and really the only negative thing you can say here is that his 1.40 HR/9 has to come down more than a little. Take that out of the equation and Gausman has been money in the bank and he is pointing himself to being even more than the low-end SP 3 he is now. It is not guaranteed of course as Gausman has wobbled in the past but right now he is pitching as well as ever and really becoming a name to watch.

2017 PROJECTION: 14-10 3.57 ERA 1.26 WHIP 179 K

Marcus Stroman: We loved Marcus Stroman coming into the 2016 season and expressed that view in last year's draft guide. A former 2012 first round pick, Stroman's vast FIVE pitch repertoire gave him the classic look of a future ace. He showed he was not there yet though in 2016 as Stroman struggled for parts of the year and finished with an elevated 4.37 ERA. The one caveat that needs to be discussed is the fact Stroman missed almost all of the 2015 season while rehabbing a spring training ACL tear and the loss of precious development time for a young pitcher likely hurt him a year ago. Keep in mind that Stroman will only be 26 in May and he made a rapid move up the Toronto Blue Jays' minor league ladder which again took away some seasoning time. Stroman actually pitched better than his numbers showed as his .308 BABIP was a bit unlucky and both his FIP and XFIP were below 3.75. We think Stroman is completely capable of approaching the low 3's with his ERA this season as his stuff is way too good for him to struggle again the way he did in 2016. The control is terrific (2.38 BB/9 in 2016) and Stroman's home run rate is solid at 0.93 despite the potency of Rogers Center. The best part about Stroman's somewhat shaky 2016 is that it will keep his draft price at an affordable rate this spring and you should absolutely jump at the chance to bring him aboard.

2017 PROJECTION: 14-7 3.42 ERA 1.14 WHIP 165 K

Matt Harvey: Wow that was ugly. There was nothing that could taken as a positive from the truly hideous season put forth by New York Mets starting pitcher Matt Harvey in 2016. Coming off a dominant return from Tommy John surgery in 2014 where he pitched like an ace (2.71 ERA/1.02 WHIP/188 K in 189.1 IP), it clearly looked like the 216 frames he threw (a high for any pitcher coming back from the UCL reconstruction) sapped his arm strength for the following season. The evidence was stark as Harvey's velocity was way down as his fastball went from an average of 97.0 in 2014 to an average of 92-94 in 2016. As a result, the hits began to pile up and the K rate dropped to a very mediocre 7.38. No longer able to consistently generate outs via the strikeout, Harvey was battered like never before to the tune of a 4.86 ERA and 1.47 WHIP. Putting the nasty topper on the cake, Harvey then was forced to undergo the very scary thoracic outlet syndrome in his pitching arm. There are some very bad end results from this procedure as guys like Noah Lowry and Jeremy Bonderman never returned anywhere near their pre-surgery form and soon were out of the game. While we are not saying this is what will happen with Harvey, he is as big a risk as there gets among the "name" pitchers in fantasy baseball. Stay away.

2017 PROJECTION: 11-8 3.88 ERA 1.29 WHIP 155 K

Danny Duffy: Sometimes the learning curve for top pitching prospects takes much longer than anticipated and often these post-hype sleepers can turn out to be extremely valuable fantasy baseball commodities. Kansas City's Danny Duffy belongs in this category since the power lefty was at times unhittable in 2016 as he struck out batters at an ace-like 9.42 clip and posted a 3.51 ERA that was inflated due to some September struggles. What perennially held back Duffy previously was downright terrible control that allowed opposing pitchers to lay off his 98-mph fastball and wait for the guy to beat himself with errant throws. It call came together at the age of 27 last season however as Duffy made a huge breakthrough with his walks in posting an impeccable 2.10 BB/9 rate. With hitters no longer being able to lay off the missed pitches, Duffy's strikeouts really ramped up and his .239 BAA was phenomenal. A .291 BABIP was only slightly lucky and so the key now will be whether or not Duffy can replicate his excellent 2016 control. That is up for debate since Duffy's numbers there a year ago were in outlier territory but he also burned so many owner before that his draft price will not go up as much as you might think. If you can snag Duffy as an SP 4, you did well.

2017 PROJECTION: 14-10 3.78 ERA 1.16 WHIP 175 K

Aaron Nola: For the first two months of the 2016 season, it certainly looked like those who used a late round pick on Philadelphia Phillies pitching prospect Aaron Nola were rewarded with a monster value play. The former 2014 first round pick (7th overall) burst out of the gates pitching like a fantasy baseball ace to the tune of a 3.55 ERA in April which was followed by a 2.31 mark in May. Even more impressive and a bit unexpected was the strikeout rate from Nola as he punched out 76 batters in those 72 innings. Unfortunately Nola couldn't keep it going as a combination of fatigue as the innings piled up and a late elbow injury conspired to make the righty a huge liability the rest of the way as shown by a 10.42 ERA in June and a 6.30 mark in July just before his shutdown. The elbow injury was diagnosed as a sprain and no surgery was needed which was the big positive result out of that disturbing development however. Overall we have to look at Nola in a few different prisms, with almost all of them positive despite the ugly final 4.78 ERA. The first two months of 2016 showed how good a pitcher Nola can be and the 9.81 K/9 rate was ace-level. Also the 2.35 BB/9 and 0.86 HR/9 rates were both very good numbers for such a young pitcher which again speak to the vast upside here. Consider also that Nola got quite unlucky with a .334 BABIP, which is revealed in a much more impressive looking 3.07 FIP and XFIP. The bottom line here is that Nola is one of the best young pitchers in fantasy baseball and the 4.78 ERA clearly does not tell the story of how good he can be. In fact that ugly ERA can only help you at the draft table as it will keep Nola's price down dramatically. Ignore and be aggressive here as Nola is going to be a good one.

2017 PROJECTION: 14-9 3.35 ERA 1.22 WHIP 175 K

Jameson Taillon: While it was an unexpectedly difficult season for the Pittsburgh Pirates in 2016, the one bright spot is that the organization was able to debut some of the prime prospects they have been accumulating over the years. One member of that club was 25-year-old righty pitching gem Jameson Taillon who was the number 2 overall pick in the 2010 draft. While it was a somewhat rocky climb up the Pirate minor league ladder (Taillon endured a Tommy John surgery and other physical ailments that wiped out his entire 2014 and 2015 seasons), the initial reviews from last year were mostly positive. Earning a promotion in June after dominating at Triple-A with a 2.04 ERA, Taillon was not overmatched in any way against major league hitters as he showed off his mid-90's fastball and knee-bending curve. In 98 innings with the Pirates, Taillon posted a 3.49 ERA and 1.14 WHIP but it wasn't all smooth sailing as he hit the DL in July with shoulder fatigue. Any problem with a pitching shoulder is never a small thing and that is especially true when you consider the massive injuries Taillon has fought through already in his young career. He is expected to be 100 percent for the start of the season but the injury risk is significant given what we already have seen on that front with Taillon. Getting back to the numbers, Taillon is not a classic power pitcher befitting his draft status and so don't pay a sticker price with that in mind. The 7.44 K/9 rate Taillon registered as a rookie was just average but on the positive side, his control as is as good as it gets (1.29 BB/9 in 2016). The ceiling could eventually go to the SP 2 floor but for now Taillon is a guy we like in the low SP 3 range with high risk attached.

2017 PROJECTION: 12-9 3.29 ERA 1.15 WHIP 146 K

J.A. Happ: Sometimes no matter how much you think you have fantasy baseball figured out, a development occurs that throws all conventional wisdom out the window. This was the story of Toronto Blue Jays lefty J.A. Happ's 2016 season as he entered the year going undrafted in many leagues and then somehow finished with 20 wins and a 3.18 ERA. It was a spectacular performance from Happ but it left almost all of us scratching our heads since this was the same pitcher who logged ERA's higher than 4.22 four straight years and who was nothing but a journeyman veteran. Obviously we have to be somewhat skeptical of Happ's 2016 performance since it was so much outside of his career norms but perhaps the guy was a late bloomer which is not totally out of the realm of possibility. Keep in mind that Happ did post a 3.61 ERA in 2015; possibly hinting at what was to come. In digging into the numbers, Happ did receive a solid boost of good luck as his BABIP of .268 came out to FIP (3.96) and XFIP (4.18) ERAs that were somewhat higher. On the plus side though, Happ has really broken through the last few years with his control after being a major liability there earlier in his career. A 2.77 BB/9 was solid and Happ also kept the ball in the park (especially crucial when Rogers Center is your home base) at 1.10 HR/9. Having turned 34 in October, there is no chance Happ will better his 2016 numbers and he is likely to slide back closer to a 4.00 ERA unless he gets some more BABIP luck. When you cut to the chase, the division is beyond rough, the ballpark is a launching pad, and you never want to buy a player coming off a career season. Let someone else have him.

2017 PROJECTION: 15-10 4.05 ERA 1.22 WHIP 159 K

Rich Hill: We all know the story by now regarding veteran starter Rich Hill pitching in Independent League baseball and then latching on with the Boston Red Sox at the end of the 2015 season. Hill shocked everyone by coming up late in the year and absolutely dominating in his four starts to the tune of a 1.55 ERA and 11.17 K/9 that looked like something out of a Clayton Kershaw book. Alas there was not a whole lot of attention given to Hill on the open market that winter which is why he signed just a one-year deal with the Oakland A's. A funny thing happened however. Instead of coming back to earth, Hill was just as dominant as ever in pitching to a 2.12 ERA and a 1.00 WHIP in a year split between the A's and Los Angeles Dodgers. Once again as well, Hill was a monster in the strikeout department as he rocked a 10.52 K/9 and all at the advanced age of 36 (turning 37 in March). Folks we are talking top ten overall numbers among starting pitchers and only a chronic blister problem held Hill back to the point he threw just 110.1

innings. Want some more incredible numbers? How about a ridiculous 0.33 HR/9 or his sparkling 2.69 BB/9. Again all ace-quality numbers. Those who snagged Hill at a discount in 2016 made one of the best scores of the season and this is really some story that has emerged. Can it continue on into 2017? That is the big question. Yes Hill is getting old but he was so dominant a year ago that it is almost impossible to doubt him. Still tread a bit carefully given the age and injury history.

2017 PROJECTION: 11-6 3.15 ERA 1.08 WHIP 156 K

Dallas Keuchel: Nailed it! Coming off a surprising 2015 Cy Young campaign (20 wins, 2.48 ERA), we screamed to the rafters in strongly suggesting you avoid Houston Astros ace lefty Dallas Keuchel for 2016 fantasy baseball. While we never buy into a player coming off a career-year, we also severely doubted the 2015 performance from Keuchel across the board since his numbers were way out of whack compared to his career norms. Throw in the likely "bounce" after making big inning jumps two years in a row and Keuchel was the poster child of our 2016 bust list in last year's draft guide. Needless to say, Keuchel was every bit the disaster we said he would be as he logged a gross 4.55 ERA, 1.29 WHIP, and saw a drop in his K/9 from 2015's 8.38 to last year's 7.71. Throw in a shoulder injury that no doubt can be attributed to the inning jumps and Keuchel was an unmitigated disaster. Turning 29 in January, Keuchel has to earn back the trust of the fantasy baseball community but he has a lot of work to do there. The shoulder injury is a major red flag on its own given the good chance the issue will pop up again as well. Keuchel's slip in K/9 last season back to his pre-2015 norms also lessen the margin of error he has. While Keuchel has every chance to better his ugly 2016 numbers, forget about seeing his 2015 performance ever again.

2017 PROJECTION: 14-11 3.89 ERA 1.23 WHIP 155 K

Adam Wainwright: This publication was well ahead of the trouble that Adam Wainwright has experienced the last two years and needless to say we have been proven spot on in our earlier assessment of him being on the decline. Already with a Tommy John surgery in his past, Wainwright was putting together another string of massive inning totals after returning from the procedure which raised the trouble meter to "high." While he posted an excellent 2.38 ERA in 2014, Wainwright was showing signs of slippage such as a drop in his K/9. A torn Achilles ruined Wainwright's 2015 which didn't give him a chance to prove us right but 2016 did the trick as he pitched to a career-worst 4.62 ERA and hideous 1.40 WHIP. Yes Wainwright's .330 BABIP was unlucky but his K/9 rate of 7.29 fell below average. Also Wainwright's fastball velocity dipped for the third year in a row which is a trend that usually is not reversible. At the age of 35 and with a ton of mileage already on his arm, Wainwright's days as even an SP 3 are finished.

2017 PROJECTION: 14-10 4.30 ERA 1.34 WHIP 155 K

Matt Shoemaker: It seems like every year we reference a pitcher who suffered the unfortunate fate of being hit in the face/head with a line drive off an opposing hitter's bat and in 2016 that guy was most starkly Los Angeles Angels pitcher Matt Shoemaker. Shoemaker wound up with a fractured skull when he was hit by a line drive during a start in early September which of course finished his season. Prior to that twist of fate, Shoemaker was having a fine year that was a sizable improvement over his sometimes messy 2015 campaign. His final 3.88 ERA was down from his high 4.46 mark the year prior and much of that drop was as a result of Shoemaker making firm inroads on his career-long struggle with giving up home runs. While Shoemaker has opened eyes in the past with his strikeouts and decent overall repertoire, his penchant for giving up home runs always made any one start a risk in terms of using him in fantasy baseball. Nowhere was this more clear than in 2015 when Shoemaker was right near the top of baseball with his horrific 1.60 HR/9. Clearly having went to work on that massive struggle prior to the start of 2016, Shoemaker's results there were tremendous as he lowered his HR/9 rate to a very solid 1.01. With home runs now no longer blowing up his ERA as much as it had in the past, the ratios dropped and Shoemaker became quite usable. On top of the drop in homers, Shoemaker's strikeouts rebounded near 2014 levels (8.14 K/9) with his 8.04 mark. A near-neutral .315 BABIP showed that Shoemaker's results last season were pretty much legit so going into 2017, he should be back in the fantasy baseball communities' good graces. Of course we do have to worry about any psychological effects for Shoemaker after the comebacker to his head but on stuff alone, he is worth using as a solid SP 4.

2017 PROJECTION: 12-12 3.75 ERA 1.22 WHIP 167 K

Vincent Velasquez: It didn't get a ton of attention but the Philadelphia Phillies committed highway robbery when they swiped hard-throwing pitching prospect Vinny Velasquez from the Houston Astros for closer Ken Giles last winter. While Giles began the 2016 season in horrid fashion that quickly cost him the closer role with the Astros, Velasquez was putting up a dominant April in posting an ace-like 1.78 ERA, 0.87 WHIP, and striking out a monstrous 33 batters in 25.1 innings (including a 16-K gem in his second start). The subsequent five months were a bit volatile though as Velasquez had ERA's over 5.00 in two of them (May and

August) but also went under the 3.00 mark in two others (June and September). The inconsistency was a product of Velasquez being a 24-year-old rookie and due to the fact he dealt with injuries (a right biceps strain landed him on the DL in June). Finishing with a composite 4.12 ERA and 1.33 WHIP before he was shut down by the Phillies in September after just 131 innings, Velasquez is quite intriguing moving forward on the strength of his power arm which stuck out batters at a very high 10.44 K/9 rate. Now like with most young power arms, Velasquez needs to curb the free passes as his 3.09 BB/9 was too high and his 1.44 HR/9 rate won't allow him to post as good of an ERA as he is capable of in his launching pad home park. Perhaps the most concerning aspect of Velasquez remains his health which has been a challenge for him ever since turning pro. Having had a Tommy John procedure already in his past, the biceps strain last season was troubling. Given the physical challenges he has faced, there is a case to be made with regard to Velasquez being a better fit for the bullpen where his extreme fastball would be a major weapon and there would be less wear and tear on his arm. The Phillies will give him another shot in the rotation for 2017 though and the high-K rate alone makes Velasquez a decent sleeper in the late rounds.

2017 PROJECTION: 10-10 3.78 ERA 1.28 WHIP 157 K

Chris Tillman: Investing in American League East pitchers not named David Price (and even that was somewhat shaky last season) is something you never want to get into the habit of doing but the Baltimore Orioles' Chris Tillman has done more than enough over the years to make himself somewhat of an asset in fantasy baseball. In four of the last five seasons in fact, Tillman's yearly ERA has come in under the 3.80 mark which is nothing to sneeze at considering the power-packed division. While his WHIP has elevated the last two years (1.39 and 1.28 respectively), Tillman has also had a knack for pitching deep into games which allows him to claim his fair share of wins (double-digit victories four straight years). Tillman's .282 BABIP was a decent help to his ERA though (4.22 FIP/4.55 XFIP) and his 3.45 BB/9 is an ugly number you can't ignore. Again we are not talking about a star here but Tillman can serve as one of the better SP 5's if you correctly draft him to fill such a role on your team.

2017 PROJECTION: 14-9 3.97 ERA 1.29 WHIP 144 K

Rick Porcello: If we were to have given you 25 or even 50 picks at the start of the 2016 fantasy baseball season and asked who would be the first pitcher to win 20 games, it would be a guarantee that Boston Red Sox veteran starter Rick Porcello would not have been mentioned. After all Porcello was coming off a truly putrid 2015 campaign where he registered a 4.92 ERA after seemingly making the stupid decision to sign into the AL East despite having a career K/9 rate that was way below average at 6.04. Talk about a bad matchup of stuff and division. Well Porcello got the last laugh by winning 22 games against just 4 losses. Porcello also showed he was not just a product of good run support as he registered a 3.15 ERA and 1.01 WHIP. It was a spectacular season no matter how you cut it and all from a guy who rightly went undrafted in many leagues. As we do with any surprising season, a trip into the advanced numbers is required to see if there was any "fluke" to what Porcello accomplished. It was there where you could see that Porcello got a fair amount of BABIP help with a lucky .269 mark. As a result, the FIP ERA for Porcello comes in a bit higher at 3.40 and his XFIP even more elevated at 3.90. Those are still good ERA's but are more indicative of what Porcello really was performance-wise last season. Now as far as the strikeouts are concerned, pitching in the AL East mean that a K/9 over 8.00 is almost a requirement and obviously this is not Porcello's strength. He did post a career-best 189 K's last season but that number was helped by the massive 223-inning Porcello posted. Still Porcello does have some of the best control in the majors as his 1.35 BB/9 shows and that helps overcome some of the strikeout shortcomings. Even though he won 22 games, the narrative should not change much here in terms of Porcello being a guy who is at BEST an SP 4 in mixers and more ideally an SP 5. Remember that wins are a fickle stat that should not even be a category in fantasy baseball 5 x 5 formats in my opinion given the luck involved there (remember Kent Bottenfield?) but give Porcello his due for getting there anyway.

2017 PROJECTION: 16-8 3.77 ERA 1.14 WHIP 165 K

Jason Hammel: One of the more pronounced first half stud/second half dud pitchers in fantasy baseball, it was a somewhat rough year for Chicago Cubs veteran Jason Hammel in 2016. While he remained a solid back-end starter both in real and in fantasy baseball, Hammel suffered elbow soreness that ended his regular season in early September. Once again the first half/second half splits were obvious as Hammel's 3.46 ERA prior to the All-Star Break was much more palatable then the shaky 4.35 mark he put up after. By now it is obvious that Hammel is a guy you sell high on in late June but keep in mind there are some other red flags to be aware of here. Specifically, Hammel's K/9 dropped from 9.07 in 2015 to a very mediocre 7.78 last season. Leaking velocity certainly is part of the reason for the slip and also for the fact Hammel's HR/9 in 2016 was tough to stomach at 1.35. Now 34 and with lots of innings under his belt, the evidence Hammel is eroding is pretty clear.

2017 PROJECTION: 14-10 3.90 ERA 1.23 WHIP 156 K

Gio Gonzalez: While he remains a useful mid-rotation fantasy baseball starter, the last two years have seen Washington Nationals veteran lefty Gio Gonzalez become quite inconsistent from one start to the next. 2016 was a down year overall for Gio as his 4.57 ERA was his highest since 2009 but at the same time he also had a slightly unlucky BABIP at .316. The ERA sailing over 4.00 did end a streak of six consecutive years where Gonzalez went under that mark so perhaps there was a bit of an outlier aspect to it. Truth be told, Gonzalez 8.68 K/9 was nearly identical to his 8.65 mark the year prior when he posted a 3.79 ERA and that bodes well for a bit of a bounce back for 2017. Also Gonzalez was able to record a career-best 2.99 BB/9 rate, which was the first time he ever went below 3.00. Considering his career-long control struggles, this was no small feat. Still young and in his prime at the age of 31, Gonzalez is a very affordable and effective SP 3 who will win a bunch of games on a great Washington team. While his WHIP will always hurt you, Gonzalez is very solid in the other three pitching categories he impacts in a standard 5 x 5 mixed league. Gonzalez has entered into a phase of his career where there is no more excitement when drafting the guy but that just makes him a good target as a value purchase in the middle-to-late rounds of your draft.

2017 PROJECTION: 14-10 3.82 ERA 1.30 WHIP 166 K

Jake Odorizzi: It was a par for the course 2016 season for the Tampa Bay Rays' Jake Odorizzi. The righthander pretty much matched his 2015 numbers, staying in the same statistical ballpark across the board. Odorizzi is one of those "solid but unspectacular" arms that can help you in an SP 4 or 5 sense but nothing more. A 3.69 ERA and 7.96 K/9 last season fell right in line with this designation and at the age of 27 this March, Odorizzi should not be graded any differently this season.

2017 PROJECTION: 11-8 3.52 ERA 1.16 WHIP 163 K

Drew Pomeranz: One tried-and-true strategy when selecting pitchers in yearly fantasy baseball drafts that almost everyone subscribers to is the targeting of arms from the much easier National League, while at the same time trying to avoid those who operate in the rougher American League. The reason is due to the fact that typically a pitcher in the NL will on average produce and ERA .50 or lower than what they would have put up in the league of the DH. Also with pitchers having to hit in the National League and even those slotted into the 8th spot in the order typically being shoddy hitters, pitchers here have much fewer lineup landmines to work against. In fact in drawing this point home, we always get firm reminders of these trends each season when a pitcher gets traded from one league into the other. Such was the case in 2016 when it came to the hard-throwing lefty Drew Pomeranz. We were on record in last year's draft guide suggesting to target Pomeranz as a late round sleeper given the fact his fastball generated a high amount of strikeouts and he would be operating in the best stadium in the game for a pitcher in San Diego's Petco Park. While we were not surprised that Pomeranz became an instant asset in fantasy baseball once April got underway, we in no way foresaw how he would pitch at an ace-like level the first half of the year. Rightfully earning a spot on the NL All-Star team, Pomeranz went into the Midsummer Classic with a sterling 2.47 ERA, 1.06 WHIP, and 115 strikeouts in just 102 innings. Pomeranz would not pitch another game in a Padres uniform though as he was dealt to the Boston Red Sox prior to the start of the second half; a trade that instantly sent his stock spiraling downward. In fact you couldn't have drawn up a more stark contrast in ballparks when it came to Pomeranz leaving the friendly confines of Petco for the offensive juggernaut that is Fenway Park. The obvious conclusion to make was that Pomeranz would start struggling in his new league and that is exactly what happened. In his 67.1 innings for the Red Sox, Pomeranz registered a gross 4.68 ERA, 1.40 WHIP, and 69 K's in 67.1 innings. Everything went in the wrong direction for Pomeranz once in Boston and the splits between his stints with the Padres to his term with the Red Sox was beyond stark. Making matters worse, Pomeranz finished the season battling soreness in his forearm which is very scary for a young (28 in November) and hard-throwing pitcher given the high caseload of Tommy John victims from this group. A free agent as of this writing, almost all of Pomeranz' 2017 prospective fantasy baseball value hinges on what team he ends up signing with. If Pomeranz goes back into the NL, feel free to target him as a low-end SP 3. If he goes back into the AL, drop him down to an SP 5.

2017 PROJECTION: 13-7 3.44 ERA 1.22 WHIP 173 K

Trevor Bauer: The annual tease that is Trevor Bauer continued on in 2016. The former third overall pick in the 2011 draft remained staggeringly inconsistent last season for the Cleveland Indians as he posted a 4.26 ERA and 1.31 WHIP. What was especially annoying about Bauer is that from one start to the next, there were often wild fluctuations in performance. A 2-hit/10-K shutout would be followed by a 5-earned run meltdown and that made Bauer impossible to trust in any one start. Even more disappointing is that Bauer's K/9 rank sank to mediocre territory in 2016 at 7.96. Since the main allure about owning Bauer centers on receiving a high number of strikeouts, this is a very troubling trend and leaves little left to make you want to invest again. We have said repeatedly not to bother with Bauer anymore as he is a seriously flawed pitcher and that is now especially true when factoring in the drop in K rate.

2017 PROJECTION: 12-11 4.11 ERA 1.30 WHIP 162 K

Ivan Nova: Sometimes all a guy needs is a change of scenery. Pittsburgh Pirates starting pitcher Ivan Nova can certainly attest to this after seeing drastically different statistical results from one team to another in 2016. What was obvious was that Nova was a terrible fit with the New York Yankees, as his soft-tossing approach was exploited constantly in the home run haven that is the team's home ballpark. Both before and after his Tommy John surgery, Nova was just a waiver guy in fantasy baseball as his ERA went over 5.00 in three of his last four full seasons with the Yankees. Nova was headed toward yet another season above that ugly mark in 2016 as he sat at 4.90 on the Aug. 1 trade deadline. It was there when Yankees GM Brian Cahsman pretty much gave Nova away to the Pirates, so desperate were they trying to get rid of him. Well as it often happens when a pitcher moves from the American League to the National League, the ratios dropped for Nova and quite sharply we might add. Joining Francisco Liriano and A.J. Burnett as other reclamation projects to suddenly turn things around with the Pirates, Nova went on a tear the last two months of the season in pitching to a 3.06 ERA, 1.10 WHIP, and striking out 75 batters in 97.1 innings. While Nova is still a liability in the strikeout department (7.06 overall K/9 last season), his plus curveball and slider were very effective in the non-DH league. There was not much fluke involved either as Nova's .306 BABIP was actually slightly UNLUCKY. Turning 30 in January, Nova looks like he is ready to settle in as a decent enough SP 5 in deeper mixed league formats for 2017.

2017 PROJECTION: 13-8 3.92 ERA 1.29 WHIP 149 K

David Phelps: It was the tale of two seasons for veteran Miami Marlins pitcher David Phelps during the 2016 season. He began the year in the team's bullpen, leaving him with little to no fantasy baseball value to speak of despite the fact Phelps pitched well there with a 2.65 ERA as the eighth inning setup man to closer A.J. Ramos. However it wasn't until the Marlins moved Phelps into the rotation at the start of August where he began to yield some very interesting value. Already possessing a fastball that reached the upper-90's and which induced a high number of K's, Phelps proceeded to strike out 32 batters in just 24.1 innings as a starter as he became a quick waiver wire darling. Unfortunately a season-ending oblique injury ruined the fun but Phelps' very good work as a starter makes him quite intriguing as a sleeper value play for 2017. The issue with Phelps has always been a lack of control (which was still a problem last season as evidenced by a high 3.66 BB/9) but his composite 2.52 ERA and dominant 11.56 K/9 are eye-opening. While Phelps is no new kid on the block at the age of 30, there is upside to take advantage of for a very cheap draft price this season. Phelps falls into that valuable and overlooked category of being a veteran arm that doesn't have the flash that younger pitchers with the same type of ability carry. That just means you can get Phelps that much cheaper at the draft table and in turn make a bigger profit. The Marlins would be foolish not to continue the Phelps as a starter experiment and so he needs to be on your sleeper list.

2017 PROJECTION: 12-10 3.33 ERA 1.17 WHIP 165 K

Jordan Zimmerman: Yeah that one was easy to see coming. You didn't have to be a psychic to predict trouble for Jordan Zimmerman entering into the 2016 fantasy baseball season as he was right at the top of our "BUST" list in last year's draft guide. The main reason for Zimmerman earning this designation was due to his signing as a free agent with the Detroit Tigers last winter. While there was no denying how great Zimmerman pitched at times during his tenure with the Washington Nationals, red flags began to crop up in 2015 when his velocity declined for the second season in a row. Never a big strikeout pitcher to begin with, moving from the National League to the American League is not what a pitcher wants to do if his fastball is losing sizzle. While Zimmerman initially had success out of the gates with the Tigers (0.55 ERA), May onward was simply brutal for the veteran. A 4.88 May ERA looked dominant compared to Zimmerman's 6.43 June, 32.40 August, and 10/13 September/October. In fact it was downright comical how bad Zimmerman was and the Tigers wouldn't let him go near a mound down the stretch of the season, save for one spot start at year's end. Once again Zimmerman's velocity declined and his K/9 has turned into a joke as it fell to 5.64. With the baseball coming in as slow as ever, opposing hitters are teeing off on Zimmerman like never before as his HR/9 went over 1.00 for the first time since 2010 at 1.20. Finally, there was no fluke to Zimmerman's 4.87 ERA as his BABIP was almost completely neutral at .304. Simply put, the only reason you should want to own Zimmerman is if your league awards a first place prize for finishing last.

2017 PROJECTION: 12-11 4.59 ERA 1.29 WHIP 146 K

Jose De Leon: The Los Angeles Dodgers saw their rotation decimated in 2016 as they went in without Zack Greinke after losing him during free agency and then saw ace Clayton Kershaw miss a huge chunk of the year with injury. That necessitated the call-up of top power pitching prospect Jose De Leon in September which served as a "run to the waiver wire" moment in the fantasy baseball community. Power is the name of the game here as De Leon put up monster K/9's at Double-A (12.33) in 2015 and then at Triple-A (11.57) last season prior to his promotion. While De Leon struggled in his four-start cameo with the Dodgers in pitching to a 6.35 ERA and 1.53 WHIP, there is no denying the fact that the 24-year-old has major ability and he should be planted firmly on most sleeper lists for drafts this spring. The initial stumble with the Dodgers didn't go according to plan but that will just help keep the price from getting out of hand at the draft table. Go get him.

2017 PROJECTION: 12-7 3.75 ERA 1.23 WHIP 152 K

Sonny Gray: There is bad and then there was the horror show that was Sonny Gray during the 2016 fantasy baseball season. Outside of maybe Matt Harvey, there was not another high-priced pitcher who so royally failed with his on-field results than the Oakland A's righty as he served as a human batting practice pitcher for large segments of the year. In fact it was staggering how bad Gray was and this from a guy who was drafted to be the ace of a fantasy baseball staff. Perhaps we should have seen this coming as Gray was leaking some velocity for a few years and his K/9 rate fell three straight years going into the 2016 season (9.42 all the way down to 7.31). With Gray no longer able to get out of trouble with the strikeout as often as he did in the past, opposing hitters went to town on him. Never was this seen in more stark terms then with the long ball as Gray's HR/9 rate soared to 1.38 last season, which dwarfed the 0.74 mark he posted in that category just a year earlier. In addition, Gray's formerly pinpoint control betrayed him as his BB/9 shot way up to 3.23 (again a sizable leap from his 2.55 rate in 2015). With the K/9 rate falling for the fourth year in a row as well at 7.23, Gray was right there as one of the worst starters in the game with his 5.69 ERA and 1.50 WHIP. So where do we go from here with a guy who is still only just 27? Well as we always say, the numbers don't lie and Gray is clearly a shell of his former ace self. Now there is a chance that Gray is crafty enough to come back with a decent bounce back campaign in 2017 but his days as an ace seem gone for good already. Visions of Matt Cain and his early decline immediately come to mind here as the two cases run parallel in terms of young starters coming up early and throwing a lot of innings with big results. Those early heavy workloads likely led to injuries and drastically slumping numbers from Cain as he approached 30 and now he is barely hanging on in the majors. While Gray's situation is not that dire, another year like 2016 and he will be close to that point. In no way, shape, or form are we suggesting you try Gray out again this season given how terrible he was in 2016 as the trends are very clear that Gray is on a major decline. Get out of the way.

2017 PROJECTION: 12-12 4.19 ERA 1.27 WHIP 142 K

Matt Moore: A previously failed prospect with the Tampa Bay Rays who hit rock bottom when he needed Tommy John elbow surgery, it certainly looked like Matt Moore was ready to finally break through at the start of 2016 upon returning from the procedure. Moore came out of the gates in April by posting a 3.86 ERA, 1.19 WHIP, and he struck out 35 batters in 32 innings. Most encouraging was the fact Moore walked only 7 batters in those 32 innings which was a terrific semi-breakthrough from a guy who had some of the worst control in the game prior to going under the knife. The old and infuriating Moore returned in May however as he blew up to the tune of a 7.36 ERA and walked 12 in 25.2 innings. Eventually the Rays had enough with Moore as they shipped him to the San Francisco Giants at the Aug. 1 trade deadline. That was a very telling move as the Rays have been lauded for their development of power pitchers over the last decade or so. The fact they gave up on Moore speaks volumes about his shortcomings. It didn't matter that Moore was pitching in the AL or the NL last season as he recorded the same exact 4.08 ERA in both locales last season. Looking at his overall year as a whole, Moore still can't harness his control as his BB/9 rate once again went over 3.00 at 3.27. Also the K/9 rate of 8.08 was below what Moore put up when he first arrived in the majors but on the plus side, a full season in the NL should boost that number upward. Turning 28 in June, Moore might have a smidge of upside remaining but we have grown tired of the walks and inconsistency. Another guy you can stop chasing.

2017 PROJECTION: 14-10 3.86 ERA 1.28 WHIP 180 K

Blake Snell: The Tampa Bay Rays have had a very impressive pipeline of power pitchers come up through their farm system over the last 10 seasons; a group that includes David Price, Wade Davis, Chris Archer, and now likely Blake Snell. The former 2011 first round pick (9th overall), Snell racked up a ton of strikeouts in the minor leagues as he posted K/9 rates of 10.30 or more at Double-A and Triple-A. The Rays couldn't keep Snell on the farm any longer last season as they called him up during the summer and had to be impressed by the small sample size of numbers in his 89 innings. The high strikeout rate traveled to the major leagues as Snell whiffed batters at a 9.91 rate and his 3.54 ERA will likely only go down as he further develops. Work needs to be done with his control as it does for most young power arms but the future looks like it will include top-end numbers before too long. Snell is going to be a good one and the positive track record of Tampa Bay developing arms is another plus.

2017 PROJECTION: 12-7 3.24 ERA 1.26 WHIP 159 K

Lance Lynn: Perhaps the first big injury to come down the pike in 2016 fantasy baseball was the Tommy John elbow surgery diagnosis for St. Louis Cardinals workhorse righty Lance Lynn. Having quietly established himself as one of the better power arms in the game prior to the surgery, Lynn was a decent-sized loss for his fantasy baseball owners right at the outset of spring training. Having suffered no setbacks in his recovery, Lynn should be ready to go sometime around mid-to-late April. Keep in mind that Lynn had a string of five MLB seasons out of five where he posted an ERA under 4.00 and in three of those campaigns, he went under 3.15. Lynn also can be considered a power pitcher as he generally resides in the 8.50 range with his K/9 and he also has a knack for coming up with wins which is always a plus from that unpredictable category. The one thing that has to be watched here is the typical control problems most pitchers have the first season back from Tommy John. This is especially troubling for Lynn because he was a poor control pitcher even before going under the knife. From 2012 through 2015, Lynn had a BB/9 rate over 3.00 which is a big negative and one assumes he will be right back there again for 2017. Still despite the lack of control, Lynn has been able to post very good ERA's and K totals to go with winning games. That is still a nice return on investment and the drastically reduced draft price is quite attractive.

2017 PROJECTION: 12-7 3.48 ERA 1.27 WHIP 163 K

Steven Wright: R.A. Dickey now has some competition in terms of being the best knuckleball pitcher in fantasy baseball and it comes in the form of 2016 Boston Red Sox All-Star Steven Wright. Just like with Dickey, Wright turned to the knuckler after seeing his career stagnate in the minor leagues and he showed some big skill with the pitch the first half of last season as he put up a 2.68 ERA and .223 BAA. Also like with Dickey, Wright picked up a decent amount of strikeouts on the pitch as he whiffed 94 batters in 114 innings. Unfortunately Wright was not able to keep the good times rolling into the second half as he began to get hit hard and then came down with a shoulder injury in August that knocked him out for the remainder of the regular season. Despite the rough ending, Wright has cemented a spot in the Boston rotation for 2017. Now when breaking down the numbers, Wright was solid in his K/9 rate at 7.30 but like most knucklers, the BB/9 was not so hot at 3.27. In terms of fantasy baseball, the 32-year-old Wright is an uncomfortable start every time out given the unpredictability of the knuckleball and the game-to-game results that go with it. Wright is just as likely to throw a 2-hit shutout as he is to surrender a 6-earned run meltdown which means you can't grade him as anything but an SP 5 in all formats.

2017 PROJECTION: 14-9 4.15 ERA 1.27 WHIP 138 K

Michael Pineda: The riddle that is Michael Pineda continued during the 2016 fantasy baseball season. Staying healthy for the first time in his career, Pineda struck out a boatload of batters throughout the year as he reached the 200-K level for the first time in his career with 207. Pineda accumulated that impressive number of whiffs in just 175.2 innings, which was good for an ace-like 10.61 K/9 rate. Still for all those strikeouts, Pineda's ERA was awful at 4.82 as he served as the AL version of Robbie Ray. Just like with Ray, Pineda wound up suffering from some ugly BABIP luck (.339) and so his 3.79 FIP and 3.31 XFIP were much better indicators of his strikeout prowess. Also on the positive side, Pineda's control remained a big asset as it has throughout his career. Turning 28 in January, Pineda's power arsenal makes him a good SP 3 candidate if his luck irons itself out and if he can stay healthy. In fact we are more concerned about Pineda's health than his 2016 ratios.

2017 PROJECTION: 12-8 3.81 ERA 1.28 WHIP 188 K

Daniel Norris: First off Detroit Tigers pitcher Daniel Norris needs to be applauded for successfully beating cancer and resuming his baseball career. When it came to Norris' 2016 performance, there was quite a bit to applaud there too as he posted a 3.38 ERA in 69.1 innings. The former 2011 second-round pick showed off the power arm that was part of his original scouting report as he posted a very high 9.22 K/9 and he also blended that with rare control for a young pitcher (2.86 BB/9). The one thing Norris has to work on is his penchant for home runs (1.30 HR/9) and there also is the strong likelihood he will struggle during the second half of 2017 as he moves into unchartered inning territory. If Norris were pitching in the NL we would be even more pumped about his potential but the upside is very good here regardless.

2017 PROJECTION: 13-9 3.52 ERA 1.33 WHIP 161 K

Hisashi Iwakuma: Since arriving in the majors in 2012 from Japan, Hisashi Iwakuma has been a favorite of these pages as a perennial value play who always gives you your draft money's worth. Iwakuma specialized in posting mid-3.00 ERA's, low WHIP numbers, and a solid strikeout rate over the last four years leading into 2016 but age began to take a toll last season. He began the season showing a drop in velocity with the fastball and it never really came around as his K/9 fell under 7.00 for the first time in his career at 6.65. The drop in velocity also seemed to affect Iwakuma's usually standout control as he upped his excellent 1.46 BB/9 mark in 2015 to last season's 2.08. Combined together, Iwakuma's season ERA went over the 4.00 mark for the first time in his career at 4.12. Turning 36 in April, Iwakuma is likely going to leak some more velocity and in turn become more hittable. This one is trending in the wrong direction.

2017 PROJECTION: 14-10 4.07 ERA 1.28 WHIP 149 K

Brandon Finnegan: With the Cincinnati Reds in full rebuild mode entering into the 2016 season, they made sure to keep a rotation spot handy for pitching prospect Brandon Finnegan whom the team acquired the year prior from the Kansas City Royals. A former 2014 first round pick, Finnegan didn't embarrass himself by pitching to a 3.98 ERA and posting a 7.59 K/9 rate. However Finnegan's story is told more clearly in his advanced numbers and that is where things turn ugly. For one thing, Finnegan's control was a downright joke as his BB/9 rate of 4.40 is pretty much as bad as it gets for a full-time starter. In addition, Finnegan's .256 BABIP was well into the "lucky" zone and when adjusted, shows a FIP (5.19) and XFIP (4.87) ERA that is very disturbing. Making matters somehow even worse, Finnegan's 1.52 HR/9 was a terrible match for a home base in Cincy that remains one of the most power-leaning ballparks in the majors. Those are a ton of negatives centering on Finnegan and it calls into question how good of a pitcher he could turn out to be. We were not impressed at any stage of his 2016 and said this constantly on the website throughout the year. The same holds true for 2017 despite the draft pedigree.

2017 PROJECTION: 4.17 ERA 1.33 WHIP 154 K

Ian Kennedy: We still are wondering why on the earth the Kansas City Royals thought it was a good idea to give a five-year free agent contract to lefty pitcher Ian Kennedy last winter. Not even a full year into the deal, the Royals were offering Kennedy all over place as the Aug. 1 trade deadline neared. While Kennedy rebounded from a tough start to finish with a solid 3.68 ERA, his underlying numbers were ghastly. For starters, Kennedy's .268 BABIP was very lucky and when adjusted, resulted in vomit-inducing FIP (4.67) and XFIP (4.67) ERA's. Kennedy also continued with his career-long struggles with the long ball; surrendering a ridiculous 33 home runs in 195.2 innings. Throw in more control woes (3.04 BB/9) and Kennedy will do nothing but harm your pitching numbers this season if you go near him.

2017 PROJECTION: 12-12 3.77 ERA 1.25 WHIP 174 K

Bartolo Colon: Just call Atlanta Braves veteran starter Bartolo Colon the David Ortiz of pitching. Similar to the Boston Red Sox slugger who went into retirement at the top of his game, you can argue that Colon was as good as ever in 2016 at the age of 43 when he won 15 games and registered a 3.43 ERA for the New York Mets. It is crazy how Colon continues to post terrific results not only at his age but also for the fact his fastball struggles to even reach 90. What makes Colon so good is not only his impeccable control (1.50 BB/9) but also for the fact he changes speeds often enough as he paints the corners. While he came up as a fireballer, Colon is far away from that stage of his career as his K/9 dropped all the way to 6.01 last season. Again the typical rules don't apply to Colon as he always needs to be given the benefit of the doubt based on the results. While we still wouldn't draft Colon as anything more than an SP 5, he still makes the grade as a good asset under that label.

2017 PROJECTION: 14-10 3.93 ERA 1.25 WHIP 122 K

Michael Wacha: We don't like to gloat when it comes to telling you all how right we were regarding the premature decline of a former top pitching prospect at a premature age but that is where we are at now with the St. Louis Cardinals' Michael Wacha. Add Wacha to the list of pitchers who were never the same after first coming down with shoulder pain; an issue that began to show up late in the 2014 season. Prior to that, Wacha was one of the most sought after young pitchers in baseball who combined top control and a K/9 that initially topped 9.0 in the majors. While Wacha avoided surgery on his shoulder, 2015 brought forth a much different pitcher as his fastball lost velocity, his K/9 sank, and home runs began to start flying out at a high rate. Last season brought nothing but more trouble as Wacha went on the DL with renewed shoulder soreness and saw his ERA enter brutal territory at 5.09. With the fastball continuing to lose steam, Wacha's K/9 rate dropped for the third season in a row to a mediocre 7.43. Yes the .334 BABIP was quite unlucky (4.05 XFIP) but Wacha's shoulder is a ticking time bomb and his K/9 rate is a shell of its former impressive self. You are asking for trouble investing in Wacha this season given all the red flags and as a result, he should be on your "Do Not Draft" list in bold lettering.

2017 PROJECTION: 12-7 4.15 ERA 1.32 WHIP 146 K

Hector Santiago: After three straight seasons of posting an ERA under 4.00 from 2012-15, Hector Santiago saw that number blow up to a terrible 4.70 mark in a 2016 campaign split between the L.A. Angels and Minnesota Twins. Having now fully converted to being a starter after initially coming up with the Chicago White Sox as a reliever, Santiago has been pretty consistent in terms of struggling with his control but at the same time striking guys out at a decent clip. It all went wrong last year however as Santiago once again walked the ballpark (3.91 BB/9) but then combined that with a HR/9 rate of 1.63 that was among the worst in the majors leagues in terms of starting pitchers. When you call the American League home, this is a very bad thing as we saw with Santiago's overall numbers. Another issue with Santiago is his tendency to be a strong first half guy but then tire badly after the All-Star break as his ERA implodes. This is not the kind of trend you want to have for any of the players you own since league are decided in September. We were never big boosters of Santiago to begin with and his putrid performance last season now suggest you strongly to avoid him altogether.

2017 PROJECTION: 11-10 4.20 ERA 1.33 WHIP 159 K

Zach Davies: While he looks like he should still be in high school, the Milwaukee Brewers' Zach Davies showed he could hang with major league hitters in 2016 as he posted a semi-breakout season. Not much was expected of Davies since he was originally just a 26th round draft pick but at the age of 23, he registered a 3.97 ERA on a bad team to go with 11 wins. With a neutral .302 BABIP, Davies' numbers were legit. The kid has a nice makeup in terms of possessing good control (2.09 BB/9) and he gets by with enough strikeouts (7.44 K/9) to keep himself out of trouble. The ceiling is not likely to go much higher then what we are seeing now though so don't draft Davies expecting a big jump from his 2016 performance.

2017 PROJECTION: 12-10 3.84 ERA 1.23 WHIP 146 K

Mike Leake: With the recent decline of former soft-tossing king Kyle Lohse, a challenger to his old throne could be the St. Louis Cardinals' Mike Leake who himself has made a solid career for himself despite not ever reaching the 7.00 mark with his K/9 rate. 2016 was a typical Leake year as he was good but not great. Yes his 4.69 ERA was very high on the surface (and ended a three-year streak where he finished with a number in that category of 3.70 or lower) but that was due to a rough .318 BABIP. When the luck was taken out of the equation, Leake's FIP (3.83) and XFIP (3.76) were pretty much in line with his standard numbers. Leake is also a classic smoke-and-mirrors pitcher who gets by with excellent control (1.53 BB/9) and with a HR/9 rate that has hovered the 1.00 mark for years despite previously operating in a prime power park in Cincinnati. You never get a feeling of excitement when you draft Leake but he will also never hurt your team as a round-out-the-rotation guy.

2017 PROJECTION: 14-8 3.88 ERA 1.22 WHIP 134 K

Taijuan Walker: It is starting to look like former Seattle Mariners top pitching prospect Taijuan Walker is never going to live up to the hype that enveloped him while coming up the team's minor league system. Classified as a power pitcher who was capable of major strikeout totals, Walker has battled ongoing shoulder trouble that seem to have taken some bite out of his stuff since arriving in Seattle. In 134.1 innings last season, Walker put up a 4.22 ERA but that number should have been even worse since he received a lot of BABIP luck at .267. When you adjust Walker's ERA based on the lucky BABIP, his FIP shoots up to 4.99 which is waiver wire territory. Even more bothersome is the fact that despite calling a spacious ballpark home in Safeco Field, Walker's HR/9 rate of 1.81 was among the highest in all of baseball. On the plus side, Walker is still very young at the age of 24 and his 7.97 K/9 has some room to grow if his shoulder stays healthy. We have seen plenty of post-hype sleepers like this eventually break through and so Walker should be given another chance as an SP 5 that could outperform his draft slot by a decent margin if all breaks right.

2017 PROJECTION: 12-10 3.90 ERA 1.23 WHIP 152 K

Colin McHugh: After shocking the fantasy baseball world by posting a 2.73 ERA and 9.14 K/9 during his terrific breakout in 2014, Colin McHugh has trended in the wrong direction the last two years almost across the board when it comes to his numbers. While McHugh gives an overall good account of himself, his 4.34 ERA last season shows that he is more a mediocre pitcher then what we saw of him in 2014. McHugh has enough oomph on his fastball to strike out guys at a decent clip

(8.63 last season) but his home run rate went up for the third year in a row in 2016 (1.22 HR/9) which is a red flag. We think McHugh can make the grade as an SP 5 who won't hurt you but you should try and get some more upside for someone priced similarly.

2017 PROJECTION: 14-11 4.10 ERA 1.32 WHIP 175 K

C.C. Sabathia: One of the more pleasant surprises in 2016 fantasy baseball was the return from the career abyss of New York Yankees aging lefty C.C. Sabathia. With vastly declining health and a fastball that barely touched 90 after years of decline, Sabathia was a fantasy baseball pariah as he posted three straight seasons with an ERA north of 4.70 from 2013-15. That is why what we saw out of Sabathia last year was so unexpected, as he won 12 games, stayed healthy enough to pitch 179.2 innings, and wound up with a 3.91 ERA. A couple of things went right for Sabathia that allowed him to post his comeback year, with the biggest being the drastic lowering of his HR/9 rate. Consider that in 2015, Sabathia had to have hurt his neck from whipping his head around so much as he gave up home runs by the boatload (1.51 HR/9). Last season not so much, as Sabathia lowered that number by a wide margin to 1.01. Sabathia also had some more life on his fastball, as the 7.61 K/9 was his highest since 2012. Still Sabathia really didn't pitch as well as his surface ERA suggested due to the fact his .288 BABIP belonged in the lucky bin. Both Sabathia's adjusted FIP and XFIP ERA's were over 4.25 and that begins to bring back some bad memories from the previous seasons. Sabathia will return for one more go-round with the Yanks in 2017 since his option year vested but he is more likely to slide back to ugly territory then approach what he did a year ago. Ignore the name brand.

2017 PROJECTION: 12-10 4.27 ERA 1.32 WHIP 151 K

Jimmy Nelson: It was nothing but a letdown year for the Milwaukee Brewers' Jimmy Nelson in 2016 after this publication hyped him up a bit in last year's draft guide. After earning some plaudits in posting a 4.11 ERA and striking out batters at a 7.51 clip in his first full major league campaign in 2015, Nelson went the other way last season all across the board. While Nelson did start strong (ERA's of 3.16 in March/April and 2.66 in May), Nelson absolutely bombed the rest of the way. Nelson's 6.10 ERA during the second half of the season left no doubt about how terrible he pitched and there were two main culprits why. The first is that Nelson became very prone to home runs in posting an elevated 1.25 HR/9. Secondly, Nelson lost all semblance of control as his 4.32 BB/9 rate was one of the worst in the majors among pitcher who threw more than 100 innings. In fact Nelson's 4.64 ERA should have even been higher if not for some slight BABIP luck. It was all one big setback for Nelson, who is a former 2010 second round pick that so far is not panning out. With the Brewers in full rebuilding mode, they will likely give Nelson another chance to right the ship but there is no way we or anyone else can offer up a recommendation here.

2017 PROJECTION: 4.29 ERA 1.33 WHIP 145 K

Junior Guerra: Not bad for a guy from the Mexican League. That was the nondescript locale that brought forth surprisingly productive Milwaukee Brewers starter Junior Guerra who was downright spectacular at times in his 2016 rookie debut in registering a 2.81 ERA, 1.13 WHIP, and .211 BAA. From the beginning, the 31-year-old Guerra performed way beyond expectations as a relative unknown and in fact there were no expectations attached to him at all given his adventurous path to the majors. Very rarely do we see such performances from a rookie at Guerra's age but he clearly looked like a missed commodity given what we saw a year ago. During the season we all kept waiting for the other shoe to drop with Guerra in anticipating that major league hitters would adjust to his stuff but it simply didn't happen. When digging into the numbers, Guerra's 7.40 K/9 rate was nothing to write home about and that makes what he accomplished even more impressive. Also on the positive side, Guerra kept the baseball in the park in posting a terrific 0.74 HR/9 and this was an especially big deal considering the offensive dimensions of his home park. Preventing home runs also helped Guerra offset any potential damage his ugly 3.18 BB/9 could have brought forth. So if you were to break it all down, a high walk rate and a low K rate would usually bring forth the assumption that Guerra would have needed some BABIP help to help maintain such a lofty ERA and that certainly was the case last season as his .250 mark was in the VERY lucky range. In fact, .250 BABIP marks are pretty much as low as it goes for a starting pitcher and thus you get the sense how sizable the fluke rate was here. When you adjust the luck, Guerra's FIP ERA jumped to 3.70 and his XFIP ERA to an even shakier 4.31. In the end, it is clear that Guerra's 2016 numbers carry a great deal of doubt regarding their validity and we saw a case just like this a year prior on that same ballclub when Taylor Jungmann came out of the blue to post big numbers and then subsequently got his head beaten in so badly at the start of 2016 that he was soon back in the minors. This very well could be the result for Guerra in 2017 as well since major league hitters will have had a winter to digest his approach and the luck will surely change. We would not go near Guerra next season as this one could blow up in a very bad way.

2017 PROJECTION: 11-10 3.77 ERA 1.16 WHIP 155 K

Yordano Ventura: When you are known more for starting bench-clearing brawls than anything you accomplish on the mound, the fantasy baseball community won't pay you much mind. That was the case in 2016 when it came to hard-throwing Kansas City Royals starting pitcher Yordano Ventura. Despite perennially residing near the top in baseball in terms of average fastball velocity, Ventura's still young career has been filled with disappointment and failing to meet expectations. For as hard as Ventura throws, his fastball has yet to translate into a high number of strikeouts. In fact Ventura was BELOW average in baseball last year as he registered just a 6.65 K/9 which was the first of many ugly numbers on his 2016 resume. For as ugly as the strikeout numbers were, Ventura's control was just as bad as his 3.73 BB/9 was among the worst in baseball when it came to starting pitchers and if not for a bit of BABIP luck (.283), Ventura's 4.35 ERA would have been much worse. When you also point out that Ventura is homer prone with his 1.18 HR/9 and seems like the next prime Tommy John victim, there really is no reason to go near him this season in fantasy baseball drafts.

2017 PROJECTION: 12-9 4.27 ERA 1.33 WHIP 159 K

Scott Kazmir: While Scott Kazmir deserves a ton of credit for fighting his way back to the majors after pitching in Independent Ball in 2012, the end could be nearing again as he comes off a terrible 2016 where he pitched to a 4.56 ERA and only accumulated 136.1 innings in an injury-marred campaign. While it was easy to respect the strikeouts that Kazmir was able to generate from such a small frame, we always tried to steer you away from him due to the guy's annual penchant both for getting hurt and annually fading badly in the second half of a season. Yes Kazmir still misses bats (8.85 K/9) but his control is starting to get nasty again (3.43 BB/9) and he also somehow managed to give up home runs at a 1.39 HR/9 clip despite calling a top pitcher's park as his home. There's no reason for us to change our negative opinions on Kazmir now.

2017 PROJECTION: 11-7 4.22 ERA 1.34 WHIP 155 K

Mike Fiers: It has been an interesting ride over the years with veteran starting pitcher Mike Fiers. From monster second-half performances in 2012 and 2014, through a truly putrid performance in 2015, Fiers has run the fantasy baseball gamut in terms of numbers. What was always intriguing about Fiers was how he was able to generate a high number of strikeouts despite possessing a fastball that only reached the upper-80's. 2016 was more on the negative side of things in terms of numbers however as Fiers posted a mediocre 4.48 ERA with the Houston Astros . Pitching in the American League for a full season also didn't agree with Fiers' K/9 rate as it fell to 7.15 (down from 8.98 and 9.54 the previous two years). A free agent as of press time, Fiers could qualify as an SP 5 if he signs back into the National League but he is entering into the "boring veteran" stage of his career.

2017 PROJECTION: 12-10 4.25 ERA 1.32 WHIP 156 K

Francisco Liriano: Few pitchers in all of fantasy baseball have elicited more negative reactions over the last ten years then Francisco Liriano. The lefty has literally run the gamut in his major league career, which began with him arriving on the scene as a dominant power arm. Tommy John surgery soon interrupted the proceedings though and once recovered, Liriano began a string of downright putrid performances that forced the Minnesota Twins to eventually cut ties with him in 2012. After the Twins dealt him to the Pittsburgh Pirates, Liriano almost overnight turned back into the ace-in-the-making he seemed destined to be when he debuted back in 2005. While Liriano's always horrible control never improved, his hit rates remained incredibly low and his strikeouts began to pop again in a Pirates uniform. After three straight years of posting an ERA under 4.00, Liriano actually became trusted again in the fantasy baseball community. Unfortunately 2016 brought forth a reminder of the ugly old days as Liriano's control somehow reached a new level of disaster, with his BB/9 rate sailing up to an unfathomable 4.69. That 4.69 mark is one of the highest numbers in that category ever recorded in modern baseball for a pitcher who threw more than 150 innings and that went a long way toward his identical 4.69 ERA. With a HR/9 that was also terrible at 1.44, it was easy to understand why the Pirates dealt him away to the Toronto Blue Jays at the Aug. 1 deadline. Through it all Liriano still misses bats at a very high rate (9.28 K/9) but good luck if you decide to tempt fate again as he turned 33 in October.

2017 PROJECTION: 10-12 4.27 ERA 1.33 WHIP 173 K

Josh Tomlin: For as dominant as the top three power arms in the Cleveland Indians rotation are with Corey Kluber, Carlos Carrasco, and Danny Salazar, someone has to pull up the rear of the rotation. That honor fell to soft-tossing Josh Tomlin in 2016 but the results were not pretty. Clearly not possessing anywhere near the heat that his three rotation mates bring, Tomlin is a guy who gets exposed eventually during the course of a season as he walks a very fine line with stuff that relies on location. While Tomlin started the season strong, he eventually suffered the inevitable beatings that caused his ERA to spike at 4.40. Outside of the 6.10 K/9 shortcoming, Tomlin's biggest bugaboo is a truly insane 1.86 HR/9 rate that makes any one start prone to a blowup due to a handful of misplaced pitches. If Tomlin were operating in the National League, maybe we could see him as an SP 5 but a weak fastball in the American League is a clear recipe for trouble.

2017 PROJECTION: 12-10 4.33 ERA 1.24 WHIP 122 K

THE REST

Joe Musgrove: The Houston Astros tried out top pitching prospect Joe Musgrove for a short spell during the 2016 season and they had to think they have something to build on as 2017 draws near. Musgrove didn't embarrass himself as he registered a 4.06 ERA in his 62 innings, showing off slid control (2.32 BB/9) and a vast pitching arsenal. The pedigree is certainly there as Musgrove was a 2011 first round pick of the Toronto Blue Jays and he seems capable of ratcheting up the strikeouts as he further comes along in his development. While we won't make it a point to make sure Musgrove is on our team at all costs, we will search him out in the last few rounds of the draft given the upside.

Drew Smyly: One guy that didn't come through for us as a 2016 fantasy baseball sleeper was the Tampa Bay Rays' Drew Smyly. Initially it did look like Smyly was going to make us look smart as he burst out of the gates in April striking out everyone (41 K in 34.2 innings) and posting a terrific 2.60 ERA. It was all downhill from there as Smyly began a three-month slog of truly horrendous pitching that got him dropped in almost all leagues well before that stretch came to an end in August. What really derailed Smyly was a pathetic 1.64 HR/9 rate that resulted in 32 long balls going out in just 175.1 innings. That really was the issue as Smyly's 8.57 K/9 rate was fantasy friendly and his 2.52 BB/9 showed solid control. Turning just 28 in June, we are almost forced to say based on the rate numbers that Smyly could be a very good late round sleeper again. Yes we are being serious for better or for worse.

Tyson Ross: Ask any pitcher what injury they want to avoid more between and elbow or a shoulder and undoubtedly the latter would win by a landslide. It has pretty much been proven over the years that shoulder trouble does so much more harm both health-wise and stuff-wise to a pitcher than does an elbow injury. There are two big issues with shoulder injuries that make them so much worse for pitchers, starting with the fact that they tend to linger and re-occur. Secondly, shoulder injuries almost always take a bite out of a pitcher's stuff. Often mileage is lost on the fastball and there can become less bite on offspeed stuff as a result of trouble in the shoulder. Look no further than recent examples such as Matt Cain, Josh Johnson, the late Tommy Hanson, and others as young ace-like pitchers who all flamed out quickly once they came down with shoulder trouble. While Cain is still pitching, he has never come close to his past skills. Meanwhile Johnson and Hanson both were out of baseball soon after coming down with initial shoulder trouble that continually re-appeared. That is why what took place in 2016 with the San Diego Padres' Tyson Ross is so troubling. One of the most talented young power pitchers in baseball, Ross came into the 2016 season with a career 3.07 ERA and 526 strikeouts in 516.2 innings as his near 100-mph fastball was a huge handful for opposing hitters. While Ross has always struggled with control, there was a ton to like about a guy who also called Petco Park home. Well Ross' 2016 consisted of just one April 4th start and then nothing else as an early bout of shoulder stiffness morphed into a series of setbacks that kept him out for the remainder of the season. As of this writing, Ross was prepping for the dreaded thoracic outlet surgery on his shoulder which means he will likely not be ready for the start of the 2017 season as well. While no one can argue with the ability, Ross is yet another in a recent long list of young pitchers who have seen their careers derailed by serious injury.

Anthony DeScalfani: For a 2011 sixth-round pick, the Cincinnati Reds' Anthony DeScalfani has developed into a very serviceable pitcher. While a dreaded and stubborn oblique strain caused DeScalfani to begin the season on the DL, he pitched very well upon returning in June. There were some September struggles but DeScalfani came home with a 3.28 ERA and he saw his K/9 rate jump slightly to 7.66. DeScalfani is able to get by with less-than dominant stuff on the strength of good control (2.19 BB/9) and that skill helps offset a bit of homer-happiness (1.17 HR/9). Again there is not much flash but you can do worse than have DeScalfani as your SP 5.

Ariel Miranda: While he is a very raw pitcher in terms of experience, the Seattle Mariners could have a decent talent on their hands in recent Cuban arrival Ariel Miranda. After coming over via trade from the Baltimore Orioles midway through 2016, Miranda opened some eyes with a decent showing for the Mariners in his 56-inning debut for the team. In fact Miranda was better than solid as he pitched to a

3.54 ERA, 1.09 WHIP, and struck out 40 batters. Yes the 6.83 K/9 was below-average but Miranda figures to improve there as he gets more experience. Miranda already shows decent control (2.79 BB/9) and that should further help him along. Not the worst way to spend a last round pick.

Tyler Anderson: Despite the obvious challenges of Coors Field, the Colorado Rockies have a genuine pair of very promising power arms in Jon Gray and Tyler Anderson on their hands. The latter was the team's 2011 first round pick (20th overall) but Anderson took some extra time to arrive in the majors after missing all of 2015 recovering from Tommy John surgery. As far as his 114-inning debut last season was concerned, there was quite a bit to like as Anderson pitched to a 3.54 ERA and recorded an impressive 7.79 K/9. What really makes Anderson intriguing going forward. and a key to his success despite the Coors Field problem, is that he showed terrific control (2.20 BB/9) and kept the ball in the park (0.94 HR/9). What was even more interesting is that like with Gray, Anderson pitched better at home (3.00 ERA) then on the road (4.71). While Anderson is older (27 in December) than most players coming off their debut years, we would actually endorse drafting him as your SP 5 given the impressive 2016.

Eduardo Rodriguez: We continue to get glimpses of impressive pitching from Boston Red Sox lefthanded prospect Eduardo Rodriguez but at the same time, he also disturbs us with just as many inconsistent outings that call into question how good he may be. The arrow pointed downward in 2016 as Rodriguez posted a terrible 4.71 ERA which overshadowed some good strikeout stuff (100 K's in 107 innings). When you call your home Fenway Park, you can't walk batters or give up home runs and on both fronts, Rodriguez failed last season. The guy will only turn 24 in April however and so he retains some solid upside going forward. We hate the division but you should be able to snag Rodriguez as a decent late round upside pick.

Dylan Bundy: At one time considered one of the best pitching prospects in the game before being forced to undergo Tommy John surgery, Dylan Bundy is already becoming a forgotten man in fantasy baseball l circles. It has been a tough road back from the surgery with some other health setbacks along the way but Bundy's 109.2-inning debut last season was pretty good as he logged a 4.02 ERA and punched out 104 batters. The K/9 rate of 8.53 shows that Bundy's stuff is almost all the way back and having turned only 24 this past November, the guy is still very young. Bundy is quite rough around the edges though as his BB/9 rate of

3.45 is no good and his 1.45 HR/9 is even more of a red flag number considering his home ballpark. There remain good upside here though but the division is a turnoff for sure.

James Paxton: For the third season in a row, we were teased with some intriguing pitching from the Seattle Mariners' James Paxton but he was never able to gain much fantasy baseball traction in any of those campaigns due to some horrific injury luck. Paxton is one of those guys whose body seems to only be able to handle 3-4 consecutive starts in a row before another physical problem develops and this is a shame since the 27-year-old has obvious ability (3.04, 3.90, and 3.79 ERA's his first three years in the majors). Driving this point home, Paxton's 120 innings in 2016 were a career-high which tells you how much time he has missed with physical problems. Getting back to the numbers, Paxton gets the requisite boost for pitching his home games at Safeco Field but he also can miss some bats as he put up an impressive 8.70 K/9 rate last year. In addition, Paxton also is skilled at not giving up home runs (0.36 HR/9) which is always a big plus. Add in the fact Paxton's 1.79 BB/9 was also excellent and a huge drop from 2015's 3.90 mark and all the tools are there for a decent breakout if he can just scratch out 150 innings. Unfortunately that seems to be asking too much.

Jeremy Hellickson: After three years of awful pitching for the Tampa Bay Rays and Arizona Diamondbacks (ERA above 4.50 in each of those campaigns), Jeremy Hellickson was surprisingly decent in 2016 for the Philadelphia Phillies in registering a useable 3.71 ERA and 7.33 K/9. Hellickson's control was also very impressive as well (2.14 BB/9) which was crucial in such an offensive park. Be that as it may, Hellickson will be 30 in April and his 2016 performance was a best case scenario which is not saying much concerning his value.

Tyler Lyons: While never considered a top pitching prospect in the always fertile St. Louis Cardinals system, Tyler Lyons has shown himself to be a serviceable back-of-the-rotation arm the last two seasons by registering ERA's of 3.75 and 3.88 in 108 combined innings. The former ninth round pick possesses some heft to his fastball as Lyons has posted a K/9 rate over 8.50 in all three of his major league seasons to go with solid control. While home runs are a major problem, Lyons has excelled enough everywhere else to get a long look as a rotation arm for the 2017 season. A stress reaction in his knee kept Lyons out for all but 48 innings in 2016 but he should be 100 percent healthy for the start of spring training. A rare opportunity to get a promising arm that carries little-to-no draft hype.

Ervin Santana: Just when everyone is about ready to throw dirt on the career of Ervin Santana, the guy goes out and puts together a very good 2016 campaign where he posted a 3.38 ERA and won 11 games on the worst team in baseball. A PED suspension the year prior really sullied Santana's name but the guy is still getting it done at 34. Still Santana's career has been filled with massive inconsistency as he seemingly alternated good and bad years; while also seeing his K/9 go all over the statistical map. He also received some BABIP help as well (.285) which when adjusted brought his ERA to a more accurate 3.80 (FIP) and 4.21 (XFIP). On the plus side, Santana kept both his walks and home runs down late season which again helped him stay relevant. At this late stage of the career game, it would be foolish to draft Santana as anything more than your SP 5 but at least by 2016's standards, it looks like the guy can still help a bit.

Brandon McCarthy: Taking most of the year to recover from 2015 Tommy John elbow surgery, the Los Angeles Dodgers' Brandon McCarthy only was able to get in 40 innings at the major league level after a brief tune-up in the minors. Just like before the surgery, McCarthy kept up with his mid-career boost in strikeouts (9.90 K/9) but his control abandoned him (5.85 BB/9) which is typical of pitchers coming back from Tommy John. McCarthy is aging as he turns 34 in July but he will be back in a spacious park with the Dodgers and retains some interesting strikeout ability. Not the worst candidate as your SP 5.

Alex Wood: While Alex Wood had some solid fantasy baseball sleeper appeal as recently as 2015, a string of injuries and statistical letdowns have conspired to make him just another name. This is a bit unfair as Wood has posted ERA's of 2.78, 3.84, and 3.73 the last three years but the fact he only threw 60.1 innings in an injury-marred 2016 have really diluted any pop that was once attached to his name. It was a bum elbow that ruined Wood's year last season but keep in mind that his K/9 rate has been over 8.90 in two of the last three years. There is some ability here but Wood needs to find some good health to restore his name. We would take a stab as a late round buy.

Sean Manaea: It didn't catch much attention given the West Coast screen but we saw a very nice debut campaign for Oakland A's pitching prospect Sean Manaea in 2016. A 3.86 ERA and 7.71 K/9 show that Manaea was not overmatched against major league hitters and his former first round draft status (2013 class) shows there is some interesting pedigree here. The lefty does a good job keeping the ball in the park (0.50 HR/9) and he was also the rare rookie pitcher to show decent control

(2.30 BB/9). This is one name that is off the fantasy baseball radar who should be on your sleeper list late in the draft.

Nathan Karns: We scratched our heads last winter when the Tampa Bay Rays made the curious decision to trade the promising power arm of Nathan Karns to the Seattle Mariners for the awful outfield bat of Logan Morrison. While Karns was no big prospect as a former 12th round pick, he put up a nice 3.67 ERA with the Rays in 2015 and paired that with an 8.88 K/9. Apparently the Rays knew something no one else did as Karns let a nice start to 2016 (5-1 with a 3.53 ERA, 57 K's in 57.1 IP) slide into a series of ugly outings that got him banished to the bullpen in late June. That move did not go well as Karns continued to get hit and then suffered what wound up becoming a season-ending back strain. Looking at his half-season as a whole, Karns' 5.15 ERA was no good but his 9.64 K/9 rate leads us to think he could possibly have some bounce back appeal. Karns does need to gets his ugly control (4.29 BB/9) in order if he wants to get to that level. Let Karns prove this to you before you make an investment.

Robert Stephenson: While Stephenson got lit up in his 37-inning debut for the Reds in 2016 (6.08 ERA), the former 2011 first round pick has had some big strikeout totals in the minors. Stephenson's control needs to be remedied however as his walks have been out of control since becoming a professional.

Vidal Nuno: While he has managed to post useful ERA's over the last two years, soft-tossing veteran starters like Vidal Nuno are a dime a dozen in fantasy baseball. Nothing Nuno does on the mound stands out, as a decent K/9 rate (7.82) is offset by a terrible 1.69 HR/9. Having only tossed 58.2 innings in 2016 as he once again battled injuries, Nuno is not even a late-round draft candidate.

Patrick Corbin: Prior to the 2016 season, there was some moderate sleeper hype attached to the Arizona Diamondbacks' Patrick Corbin. A Tommy John elbow victim who missed all of the 2014 season, Corbin came back throwing HARDER than he did before he surgery, which led to a very interesting 3.60 ERA and 8.26 K/9 rate in his 85-inning return in 2015. Unfortunately the good vibes didn't carry over for Corbin as he ruined any sense that he was headed for a breakout by getting shellacked in March/April (4.88 ERA) and then somehow pitched WORSE in each of the following months as his number there went over 5.00 in each. A final composite 5.15 ERA showed just how bad Corbin pitched and trusting him for 2017 is going to take a deep level of optimism we just don't have.

Luis Severino: Both the New York Yankees and fantasy baseball owners of Luis Severino had to be incredibly frustrated with the 22-year-old in 2016 as he bombed in spectacular fashion when pitching in the team's rotation. Severino looked as polar opposite as could be to the poised kid who threw like a future star in pitching to a 2.89 ERA in 11 starts during the heat of a pennant race when he debuted in 2015. Severino in fact couldn't pitch any worse than he did at the start of last season as his 6.86 March/April ERA was followed by an 8.22 mark in May that got him demoted back to the minor leagues. He would return in late July with a new role as Severino was placed in the Yankee bullpen and almost overnight the kid began to excel. In fact Severino was a pure lock-down arm as a reliever since he could rely more on his potent fastball and the strikeouts began to flow in earnest, along with a string of scoreless appearances. He would still wind up getting a few more spot starts in between but once again Severino was hit hard. So as the 2017 season approaches, one has to wonder if Severino could be another Mariano Rivera in terms of being an arm that fails as a starter but at the same time works very well as a reliever. The plan for Severino should be to monitor what his status will be in the spring and then react from there. Being assigned to setup man would remove almost all of Severino's value but if he sticks in the rotation, he should at least be drafted as an upside SP 5 play.

Wei-Yin Chen: When the Miami Marlins signed free agent pitcher Wei-Yin Chen last winter, the thought was that they were adding a guy to their rotation who can help the youngsters, while also putting up another mid-3.00 ERA as he had done both in 2014 and 2015. Well nothing went right for Chen last season as he missed two months with an elbow sprain and was hit hard when on the mound as he posted an ugly 4.96 ERA. The biggest issue Chen had besides ill health was a HR/9 rate that was out of hand at 1.61. 22 home runs given up in 123.1 is a huge problem and makes every Chen start a roller coaster. Outside of that, Chen's other rate stats were pretty good as he struck out batters at a solid 7.30 K/9 clip and he showed tremendous control (1.75 BB/9) as well. If he can knock down the HR/9 even just a bit, Chen could go right back to the mid-3.00 ERA range. Possible SP 5 but a shaky one at that.

Tom Koehler: The pride of Stony Brook University on Long Island, Miami Marlins starter Tom Koehler was once again good but not great in 2016. While Koehler throws hard and is capable of reaching the upper 90's with his fastball, his secondary stuff is lacking and that is why his 4.33 ERA last year was not far off the 4.08 mark he posted in 2015. Koehler hurts himself with too many walks (4.23

BB/9) and his 1.12 HR/9 is not great either considering his spacious home ballpark. Turning 31 in June, Koehler is not going to get any better than what he is now and that is not saying much.

Mike Montgomery: We are well past the point now where Mike Montgomery can't be considered anything but a draft bust after he was the number 36 pick back in the 2008. Almost from the start Montgomery was hit hard at all levels of the minor leagues and his K/9 struggled to stay above the mediocre line even against much weaker hitters. While he finally broke through with the Seattle Mariners in 2015, the results were unimpressive as he posted a 4.60 ERA. He would get another shot with the Mariners filling in for rotation injuries on the big league squad and Montgomery threw pretty well in his 100.0 innings. A 2.52 ERA was encouraging and so was Montgomery's 8.28 K/9. Beneath those numbers though resided trouble as Montgomery's .267 BABIP was very lucky and showed that there really was not some sort of magical breakthrough here. He still showed zero control in walking guys at a 3.42 BB/9 clip and the K/9 rate was in major outlier territory. After excelling out of the bullpen for the Chicago Cubs in the postseason (earning the clinching Game 7 saves), Montgomery is now looking like he is destined for bullpen duty in 2017.

Colby Lewis: Texas Rangers veteran starter Colby Lewis ended a two-year streak of seeing his ERA go over the 4.50 mark in 2016 by finishing at a solid 3.71 in 116.1 innings. The low inning total was due to some injury issues that kept Lewis out of commission but ill health at his advanced age of 37 is no shock. While the surface ERA was decent, the underlying numbers were filled with red flags as Lewis' .241 BABIP was extremely lucky and his K/9 rate has tumbled all the way down to a below-average 5.65. When Lewis' ERA is adjusted to remove the luck, his FIP (4.81) and XFIP (5.14) numbers were abysmal. For that reason alone, Lewis should not be drafted this season.

Adam Conley: While not the worst pitcher in the world, Miami Marlins lefty Adam Conley leaves a bit to be desired when it comes to his fantasy baseball impact. His 2016 3.85 ERA was a fluke due to some BABIP luck (FIP-4.20, XFIP-4.84) and his 4.19 BB/9 in 133.1 innings was pathetic. Yes there is some strikeout ability here (8.37 K/9) but Conley is only an SP 5 at best.

Jaime Garcia: St. Louis Cardinals pitcher Jaime Garcia was always a fun guy to own due to the fact he annually posted ERA's under 4.00 (5 times in 7 previous years) and he never cost much more than a few pennies at the draft table. His usefulness began to run out in 2016 though as Garcia struggled to the tune of a 4.67 ERA; a performance that got him kicked out of the rotation late in the season. While it was a rough year no doubt, we like to think it was just a bad year for Garcia who is still young at the age of 30. Again he will cost literally nothing to own and his floor numbers are usually very useful.

Anibal Sanchez: Rampant injuries have really taken a firm bite out of the former top-shelf power stuff of Detroit Tigers starter Anibal Sanchez the last few seasons. As recently as 2013 Sanchez struck out 202 batters for the Tigers, which helped him overcome some pronounced control problems going back to his early Florida Marlin days. Already with a Tommy John surgery in his past, Sanchez is now dealing with chronic shoulder trouble that has made him yet another victim of that ailment in terms of seeing his stuff begin to erode. While Sanchez still struck out a decent amount of batters last season (7.92 K/9), his control is as bad as ever (3.11 BB/9) and the home run rate is going through the roof. In fact over the last two years, Sanchez is right there as one of the worst pitchers in baseball in terms of giving up long balls, with a HR/9 rate going over 1.60 in both seasons. Turning 33 in February, Sanchez is likely to see more erosion to his stuff going forward and thus, some more overall decline.

Aaron Blair: Part of the ridiculously great package the Atlanta Braves received from the Arizona Diamondbacks in the Shelby Miller trade, it looks like it may take some time before Aaron Blair finds his major league footing. Blair was clearly not ready for the bigs last season as he was hit very hard in accumulating a 7.59 ERA and walked batters at a 4.37 BB/9 clip in 70 late-season innings. Still there is pedigree here as Blair was the number 3 pick overall in the 2013 draft and so that alone makes him one to at least monitor his progress. Just don't automatically think Blair is a major strikeout guy for being picked that high because the fact of the matter is that he is anything but. While Blair is capable of a K/9 north of 7.00, he is more of a location guy who keeps the ball on the ground. This is more of a story for 2018 and not next season.

Jose Berrios: Not every young fireballing pitcher who comes up to the majors succeeds right away as we saw in the 2016 performance of the Minnesota Twins' Jose Berrios. The 22-year-old was blasted in almost every one of his 58.1 innings; a clear victim of both nerves and some horrific control (5.40 BB/9). Berrios also somehow managed to give up home runs at a 1.85 HR/9 clip despite the advantages of pitching in Target Field. As bad as Berrios was in his cup of coffee debut, keep in mind he was a strikeout machine on the farm (9.00 K/9 or higher at both Double-A and Triple-A since 2014). With many focusing on his ugly 8.02 debut ERA, Berrios has plenty of remaining upside to try and steal him at a very cheap cost in drafts this spring.

Tyler Chatwood: It is a clear understatement to point out that investing in Colorado Rockie pitchers is mostly a fruitless endeavor but an exception could have been made for Tyler Chatwood in 2016. After not pitching in the majors the previous year (and overall hardly at all due to injury), Chatwood claimed a rotation spot with the Rockies for the 2016 season and surprised many by posting a 3.87 ERA and winning 12 games on a bad team. The surface ERA was solid but the underlying numbers were marked with a slew of red flags. Also one only had to look at Chatwood's 1.37 WHIP to understand that there was some fluke attached to the ERA. This was seen in Chatwood's lucky .286 BABIP, which when adjusted for good fortune came out to a more accurate 4.32 FIP/4.37 XFIP. In addition to receiving batted ball help, Chatwood's rate numbers were ugly as his 6.66 K/9 is a terrible number to have in Colorado where it is imperative to miss bats and his control was brutal throughout most of the season (3.99 BB/9). Thus it was a minor miracle Chatwood's ERA came in under 4.00 and all of these issues should serve as a warning against doing something foolish when it comes to using him for 2017.

Mike Foltynewicz: With the Atlanta Braves needing to fill out innings in the second half of the 2016 season, 24-year-old righty Mike Foltynewicz got a second chance with the team after he absolutely bombed the year prior (5.71 ERA/1.63 WHIP). While he was better the second time around, that was not saying too much as Foltynewicz was still quite hittable as shown by his 4.41 ERA and putrid 1.37 HR/9 rate. The HR/9 was even more disturbing when you consider that Foltynewicz' home ballpark favors pitchers but honestly we are just talking about a borderline major league hurler here.

Shelby Miller: Yes the Arizona Diamondbacks actually traded not only top infield prospect Dansby Swanson for veteran starter Shelby Miller but they also included top pitching prospect Aaron Blair and useful everyday outfielder Ender Inciarte. All of that for a guy who was arguably the worst starting pitcher in baseball for 2016 as he registered a 6.47 ERA, 1.70, and a laughable 6.09 K/9 rate. Those beyond hideous numbers also got Miller sent back down to the minors which made the deal look even worse. Clearly pitching in an offensive park for the first time in his career was a big problem for Miller but truth be told both the D-

Backs and his fantasy owners should have known trouble was coming. After all we warned you that the 3.02 ERA Miller put up in 2015 with the Atlanta Braves was a giant fluke due to the guy receiving a big BABIP assist (.285) and his 4.07 XFIP more told the story in terms of the true ability. Still what Miller put forth last season was insanely bad and his 1.31 HR/9 is a problem of epic proportions in Chase Field. There is no reason on earth to draft Miller this season given the abomination we just saw and that goes for anyone who thinks there is any bounce back appeal here as a late round pick.

Zach Wheeler: We are now up to two full missed seasons and counting for one-time top New York Mets pitching prospect Zach Wheeler. Tommy John surgery did him in during spring training of 2015 and a series of setbacks that included a flexor strain in his pitching elbow took out 2016 as well. By now Wheeler is almost a forgotten man amid concerns he may never make it back from the surgery. The problem with Wheeler always has been his rough delivery which adds a high amount of stress to the elbow and that makes his future very murky. While there is no denying the power pitching talent, Wheeler should only be touched if the spring training reports are positive.

Garrett Richards: It has all gone so wrong lately for the Los Angeles Angels' Garrett Richards. After bursting out with a huge career-year in 2014 when he posted ace-like numbers (2.61 ERA/1.04 WHIP/164 K in 168.2 innings), Richards suffered a gruesome knee injury that September which put a damper on his big season. Having rehabbed the injury all winter, Richards made it back for 2015 where he pitched decently but a clear level below where he was the season prior (3.65 ERA/1.24 WHIP/176 K in 207.1 innings). While 2014 looked like a bit of an outlier, Richards was still being viewed as a rock solid SP 3 for 2016 fantasy baseball. More misfortune struck though as Richards began experiencing pain in his pitching elbow in May which soon led to a Tommy John surgery recommendation. Richards instead chose to rehab the injury a la Masahiro Tanaka but he never made it back to the Angels by the end of the season. In total, Richards was only able to toss 34.2 innings and his outlook is very dicey for 2017 given the fact his elbow could snap on any pitch. While Richards has done some nice things in the past, you seriously don't want to get involved with the headaches that will likely be a part of this investment.

James Shields: The San Diego Padres finally found a sucker to take on the remaining two-plus years of James Shields' contract last season; sending him packing to the Chicago White Sox at the start of June. Almost from the minute they signed Shields to a four-year deal prior to the start of the 2015 season, the Padres realized they had a pitcher on their hands who was fully into the decline phase of his career. Once considered almost ace-worthy due to his string of 200-K seasons with the Tampa Bay Rays (to go with solid ratios), Shields started losing velocity in 2014 due to all the massive inning totals he had accumulated to that point (9 straight 200-plus inning totals from 2007-2015 overall). A pitching arm only has so many frames in it before irreversible fatigue and a loss of fastball power take hold and Shields was now fully into that trend last season as he was beaten to a pulp all year. A 4.28 ERA with the Padres was followed by some of the worst pitching we have seen in years as Shields saw that number go up to 6.77 with the White Sox after the trade. The biggest red flag with Shields is the fact his K/9 rate fell all the way to 6.69 and his walk rate went the other way to 4.06. Having turned 35 in December, Shields is as close to an automatic avoid as one can get.

Edinson Volquez: The unwise move of Edinson Volquez leaving the Pittsburgh Pirates for the Kansas City Royals prior to 2015 fully showed itself last season in a very ugly year for the veteran. After looking like he had finally found a home with the Pirates in 2014 when he pitched to a terrific 3.04 ERA, Volquez took the money in free agency that winter and jumped back into the rough American League with the Royals. With a vastly diminishing fastball, it was only a matter of time before the struggles ensued. While Volquez skated by in 2015 (3.55 ERA), everything fell apart last season as his ERA spiked to 5.37. Pretty much everywhere you looked, Volquez showed nothing but nasty numbers as his K/9 rate finished under 7.00 for the third season in a row (6.61) and his always terrible control grew worse (3.61 BB/9). Once a guy who could blow opposing batters away with a 98-mph fastball, Volquez now struggles to say above the 90 mark. Throw in the terrible control while operating in the DH-league and it becomes impossible trying to find anything to say about the guy that is a positive.

R.A. Dickey: Knuckleballer R.A. Dickey continued onward with pitching into his 40's during the 2016 season but the results have become quite shaky at this very late stage of his career. While Dickey won a Cy Young Award using the knuckler as his main pitch back in 2012, his results since then (coinciding with his trade to Toronto and the much tougher American League) have not been very good. His 4.46 ERA in 2016 was his highest since that magical season with the Mets and almost all of Dickey's rate stats are nothing but big negatives (3.34 BB/9 and 1.49

HR/9). However he signed back into the National League early in the winter by agreeing to terms on a free agent deal with the Atlanta Braves and that alone should help lower the ratios a bit. Still Dickey is nothing but an SP 5 despite the improvement in ballpark and location.

Homer Bailey: We can't think of many more aggravating players to have owned over the last ten years then perennial tease and ultimate underachiever Homer Bailey. The former first-round pick has never lived up to his draft status and his more recent semi-breakthrough has been thoroughly derailed by serious injuries. Enough.

Ubaldo Jimenez: Having turned 33 in January, we are clearly on the career back nine of the Baltimore Orioles' Ubaldo Jimenez. In short, Jimenez has been nothing but an epic disaster in his three years with the team, posting ERA's of 4.81, 4.11, and 5.44. You won't find many pitchers who threw worse than Jimenez did last season and if anyone needs to be told not to draft him, maybe they should be doing something else.

A.J. Griffin: While A.J. Griffin has been good to spot start on occasion when he is pitching at home, his 5.07 ERA in 2016 showed what a disaster he has become since returning from Tommy John surgery. You can do a million times better.

Scott Feldman: With four straight years posting an ERA under the 4.00 mark, Scott Feldman is a guy who has done a nice job on the mound in his career with virtually no one noticing. This is what happens when you have a below-average K/9 rate and are a guy who seems to have a new team each season as a classic journeyman. If you need Feldman at any point during the 2017 season, he should be waiting there on the waiver wire.

Andrew Cashner: When you struggle to post good numbers when calling Petco Park as your home base, we have little use for you. In fact the entire career of Andrew Cashner has been one big disappointment as rampant arm/shoulder injuries have destroyed his stuff and turned him into a major liability in fantasy baseball. Cashner outdid himself in the ugly numbers department last season as he pitched to a 4.76 ERA with the San Diego Padres and then was even worse in registering a 5.98 mark with the Miami Marlins after coming over via trade. At one time Cashner was able to get his fastball to the upper 90's but now he is around the 90-92 range and is walking everyone (4.02 BB/9 last season). Also Cashner somehow managed to give up home runs at a very high 1.30 rate despite operating in two of the most spacious ballparks in the game. Stop chasing potential that is simply not there.

Matt Cain: Stick a fork in him. Matt Cain is the poster child for what happens to a pitcher who is allowed to throw a ridiculous amount of innings with little oversight prior to the age of 27. With the San Francisco Giants promoting Cain at a young age and having him throw 6 straight seasons of 200-plus innings, it is no shock that his arm is now on life support at the age of 32. In fact Cain has been garbage since 2014 and his health is so bad that he has thrown for just 150 innings total the last two years. Add in the 5.64 ERA in 2016 and Cain should not be drafted.

Phil Hughes: It always seems to be something when it comes to veteran hurler Phil Hughes and his health. This time around, it was a live drive that broke his femur that interrupted things during the 2016 season. Then while trying to come back from that bout of misfortune, Hughes began experiencing weakness in his pitching shoulder that soon was diagnosed as thoracic outlet syndrome which required season-ending surgery. In other words, 2016 was a complete disaster for Hughes and his future both in the majors and as a fantasy baseball asset are very much in question. While still young at the age of 30, Hughes' last full major league season was a disaster when he posted a 4.40 ERA and a pathetic 5.45 K/9 rate in 2015. With so many injuries and health woes in his past, Hughes' stuff is now well below-average. Avoid this mess altogether.

Henderson Alvarez: In just two short years time, Henderson Alvarez has gone from an intriguing young pitcher who put up a 2.65 ERA in 2014, to a guy who is nothing but a major league rumor after he missed all of last season with a shoulder injury that eventually required surgery. Over the last two years, Alvarez has tossed just 22.1 major league innings and so on ill health alone, he only at best is a last round pick.

Jason Vargas: There was not much to say about Jason Vargas in 2016 as he pitched only 12 innings after coming back from Tommy John elbow surgery. Prior to the injury, Vargas was a guy you could round out your fantasy baseball rotation with as he posted mid-3.00 ERA's every year from 2012 through 2015. The caveat was that you only wanted to start Vargas at home as his numbers rose sharply when on the road. Also Vargas was a big negative in strikeouts as his K/9 rate historically came in below the major league average. He will be 34 when the 2017 season gets underway and so ultimately you want to do better now with your SP 5.

Matt Boyd: While Matt Boyd got 97.1 innings from the Detroit Tigers last season, he shouldn't net even 1 on any given fantasy baseball team in 2017. A 4.53 ERA last season was quite ugly and Boyd's 1.57 HR/9 while calling spacious Comerica Park home should really drive home the point he should not be drafted.

Derek Holland: When you are a lefty pitcher in the power-leaning Texas Rangers ballpark, you are already are at a distinct disadvantage due to the high incidence of fly balls going out of the place when a southpaw is on the mound. Combine that with rampant injuries and we present to you Derek Holland. All Holland did in 2016 was pitch so poorly (4.95 ERA which followed a 4.91 2015 campaign) that he was kicked out of the team's rotation and exiled to the bullpen. Well past the prospect stage as he turned 30 this past October, Holland is another failed pitcher who should not be drafted.

Brett Anderson: Some guys just can't ever escape the injury-prone label and perhaps the most shining example of this among pitchers is lefty Brett Anderson. At one time a very hyped prospect with the Oakland A's who combined a good K rate with a vast four-pitch arsenal, Anderson has had two Tommy John elbow surgery and a slew of other major injuries that have derailed his career. 2016 would have been rock bottom as Anderson pitched just 11.1 innings with the Los Angeles Dodgers but we have reached that low seemingly too many times to count with the guy already. Don't give yourself aggravation.

Jake Peavy: The end is likely near for former ace pitcher Jake Peavy but that should be no shock after the 35-year-old fooled nobody last season in registering a 5.54 ERA while calling a spacious ballpark home in San Francisco. While Peavy's career was a bit of a disappointment after his big start with the San Diego Padres, he was still a decent arm for a number of years. That is clearly no longer the case however as Peavy may not even be in the majors next season.

Luis Cessa: After rampant rotation injuries forced the New York Yankees to dip into their farm system for reinforcements, 24-year-old righty Luis Cessa got his chance to show the big club what he could do. While he wasn't terrible in posting a 4.35 ERA, Cessa seems like a very bad fit for Yankee Stadium due to his massive fly ball rate that resulted in home runs going out at a 2.05 HR/9 clip in his 70.1 innings. Cessa also is held back by the fact he doesn't miss many bats (5.89 K/9) and this is fantasy baseball death when you again factor in the ballpark.

Ty Blach: When the San Francisco Giants needed an emergency starter to fill some innings during the last month of the 2016 season, lefty prospect Ty Blach was called on to stem the bleeding from the team's foundering postseason aspirations. Blach surprisingly did the job as he pitched to a 1.06 ERA in 17 innings and 2 starts for the team in the heat of a pennant race. A former fifth-round pick in 2012, Blach was ordinary at Triple-A prior to the promotion (3.43 ERA and 6.25 K/9). Still he opened some eyes with his clutch performances at the end of last season and that should at least net him a shot to stick in the rotation for 2017. Despite all this, there are pretty much no fantasy baseball prospects to speak of.

Yovani Gallardo: It has become almost a reflexive habit now to criticize the Baltimore Orioles' Yovani Gallardo in these pages. At one time a 200-K power pitcher who had terrible control, Gallardo is now a soft-tosser who still gives up a ton of free passes. That is a terrible combination when it comes to fantasy baseball and 2016 gave further proof that Gallardo should not even be owned anymore after he posted a ghastly 5.42 ERA and 4.65 BB/9. Again Gallardo has leaked strikeouts for years and he is now down to a way below-average 6.48 K/9 rate. Stop living in the past.

Robert Gsellman: When the New York Mets lost Matt Harvey, Jacob DeGrom, and Steven Matz to season-ending injuries, it was assumed the team was sunk in terms of getting back to the postseason after enduring such a colossal hit to their rotation. Flying in on his cape to the rescue was the unknown Robert Gsellman who had people looking up who he was after helping to save the Mets' season in pitching to a 2.42 ERA and winning 4 games in 44.2 innings. This after Gsellman was battered at Triple-A (5.73 ERA) and whose status as a former 12th round pick barely made him a noteworthy prospect. Clearly Gsellman was pitching over his head as his minor league numbers were nothing but average and expecting him to sustain his performance down the stretch of 2016 is beyond foolish. In fact Gsellman is more likely to be back in the minors to begin 2017 as the Mets expect to have their full rotation back in working order.

Josh Collmenter: Nobody ever wants to own the guy but Josh Collmenter made it six seasons out of six at the major league level in terms of pitching to an ERA below 4.00. Try seeing if anyone else knew that statistic. Collmenter only tossed 41 major league innings in 2016 in a season split between the Atlanta Braves and Arizona Diamondbacks but the guy has proven that he can still get opposing hitters out. The D-Backs tried to use Collmenter as a reliever but that experiment failed miserably as he pitched to a 4.84 ERA but once back in a rotation with Atlanta, that number dropped to 2.37 in three starts. Overall though, Collmenter is a smoke-and-mirrors guy who struggles to strike batters out and that makes him such a spot start guy at best.

Kendall Graveman: While the cool last name draws quite a bit of attention, Oakland A's starter Kendall Graveman has shown some ability in pitching to a 4.05 and 4.11 ERA the last two years for the team. He is the epitome of a soft-tosser though, as Graveman failed to crack even the below-average 6.00 mark in his K/9 in both campaigns which pretty much kills any chance he gets drafted in fantasy baseball.

Doug Fister: Not since 2014 has Doug Fister been useful for an extended time in fantasy baseball as injuries and stuff that has become quite hittable the last two years (4.19 and 4.64 ERA's in that time frame) have moved him toward the edge of SP5/waiver wire territory. Now at one time Fister was a favorite of this space due to the fact that despite not possessing impressive strikeout stuff, the guy was able to reel off four straight years with an ERA under 3.70 (three of them in the American League). While his mid-6.00 K/9 during that run was below average, Fister's secondary stuff and top-flight control helped him succeed. Unfortunately over the last two years Fister's K/9 has sank to the mid-5.00 range and the control betrayed him for the first time in 2016 as his BB/9 shot up to 3.09. With health becoming a yearly problem, those are very bad trends for a guy who is now 33.

Clay Buchholz: Three may not be a pitcher we have enjoyed hammering more than the Boston Red Sox' Clay Buchholz. After all it is not a very difficult thing to do as Buchholz has been simply pathetic at times and that especially goes for recently as he has recorded an ERA of 4.75 or higher in 2 of the last 3 years. Far from his early days as a top pitching prospect capable of a high number of K's, Buchholz will be 33 in April with a growing rate of getting injured. One only has to look at the swan dive Buchholz took in his K/9 last season (6.01) to realize how lifeless his stuff has become. Act like he is not even in the majors anymore.

Miguel Gonzalez: We can bet that you had no idea veteran starter Miguel Gonzalez had pitched to an ERA under 4.00 every year from 2012 through the 2014 season. That is exactly what Gonzalez accomplished with pretty much no attention paid to his performance as he combined good control and enough movement on his secondary stuff to keep hitters off balance. Still Gonzalez always walked a fine line on the mound due to a below-average K/9 rate that sat mostly in the mid-6.00 range and trouble began to show up in 2015 as he settled into his 30's.

A 4.91 ERA resulted in the Orioles bidding Gonzalez adieu but he got a fresh start with the Chicago White Sox for the 2016 season. Serving mostly as pitching insurance in the minor leagues which surely was not what Gonzalez had anticipated, he impressed again in a 135-inning run with the team during the second half of the year when he pitched to a 3.73 ERA. Alas at the age of 33 in May and with fading stuff, Gonzalez is nothing but a waiver guy now.

Chris Heston: From throwing a no-hitter (and almost a second one) one year to being demoted to the minors and suffering a serious oblique injury the very next season, it has been a whirlwind ride for the San Francisco Giants' Chris Heston. The Giants have to take some of the blame for Heston's predicament last season though as they put him into the bullpen to begin the year despite the fact he was very good at times in 2015 when he registered the no-no and a 3.95 ERA. Heston quickly showed that he was not a bullpen arm as he was hit very hard to begin the year to the tune of a 10.80 ERA in 5 innings, which was a performance that got him sent back to the minor leagues. It was back on the farm where Heston suffered the oblique injury that cost him the last five months of the season and thus made 2016 a year to forget. As far as 2017 is concerned, Heston will have a tough time cracking the Giants rotation again and so he can safely be left on your league's waiver wire.

Rubby De La Rosa: Whether you are Jorge or Rubby De La Rosa, you carry minimal fantasy baseball value given the level of mediocrity we are talking about here. Just like with Jorge, Rubby De La Rosa blended good strikeout stuff last season (9.59) with horrible control (3.55). In addition De La Rosa gives up home runs at a very high 1.42 clip which is a terrible matchup for the offensive dimensions of Arizona's Chase Field. Having been shut down in September with a sprained UCL in his elbow after posting a mediocre 4.26 ERA but a better 1.24 WHIP, De La Rosa is nothing but an NL-only late round pitcher.

Dan Straily: Now a clear journeyman pitcher at the age of 28, southpaw Dan Straily actually comes off his best season in 2016 when he registered a 3.76 ERA and won 14 games on a bad Cincinnati Reds team. There were zero expectations attached to Straily coming into the year as the Reds were already his fourth major league organization and he had already been hit very hard in previous cup of coffee stints with the Houston Astros and Chicago Cubs. Straily did have some initial intrigue in the minors due to some double-digit K/9 rates early in his professional career but those numbers never made the jump to the majors. In dissecting

Straily's 2016 performance, there was a huge amount of "fluke" attached to the numbers; with his very lucky .239 BABIP being the primary red flag. With .300 being average when it comes to BABIP, Straily was nowhere near as good as his 3.76 ERA suggested. In fact his FIP of 4.88 and XFIP of 5.01 would have made Straily just as much a fantasy baseball pariah he always has been. Look past the ERA and understand this will likely go very wrong if you make an investment here.

Hyun-Jin Ryu: Over the last two years, the Los Angeles Dodgers' Hyun-Jin Ryu has thrown a grand total of 4.2 major league innings. Allow that to sink in for a second and then realize that any initial attractiveness that Ryu had when he posted a 3.00 ERA as a rookie in 2013, have long since faded away. You simply can't depend on the Korean as anything but a last round lottery ticket.

Alec Asher: With the Philadelphia Phillies playing out the string on another lost season in 2016, the team gave a quick look to former 4th round pick Alec Asher for a 5-start cameo. The results were actually pretty good on the surface as Asher posted a 2.28 ERA. Asher's performance was one giant fluke however as his .231 BABIP was as lucky a number as a pitcher can get and you only need to look at his 5.09 XFIP ERA to understand how much good fortune he received. His 4.23 K/9 rate was also laughable and it was not much higher in the minors either.

Henry Owens: The Boston Red Sox already seem to be running out of patience with lefty pitching prospect Henry Owens as they could stomach just ugly 22 innings out of him in 2016. The former third overall pick in the 2011 draft was hit very hard to the tune of a 6.95 ERA and that comes on the heels of his 2015 flameout when a 4.57 ERA had Owens fast-tracked back to the minor leagues. While Owens has shown a knack for missing bats at all levels, his control is brutal and he also tends to give up home runs. That can be deadly in the American League and especially the AL East. Owens is in no way guaranteed anything for 2017 so there really is no reason to chase this quickly fading prospect.

Jered Weaver: We are well past the point now where Jered Weaver is nothing but waiver wire rot, with his fastball now barely touching the upper 80's. The very slight and lanky Weaver at one time was a 200-plus K fantasy baseball ace but very high usage earlier in his career sapped strength in his arm and began the velocity leak as early as the 2011 season. As a result, Weaver is down to a 5.21 K/9 guy, which is one of the worst marks in the major leagues among pitchers who threw more than 10 innings in 2016. Another fallout of the velocity erosion is the fact Weaver gives up home runs like a batting practice machine (1.87 HR/9) and that went a long way toward his ERA spiking to 5.06 a year ago. Having turned 35 in October, Weaver is completely finished when it comes to usage in fantasy baseball.

Matt Garza: At one time during his early years with the Tampa Bay Rays, Matt Garza was a very good pitcher who couldn't stay healthy. Now Garza is a very bad pitcher who can't stay healthy. Let's move on.

Archie Bradley: While he has gotten hit very hard when appearing in the major leagues in 2015 and '16, the one thing Archie Bradley can do that is interesting is strike batters out. The 5.80 and 5.02 ERA's Bradley has put up with the Arizona Diamondbacks the last two seasons are beyond hideous but his 9.08 K/9 a year ago show that his fastball has juice to it. While Bradley will likely get yet another chance to stick in 2017, you can get those strikeouts with some much better ratios in a million other places.

Wily Peralta: Serving as nothing but an innings-filler on some bad Milwaukee Brewer teams the last two seasons, Wily Peralta is about as negative a place to look for fantasy baseball pitching help as you can get. ERA's of 4.72 and 4.86 the last two seasons make Peralta a non-story.

Chad Bettis: When you pitch for the Colorado Rockies, post ERA's north of 4.20 during your first two seasons, and struggle to be even average in strikeouts, there is really not much else to say. These three designations center on the Rockies' Chad Bettis who is just a below-average starter operating in arguably the worst park for pitchers in all of baseball. Should not be drafted even in NL-only formats.

Wade Miley: It was a beyond brutal season for Wade Miley in 2016 as he was hit very hard both when he was with the Seattle Mariners and then later with the Baltimore Orioles. After posting a gross 4.98 ERA with the Mariners, Miley somehow figured out a way to pitch worse with the Orioles as his number there shot up to 6.17. Miley has posted an ERA north of 4.30 for three straight years now and his lack of flash in any other category makes him a completely radioactive name in fantasy baseball.

Kyle Gibson: Minnesota Twins righty Kyle Gibson has never come close to his 2009 first round status (22nd overall) and he can be grouped into an ugly fraternity with Luke Hochevar and Mike Pelfrey as prospects who have failed in very ugly fashion in the majors. Having turned 29 last October, Gibson is one of the worst starting pitchers in the game today as he comes off a 2016 campaign that included a 5.07 ERA. With a 6.36 K/9 rate that is way below the major league average and with ugly control (3.36 BB/9), Gibson is a complete disaster of a pitcher.

Chase Anderson: When you are known for being just an innings-eater, there is not much to say from a fantasy baseball perspective. This is a status that belongs to Chase Anderson who is a mid-4.00 ERA guy who struggles keeping the ball in the park and especially in 2016, has issues with walks. Nothing happening here.

Ricky Nolasco: It is hard to believe that at one time very early in his career, we actually had some upside interest in Minnesota Twins starting pitcher Ricky Nolasco. Soon after he broke in with the Florida Marlins in 2008 however, Nolasco has annually been on the short list of being the worst starting pitcher in the game. With his season ERA's coming in over 4.40 in 7 of the last 8 years, Nolasco would be about the last pitcher we would ever draft.

Martin Perez: Having successfully come back from Tommy John elbow surgery, the Texas Rangers' Martin Perez has shown that he is not deserving of our fantasy baseball attention as he has posted ERA's of 4.46 and 4.39 the last two years. While we can sometimes overlook ugly ERA's if there are a high number of strikeouts, Perez fails badly here as well since he was only able to manage a 4.67 K/9 last season. In fact ,that K/9 rate is downright laughable and disqualifies Perez from being worthy of inclusion in 2017 fantasy baseball.

Adam Morgan: In his first two years in the major leagues, the Philadelphia Phillies' Adam Morgan has put up ERA's of 4.48 and 5.57, while also giving up home runs by the boatload. With an ordinary fastball and a repertoire that scares no one, Morgan should never come off your league's waiver wire.

Matt Andriese: While you always want to take an extra second to evaluate any pitcher that the Tampa Bay Rays operate with, Matt Andriese is a guy who shouldn't require a second look. An ERA north of 4.00 in both of his MLB seasons and a struggle with home runs despite operating in a pitcher's park put Andriese in waiver territory.

Tyler Duffey: It is amazing that the Minnesota Twins gave 26 starts to Tyler Duffey last season as he was right there as one of the worst pitchers in baseball as evidenced by his 6.43 ERA. While it says little about how the Twins view their players, what should not be unclear is that Duffey should not go within a mile of a fantasy baseball roster.

Charlie Morton: While Charlie Morton has had some decent stretches in his career in terms of being a capable SP 5 in non-inning capped leagues, those days appear to be over as his last full season in 2015 saw his ERA soar to an ugly 4.81 and then he followed that up by missing most of 2016 with injury. Always a soft-tosser whose K/9 struggled to escape the 6.00-range, the 33-year-old Morton is no longer worth your time in fantasy baseball.

Bud Norris: Quite intriguing early in his career due to a fastball that brought forth a high number of strikeouts, Bud Norris is now just a bad journeyman pitcher who failed in two locales (Atlanta, Los Angeles Dodgers) in 2016. Norris never solved his career-long control woes and now he is an aging pitcher who is leaking velocity. Ignore.

Robbi Erlin: Erlin became yet another young pitcher who succumbed to Tommy John surgery last May and if he even does pitch in 2017, it won't be until September. Check back for 2017.

Nick Tropeano: Tropeano suffered a total UCL year in his elbow last summer that required Tommy John surgery. He will likely not pitch at all in 2017.

Matt Wisler: After registering ERA's of 4.71 ERA and 5.00 during his first two MLB seasons, the Atlanta Braves' Matt Wisler is a comically bad pitcher. Not even guaranteed to be in the major leagues to start the year, Wisler should be a permanent member of the waiver wire.

Alfredo Simon: Over the last two years, Alfredo Simon has been arguably one of the worst starting pitchers in baseball as he posted ERA 's of 5.05 and 9.36 in that span. While he did actually earn and deserve an All-Star berth in a shockingly good first half of 2014, it has all gone downhill since in a hideous manner. Given how pathetic Simon has pitched the last two years, he shouldn't even be in the majors anymore.

Mike Pelfrey: A 5.07 ERA for Mike Pelfrey in 2016 was par for the course as the guy has now gone over that very nasty mark in three of the last four seasons. There may not be a more overpaid and truly awful starting pitcher in the game today.

Trevor May: Having failed as a starting pitcher when coming up the minor league ladder and in his initial foray into the majors with the Minnesota Twins, lefty Trevor May's high-powered fastball was that much more effective in the team's bullpen during the 2016 season. Racking up an extreme 60 strikeouts in

42.2 innings, May began the year by posting an encouraging 2.57 ERA in April. It all went downhill from there though as May walked everyone (3.59 BB/9) and saw home runs fly out at an alarming rate (1.48 HR/9). The Twins will stretch May out for one last shot to grab a rotation spot but there is nothing to see here from a fantasy baseball perspective.

Jon Niese: While Jon Niese at one time was a useful SP 5 in mixed leagues (posting an ERA under 4.00 three straight seasons from 2012-2014), he has been nothing but a colossal liability in any fantasy baseball format the last two years. Things got downright hideous for Niese in 2016 as he was banished to the bullpen by the Pittsburgh Pirates after his ERA soared over 5.00 while in the rotation and then was dumped onto the New York Mets (who originally traded him to the Pirates in the deal for Neil Walker the previous winter). Niese was even more pathetic with the Mets as he posted an 11.45 ERA before requiring season-ending knee surgery. It is likely Niese will need to accept a minor league deal to get another shot in the majors for 2017 and that obviously means he has zero fantasy baseball value.

Nathan Eovaldi: Nathan Eovaldi must have been a big fan of former Major League reliever Kyle Farnsworth because never before have we seen a guy throw as consistently hard as Eovaldi does but at the same time give up more hits and induce way too few strikeouts considering the velocity. That has been the story of the annually disappointing Eovaldi's career as his 4.76 ERA in 2016 could attest despite residing around the top five in all of baseball in average velocity with the fastball. Alas Eovaldi hit rock bottom in August when it was revealed he completely tore the UCL off the bone in his elbow which threatens to keep him out for all of 2017. Chalk Eovaldi up as another classic victim in terms of being a young and hard-throwing hurler who fell prey to Tommy John.

Andrew Heaney: The Tommy John epidemic continued in 2016 as it claimed Los Angeles Angels southpaw Andrew Heaney during this past summer. The former 2012 first round pick was just starting to show the talent that made him a lauded prospect in the Miami Marlins system before the UCL went bad and now he is likely out until late in 2017. In fact there is no guarantee we will see Heaney at all next season so it is safe to ignore him.

CLOSER OVERVIEW

Nothing new to add here that we haven't already espoused on for the last ten-plus years in publication. The specialized nature of your fantasy baseball closer (where the lack of total innings pitched results in an impact in just one standard 5 x 5 category) and the massive amount of turnover among the closers who begin each season in the role, means that you would be absolutely foolish to address this group until the middle rounds at the earliest. In fact you can go so far as to not pick a single closer in your draft and still be able to be competitive in saves just by staying active on the wire and being there to pick up new stoppers along the way due to injuries, demotions, and what not. The turnover is non-stop here as some teams change their closer 2-3 times during the season which means this position should be the least of your concerns.

*****KEEP IN MIND THAT AS OF THIS WRITING, TOP TIER CLOSERS AROLDIS CHAPMAN, MARK MELANCON, AND KENLEY JANSEN ARE FREE AGENTS.******

New York Yankees (Dellin Betances): With the New York Yankees having first dealt Aroldis Chapman and then Andrew Miller leading up to the Aug. 1 trade deadline last season, fireballer Dellin Betances finally got the chance to close games late in the 2016 season. Already having been selected for his third straight All-Star Game as Betances once again performed like one of the most dominant relievers in the game, his performance in the closer role was somewhat of a mixed bag. While he dominated in August (0.68 ERA), Sept./Oct. was another story altogether. Looking like he was on fumes, Betances registered a frightening 9.64 ERA in his last 9.1 innings; a performance that might have shaken the Yankees' confidence in him moving forward as the closer. On stuff alone, there are few relievers who can say they have pitcher better overall then Betances the last three seasons (K/9 rates of 13.50 or higher in all four of his MLB campaigns) but closing games is a whole different story mentally which at least is somewhat of a concern here. In addition, there is more than a little chatter that the Yanks and Chapman mutually want a reunion and that would obviously put Betances back in a setup role which carries little fantasy baseball value. This is a setup that needs to be watched during free agency but for now Betances' insane K rate and overall dominant stuff makes him a firm top ten fantasy baseball closer.

Boston Red Sox (Craig Kimbrel): Boston Red Sox closer Craig Kimbrel had become somewhat of a hired gun the last few season as he found himself being traded twice during that span. Kimbrel has a bit more stability this season though as he is back pitching the ninth inning for the Red Sox for 2017 but his debut campaign for them a year ago was far from impressive. We have been saying for a few years now that Kimbrel is starting to lose his stuff a bit and that showed last year when his 3.40 ERA ended up being a career-high by a mile. In addition, Kimbrel is fighting his stuff like never before as his 5.06 BB/9 was downright hideous and a major problem for any closer. Kimbrel still can bring it with the fastball which nets him a very high amount of strikeouts (14.09 K/9) but his overall performance is a clear shade or two below his old Atlanta Brave days. Add in some recent elbow/shoulder scares and Kimbrel is a closer we suggest avoiding this season.

Baltimore Orioles (Zach Britton): While he hasn't reflexively been mentioned as a top tier closer in the past, this needs to change for Baltimore Orioles stopper Zach Britton after he just got done putting up the finishing touches on a 2016 performance for the ages. It was downright insane how dominant Britton was as he gave up just FIVE earned runs all season, resulting in a nearly spotless ERA of 0.54. While Britton was not a big strikeout guy when he first started closing games in 2014, that number has really ramped up the last two years (10.83 and 9.94 K/9 rates). Possessing excellent control and a HR/9 rate that came in at just 0.13 last season, you can make the case Britton should be the top closer off the draft board in 2017.

Tampa Bay Rays (Alex Colome): Even the Tampa Bay Rays had to be pleasantly surprised how good new 2016 closer Alex Colome performed in the role. While he battled some injuries, Colome proved to be a natural stopper in nailing down 37 saves with a 1.91 ERA and sky-high 11.28 K/9 last season. Another struggling minor league starter who converted into a top reliever, Colome looks like a very safe 2017 fantasy baseball investment since both his BB/9 (2.38) and HR/9 (0.95) rates were very good. Yes he is legit.

Toronto Blue Jays (Roberto Osuna): While the Toronto Blue Jays didn't take our advice right away when we said Roberto Osuna should be the closer for 2015, they eventually figured out that the hard-throwing youngster was by far their best option to finish games last season. Showing incredible poise for a 21-year-old pitching on a prime American League contender, Osuna locked up 36 saves with a 2.68 ERA. Needless to say, the Blue Jays have found their closer of the present and the future.

Detroit Tigers (Francisco Rodriguez: It is almost certain the Detroit Tigers will pick their option on ageless closer Francisco Rodriguez for 2017 but even if they don't, the guy showed last season that he still has the ability to finish games (3.24 ERA and a total of 44 saves). Keep in mind though that Rodriguez will be 35 when the 2017 season gets underway and he is far from dominant as his 3.24 ERA in 2016 is getting high for a closer. He continues to leak velocity and Rodriguez' 8.02 K/9 rate really shows how the margin of error is decreasing drastically. Having also struggled with control (3.24 BB/9), it is clear that Rodriguez is quite risky and not lock to hold a closer role for the entirety all of 2017.

Chicago White Sox (David Robertson): While the Chicago White Sox have openly offered up for trade closer David Robertson almost from the moment they signed him as a free agent prior to 2015, the veteran did his job in finishing out 37 games for the team in 2016. It should be pointed out that Robertson's' ERA has shot upwards the last two years (3.41 and 3.47) and that is not such a great development when it comes to a closer. Robertson still misses bats (10.83 K/9) but also keep in mind 2016 was the third year in a row he showed a decline in that category. A major reason Robertson struggled for stretches last season was that he fought control like never before (4.62 BB/9) and that needs to be remedied. While the name brand means Robertson will still carry a decent price on draft day, the reality is that he is now on a two-year run of trending in the wrong direction.

Cleveland Indians (Cody Allen): Yes Andrew Miller is also returning to the Cleveland Indians for 2017 but manager Terry Francona has shown he is more apt to use his fireballing lefty in a setup capacity. That leaves the very capable Cody Allen to man the ninth inning again and he should be up to the task since 2016 was the fourth season in a row he registered an ERA under 3.00. Allen is also one of the best strikeout arms in the ninth inning, going above 11.25 K/9 during that same four-season span. While Miller might steal a save here or there, Allen is the guy to own this season in the ninth inning for Cleveland.

Kansas City Royals (Wade Davis/Greg Holland): By the time you read this, the Kansas City Royals might have traded away All-Star closer Wade Davis. Having endured a Tommy John elbow scare in 2016, the Royals are likely trying to get out from under the ticking time bomb in his arm/elbow. Even through his health struggles last season, Davis' 1.87 ERA was the third year in a row he has registered a mark there under 2.00. That is some serious ability for sure but Davis has to be considered a prime injury risk going into 2017. What also could complicate the ninth inning setup here is the return to action of former All-Star closer Greg Holland who underwent Tommy John elbow surgery early in 2016. At one time a firm challenger to Craig Kimbrel as the top closer in the game back in 2014, a healthy Holland is surely going to be a factor again in the ninth inning.

Minnesota Twins (Glen Perkins/Brandon Kintzler) : A torn labrum that completely detached from the bone kept Minnesota Twins closer Glen Perkins out for all but 2 innings during the 2016 season. Already showing signs of slipping going into the year, Perkins' outlook if very murky at the moment since there is no guarantee he will even be ready to go when the 2017 season gets underway in April. Prior to the 2016 troubles, Perkins had seen his K/9 erode for three straight years from 2012-15 and his ERA settled over 3.00 as well the latter two years in that same span. In Perkins' place last season, career setup man Brandon Kintzler locked down 17 saves in 20 chances with a 3.15 ERA. Kintzler has decent stuff but a full season at closer could get him exposed since he struck out just 35 batters in 54.1 innings. That type of below-average K rate is not anywhere near what you want in that category while pitching the ninth inning and so this whole messy closing situation in Minnesota should not be touched.

Seattle Mariners (Edwin Diaz): Once the Seattle Mariners went through the expected disaster that was Steve Cishek at closer, they soon turned to a nuclear-armed youngster who looks like he can be a top tier stopper for many years to come. We are of course referring to righty Edwin Diaz who earned some Rookie of the Year attention by pitching to a 2.79 ERA and locking down 18 saves in a trial run debut at closer for the Mariners last season. Other then Aroldis Chapman, there may not be a more potent strikeout artist in the ninth inning as Diaz whiffed batters at an unfathomable 15.33 K/9 mark as a rookie. That sets Diaz up nicely to be a huge closing force for 2017 and the fact he is not yet a well-known commodity means some major profit can be made here.

Oakland A's (Ryan Dull-Sean Doolittle): With Ryan Madson and Sean Doolittle both proving not to be dependable closing options for the Oakland A's in 2016, the job ultimately fell to second-year man Ryan Dull with decent results. While Dull is far from a hard-thrower (8.84 K/9), he kept enough hitters off balance to put up a tidy 2.42 ERA. Treat very carefully here though as Dull's 2.09 BABIP was incredibly lucky and his 1.21 HR/9 is high for a guy who called a spacious park home. There is tremendous volatility here as Dull doesn't look anywhere near like a long-term closing solution for the A's and the team may very well bring someone else in by the time you read this. Also don't discount Doolittle getting another shot as it was just 2014 when it looked like he was developing into one of the best stoppers in the game.

Los Angeles Angels (Huston Street): The end is coming for longtime closer Huston Street by the looks of his truly putrid 2016 campaign for the Los Angeles Angels. Already an annual annoyance due to some of the worst injury problems in the game, Street couldn't get anyone out last season as his ERA shot up to a laughable 6.45. No matter where you looked, red flags abounded as Street's K/9 sank to a very below-average 5.64 and his control completely abandoned him (4.84 BB/9). Still under contract for another year with an option, the Angels might very well cut a check in telling Street to go away. Turning 34 in August and with major wear-and-tear on his arm, Street should not be drafted in any league.

Texas Rangers (OPEN): The ninth inning has been a major source of frustration for the Texas Rangers over the last few seasons. From seeing Neftali Feliz fail to close out the World Series, to his eventual struggles and release, followed by the meltdown of Shawn Tolleson early in 2016, closing games has been a major adventure here. The latest to try and become the solution to this annual problem for the Rangers was Sam Dyson, who successfully finished off 38 saves in 2016 with a 2.43 ERA. While the on paper results were good, Dyson left a lot to be desired in the strikeout department (7.04 K/9) which is not what you want from your stopper. Unable to consistently get outs via the whiff, there is a major blowup risk when it comes to investing in Dyson for 2017. That is if Dyson returns to the Rangers as he is a free agent as of press time. The Rangers are likely going to try and address the closer spot in free agency where major arms like Kenley Jansen, Mark Melancon, and Aroldis Chapman all await.

Houston Astros (Ken Giles): The Houston Astros better hope that Ken Giles pitches a whole lot better in 2017 or else they will rightly get destroyed for trading away talented power-arm Vincent Velasquez to the Philadelphia Phillies in order to acquire the hard-throwing reliever r last winter. While no one doubts the strikeout stuff that Giles possesses, he was an utter disaster at times closing games for the Astros in 2016. After tossing away the gig soon after the year got underway, Giles eventually re-claimed the closer role during the late summer. That too ended in disaster as Giles logged a 7.15 ERA in Sept./Oct. and thus opened up questions whether or not he will be closing in 2017. The big issue here is that Giles' 3.43 BB/9 was a mess and struggles there are never a good match for the ninth inning.

On the flip side though, Giles had a very unlucky .349 BABIP that showed he was not pitching as bad as his subsequent 4.11 ERA presented. Remember that Giles was an extremely attractive closer prior to the start of last season given how well he pitched in Philly but we were not on board there as we said in print due to the control woes. A fresh start this season could help unleash the old dominance and Giles' 13.98 K/9 rate in 2016 really couldn't get much more impressive. Still this looks like too volatile a situation right now and that means taking a pass on Giles when you are at the draft.

New York Mets (Jeurys Familia): Thank goodness the fantasy baseball season ends prior to the playoffs as New York Mets stopper Jeurys Familia would see his value sink. While Familia is undeniably one of the best closers in the game from April-September, the postseason is another story as he struggled for the second year in a row on that front in 2016. Be that as it may, Familia was terrific when the fantasy baseball season was in play, as he reached 50 straight converted saves at one point. Registering a 2.55 ERA and 9.73 K/9 rate, Familia's numbers can hold up against any other closer in the game. The one knock on Familia is that he gets in trouble at times with walks (3.59 BB/9) but with a very low hit rate, his struggles there don't hurt him much. More concerning was Familia being charged with domestic violence this past Halloween. While the chargers were soon dropped, a suspension is likely. That means Addison Reed will have to be handcuffed to Familia at the draft.

Philadelphia Phillies (Hector Neris): While he held the role longer than anyone could have imagined, Jeanmar Gomez' poor strikeout rate eventually led him to being exposed in the closer role. Gomez would ultimately cede the ninth inning in September and that allowed the very intriguing Hector Neris to get a short cameo finishing games. For the season Neris was very good overall as he pitched to a 2.58 ERA and his 11.43 K/9 rate is tailor-made for closing games. We actually said in last year's draft guide that Neris should be the closer from the start of 2016 (like our correct hedge on Roberto Osuna for Toronto the year before) but his ascension took a bit longer than expected. There is no reason Neris shouldn't be finishing games from the jump in 2017 and the fact he pitches for the rebuilding Phillies should make him a very cost-efficient upside play.

Atlanta Braves (Arodys Vizcaino): While he came into the 2016 season with some sleeper hype at the closer position, nothing went according to plan for the Atlanta Braves' Arodys Vizcaino. While he quickly beat out Jason Grilli in the ninth inning, Vizcaino was hit hard for long stretches and was undermined by horrible control (6.05 BB/9). While Vizcaino still struck out batters at a very high rate (11.64 K/9), his 4.42 ERA was as bad as it gets among those who earned saves last season. Perhaps even more concerning was the fact Vizcaino hit the DL with soreness in his pitching shoulder and that lasted into the early fall. While Vizcaino is expected to be ready for the start of 2017, shoulder injuries tend to re-occur and he also may have to win the job back again during spring training. Ageless veteran Jim Johnson (3.06 ERA/9.46 K/9) could also be brought back as closer insurance which make the setup here quite murky.

Miami Marlins (A.J. Ramos): It was a roller-coaster ride of a season for Miami Marlins closer A.J. Ramos in 2016 to say the least. Having earned the role to begin the year, Ramos' ongoing control problems eventually led to trade acquisition Fernando Rodney taking over for a spell. As Rodney himself threw the gig away, Ramos was given the chance to save his season. His overall performance was a mixed bag as the 2.81 ERA was excellent, but Ramos really needs to do some major work on his 4.92 BB/9. There is no way any closer can succeed long-term when walking that many batters and that alone makes Ramos quite risky for 2017. His 10.27 K/9 remained imposing though and Ramos has now been in double-digits there in three straight seasons which show the potential he carries. As long as you keep the price in mind, Ramos could be a decent rebound candidate.

Washington Nationals (OPEN-Mark Melancon?): With Jonathan Papelbon finally revealing his age as he tossed away the closer role in Washington (and then was outright released), the Nats' move to acquire Mark Melancon was deemed a potential World Series-winning transaction. Of course the Nationals went out in the divisional round yet again but Melancon was dominant to the tune of a 1.64 collective ERA. In fact there is more than enough evidence that Melancon is arguably the best closer in the game today as his ERA has been under 2.00 in three of the last four years, despite the fact his K/9 rate is not exactly imposing. A free agent as of press time, it makes too much sense for the two sides not to have a reunion.

Chicago Cubs (Hector Rondon): This is another volatile closer situation going into the winter as Aroldis Chapman enters into free agency and reportedly is interested in reuniting with the New York Yankees. If Chapman and his number 1 overall closer tag decided to jump ship, old friend Hector Rondon would likely go right back into the ninth inning. While no one would ever question Chapman taking over the closer role as soon as he was acquired last summer, Rondon did nothing to lose the job as he put up a 3.53 ERA and struck out batters at a 10.24 clip. Also possessing excellent control, Rondon just has to keep his tendency to give up home runs in check. As far as Chapman is concerned, there is no argument he is the number 1 closer by a mile in fantasy baseball as his strikeout rates are stuff of legend. Wherever Chapman ends up during the winter, he is locked-in as the top closer in the game.

St. Louis Cardinals (Seung Hwan Oh): Already the St. Louis Cardinals organization have publicly endorsed Seung Hwan Oh as the team's closer to begin 2017 and no one would dare question that decision after the Korean rookie dominated from the start in pitching to a 1.92 ERA and striking out batters at an 11.64 clip. Oh is also a ground ball pitcher who possesses good control, which pretty much checks all the boxes in terms of being a high-end stopper.

Pittsburgh Pirates (Tony Watson): With Mark Melancon having been traded to the Washington Nationals last summer, the Pittsburgh Pirates didn't hesitate in naming lefty Tony Watson as the team's new closer. Watson had his worst stretch of the season after ascending to the job though, as his September 5.06 ERA showed. Whether it was fatigue or mental troubles closing games, the Pirates ninth inning situation might not be set in stone at the start of spring training. While Watson didn't have the finish he would have liked, the fact of the matter is that the veteran has been one of the better relievers in baseball going back to 2012. While Watson has good control and keeps the ball in the park, his mediocre (7.71) K/9 is a potential issue in the ninth inning. This is another closing situation to monitor in spring training given the uncertain current setup.

Milwaukee Brewers (Tyler Thornburg): When the Milwaukee Brewers dealt veteran closer Francisco Rodriguez to the Detroit Tigers midway through the 2016 season, an opportunity presented itself to hard-throwing setup man Tyler Thornburg. All in all, Thornburg did pretty well as he logged 13 saves with a sparkling 2.15 ERA. Better yet, Thornburg proved to be a good fit in the ninth inning due to his massive 12.09 K/9 rate. A former third-round pick of the team, Thornburg is set to open 2017 as the Brewers' closer where he presents some good value since he is still quite unknown. Yes there are some control issues (3.36 BB/9) but Thornburg is the type of upside closer who comes with a nice price tag this season.

Cincinnati Reds (Tony Cingrani): Already a failed starting pitcher with the Cincinnati Reds, the team turned to the lefty when an opening arose in the ninth inning midway through the 2016 season. While Cingrani was able to lock down 17 saves, his advanced numbers were gross as his hideous control (5.29 BB/9) was a big problem and he also doesn't strike out nearly enough batters to overcome that negative With the Reds in rebuilding mode, their closer role is not likely to be a high priority for the front office during the winter. That means Cingrani or Jumbo Diaz could battle it out in the spring. Neither guy is worth going after.

Colorado Rockies (Adam Ottavino): It was a successful return from Tommy John surgery for hard-throwing reliever Adam Ottavino in 2016. Soon after his activation from the DL after completing rehab early in the year, Ottavino went right back into the closer role he left behind when his UCL tore back at the start of 2015. What was encouraging to see was Ottavino's high K rate staying intact, as he whiffed batters at a very high 11.67 in his 27-inning return to the Rockies. Nailing down 7 saves in the process, Ottavino will begin 2017 in the closer role. While Ottavino struggles a bit with control, his annually high strikeout rate makes the guy a good bet to yield solid value this season since the name brand is quite muted after missing so much time from elbow surgery.

San Francisco Giants (OPEN): Whether it was Santiago Casilla, Sergio Romo, or Hunter Strickland, the San Francisco Giants had arguably the worst ninth inning results in the major leagues in 2016. It was a gigantic issue that followed the team into the postseason where more blown saves cost them the divisional round series versus the Chicago Cubs. You would have to think the Giants will be in play for the top free agent closers in the market this winter or maybe they will address the position via trade. What we do know is that Casilla, Romo, and Strickland should be avoided in drafts this season.

San Diego Padres (Carter Capps): As the San Diego Padres completely tore down the team in 2016, they made an under-the-radar deal with the Miami Marlins for hard-throwing bullpen arm Carter Capps which didn't catch much of the public's attention. That was probably due to the fact Capps was in the process of recovering from Tommy John elbow surgery but it was obvious the Padres were making a buy-low deal to acquire their future closer. Prior to the surgery, Capps was an instant curiosity given his unorthodox jump-step to the mound before unleashing his 100-mph fastball. That helped Capps put up a truly insane 16.84 K/9 in 2015 as he pitched to a 1.16 ERA. That is the type of lockdown dominance that the ninth inning is made of and with Capps expected to be ready for the start of spring training, the upside is massive.

Arizona Diamondbacks (Jake Barrett): The Arizona Diamondbacks failed on multiple levels in their very disappointing 2016 campaign and that led to them unloading closer Brad Ziegler early enough in the season which signaled the waving of the proverbial white flag. After trying out some Ziegler replacements that didn't pan out, the team turned to Jake Barrett late in the year and saw him perform pretty well in recording 4 saves with a 3.49 ERA. The ceiling is not very high here though as Barrett doesn't strike out enough batters to be a prime ninth inning guy (8.49 K/9) and his control is terrible (4.25 BB/9), which are two major negatives for any prospective closer. Unless the D-Backs make a big move in free agency or via trade to address the situation, the team's ninth inning setup looks like one to avoid altogether.

Los Angeles Dodgers (OPEN): With Kenley Jansen a free agent as of this writing, it is tough to pin down what the Dodgers will look like in the ninth inning for 2017. As far as Jansen is concerned, the fireballer is a rock solid top five fantasy baseball closer with no debate. Since entering into the majors in 2010, Jansen's highest ERA was 2.85 back in 2011. Over the last two years? Try 1.83 and 2.41. Want some more glowing numbers? Try K/9 rates that have never gone below a massive 13.00 in his entire career. Few do it better than Jansen and whether he returns to the Dodgers or goes elsewhere, the veteran should be picked no latter then fifth among closers. Meanwhile if Jansen were to depart, the Dodgers could bring back Joe Blanton, whose full transition from starter to reliever was a smashing success in 2016 (2.48 ERA/9.00 K/9).

THE LAST WORD

So as we always do in this space once you have digested our massive draft guide, it is time to reiterate the fact that your work has really only just begun once you assembled your initial roster of players. The six-month slog that is the fantasy baseball season tests your patience, will, and determination to win given the daily moves that need to be made to stay on top but we try to make the process so much less stressful for you the reader. Once again our staff will cover every inch of the game through our website (www.thefantasysportsboss.com), starting with our daily "Wrap Up" feature where we report on all of the performances and news items from the night before. In addition, we post injury updates, lineup changes, and daily features to keep you on the path to success. While we can't promise that you will win your league, we CAN guarantee you will get every chance to do so by following our expert advice. As always good luck for the start of the season and we hope to see you six months later with a league title in your grasp.

38131290R00128

Made in the USA
Middletown, DE
15 December 2016